Sadly, innovation still mainly consists of misused and misunderstood buzzwords, well-intentioned yet fruitless initiatives and snake-oil peddlers promising the panacea for all innovation ills. *Innovation Sucks* shines a uniquely bright light into the four corners of innovation rethinking innovation itself and providing novel frameworks that systematise successful commercialisation. A must-read for those bored with the hype who believe we need to revolutionise innovation.

Jordan Schlipf, *Founder Rainmaking*

I have said for years how we need to PULL customers with branding and emotion rather than PUSH to them with deals and discounting. This book blew my mind on how to create that pull. It literally rewrites how our brains see innovation. I have insisted it's read by my entire team.

Simon Beard, *CEO Culture Kings*

Imagine a book that will help you truly transform your business, navigate the smoke and mirrors plus give you a recipe for real innovation and growth. This is that book. In my business the early results are incredible.

Simon Leslie, *CEO Ink Global*

Innovation often fails because the corporate funnel or filtering machine and the people who put the ideas into the machine fail. In too many businesses the strategy department and the leadership team aren't representative of their customers. This book reveals how we change the innovation machine and the machine operators to deliver a genuine business transformation.

Jeff Dodds, *COO Virgin Media*

You could spend thousands of hours researching innovation and leadership or you could let the masters do it for you and read this book.

Christina Bognet, *CEO Platejoy*

This book is brilliant in showing the value of all people, including those that think differently about things. I will be sending a copy to the CEOs of my top 10 pension fund holdings! It will be the soundest investment I've made all year!

Peter Needle, *CEO Segura*

I loved this book! Really thought provoking, compelling and insightful and while I started off trying to skim read it, I found myself reading every page. If we can apply the ideas offered in this book, we could significantly increase our organizational efficiency.

Chris Parsons, *President Mayborn NA*

I've become an ardent fan of Alan's books and I think this may be his best yet! Essential reading for any company that sees creativity as part of competitive advantage.

Jason Foo, *CEO BBD Perfect Storm*

Innovation has always been the key to solve the world's problems. But it has stagnated and become formulaic. Innovation itself therefore is in dire need of Innovation! This game changing book provides multiple ways to transform and align it with aspirations of the millennial generation who will play a key role in the Workplace of the future. With insights and takeaways on practically every page, the book is not only about thinking but also doing Innovation differently.

Alex Rocha, *MD ITP*

2020 has highlighted how uncomfortable businesses are in the face of change. Under pressure most retrench and go back to basics. This book shines a light on how the winners in the future will be those that innovate the way they innovate and embrace change.

Peter Janes, *CEO Shieldpay*

The word innovation is often over-used or used incorrectly and for some companies, it represents new product development only. But we know the truth – that innovation is all encompassing. It requires depth of empathy, diversity of thought and critical thinking. No amount of funding and resources can compensate for a lack of robust and varied insight and reasoning. This engaging book will become your new 'innovation manual' – unlocking hidden potential, resident in all organisations.

Lara Ramdin, *CIO Dole International*

This book comes at the right time and turns worry into courage. It provides answers and guidelines to build a new future with a real competitive advantage.

Wei Tze Ooi, *Director of Strategy Dole International*

There are many reasons why organisations find innovation so difficult. It requires both art and science. Of course, all artists and scientists are human beings. What this book brilliantly reveals is how humans can develop their ability to innovate, thereby unlocking all organisations' ability to transform their own futures.

Garri Jones, *Managing Director Lazard*

If you want to innovate better read this book. It goes right to the heart of what is most often overlooked in innovation – the role of the adult development, mindset, and values systems. Now, more than ever, we need leaders who develop themselves, so they can shape and nurture more effective innovation systems.

Joe Boggio, VP Innovation, Capgemini

Why did the iPod beat the Walkman and Dyson beat the Hoover? Innovation. It wins every single time. Study it, understand it and put it right at the core of your business. This book shows you how to innovate your way to success."

Jesse Swash, *Co-Founder, Structure*

In 1969 NASA demonstrated that people could walk on the Moon. In 2020 we are just beginning to answer the question "why" with the discovery of water molecules on its sunlit surface. There is never just one question and certainly never just one answer. The impeller approach acknowledges this most critical driver for innovation and advocates creating a vacuum into which multiple questions and answers are drawn, enabling innovators to collaborate, co-create and integrate innovation that is meaningful and endures. The platforms of tomorrow will be born out of innovation that sucks.

Trevor Didcock, *Director, Futurice Oy and ex-CIO easyJet*

If you think you know everything you need to know about innovation, you´re not innovating! Read this book and stimulate to innovate!

Simon Matthews, *Chief Product & Technology Officer, Hotelbeds*

Who would have thought that innovation itself needs to be disrupted. At a time when all businesses see innovation as a way to thrive and grow this remarkable book turns the whole process on its head. Like all the best disruptive ideas you wonder why nobody had thought of it before.

David Robinson, *COO, Pets at Home*

Carefully reading this book changed my working mindset entirely, transforming my appreciation of the value that experience and an enquiring mind can bring to businesses plus a deeper appreciation of the skills and strengths of the people in my network and of course the value of that network.

Al Sherrif, *CEO CBoxx Ltd*

It's about time we became more innovative about innovation. The impeller approach, outlined in this book, is the start of such a shift and builds on the idea that you must fail fast and learn even faster. The problem for many organisations is that innovation is simply a bolt on or, at worst, an over-used buzzword. If you're serious about changing the way you innovate then this means a change in mindset and culture. This book is a start, the rest is down to you.

Professor Mark Jenkins, *Cranfield School of Management*

Reading this book during a global pandemic illustrates what can be done when starting with the solution. In this case, a safe and effective vaccine for SARS-Cov-2! Science has moved at an unprecedented rate; governments have shredded masses of red tape and regulatory agencies are working hand in hand with manufacturers. This important book is a "how to" manual for such an enterprise.

Paul Kemp PhD, *Co-Founder, Chief Executive Director HairClone*

A peek into a fascinating world, populated by bees, meadows and jokers who offer the potential to revolutionise innovation. A book that points to a future where digital technology and new ways of thinking, working and innovating might effectively address the apparently intractable issues faced by industry, government and the third sector. An intriguing challenge to traditional innovation approaches. The authors have produced a short and practical guide to their unique approach to innovation, which is an easy read and highly recommended for anyone in industry, government or the third sector with an interest in this challenging subject.

John Jeans CBE, *Ex Chair GE Healthcare UK, Ex Deputy CEO Medical Research Council, Non-Executive Director and Mentor, Chair Digital Health and Social Care Innovation Centre*

We only notice innovation when it succeeds: and, in truth, it very rarely does. This book redresses this survivorship bias with a long-overdue enquiry into the causes of failure, and what we can do to avoid them.

Rory Sutherland, *Vice Chairman Ogilvy*

Much of what we call innovation these days does indeed suck and faced with a growing list of problems it's time to consider a radically different approach. The impeller approach offers an intriguing and exciting glimpse of what could be achieved if we dared to think and do things differently.

Adrian Swinscoe, *Best-selling author, Forbes contributor and strategic advisor*

It's really exciting to understand the role that just one person with a unique set of skills can play within the setting of innovation if you hunt them down and give them a platform to be themselves. The 'honeybee' truly goes beyond process and brings something quite unique. If you don't know who your bees are, find them! I encourage anyone reading this book to prioritise identifying these individuals to realise their true potential.

Debbie Bevan, *Executive Coach and freelance Marketing Director Debbie Bevan, Executive Coach and freelance Marketing Director Academie Ltd*

An insightful and well-evidenced overview of how and why we're getting innovation wrong through following an 'innovation funnel' approach and have done for the last decade at least. Watkins and May present a fresh, and in itself novel, approach to innovating, a paradigm shift in how to innovate in this very cleverly titled book, revealed early in the book and making perfect sense.

Dr John L Collins, *Disruptive Technologist Innovation Foundry Ltd*

I would recommend it to anyone who wants to understand what innovation is (and is not) and why to truly innovate we must think and act differently.

Marco Mohwinckel, *Healthcare Executive and Advisor*

This book challenges conventional thinking about how we innovate – the concept of the impeller, its wide application and its focus on the acceleration of progressive commercial ideas and early exposure of failures is a game-changer. It brings into focus the waste of talent, innovation and ideas created by traditional sequential methods of screening, reviewing and judging – instead the impeller approach improves, nurtures and delivers innovation by bringing ideas to life quickly, effectively and concurrently. It is an inspiring read.

Mark Sismey-Durrant, *Chair Cashplus*

Innovation needs to be re-invented before it becomes a dirty word because in the current environment, we really need to do something different and we need it quickly.

Phil Smith CBE, *Chairman IQE*

I think this an important book which highlights an issue that organisations need to address and may not even appreciate is there. In this sense, the book names a "naked emperor" and offers a response to those who accept the emperor needs dressing.

Stuart Turnbull, *Head of International Consulting Mannaz*

In this book, the authors propose that new approaches are needed and describe two methods which they believe will make a difference by 'impelling' innovation rather than by 'pushing' an idea. Recognising the desired outcome rather than excess concentration on up front detail required to get there. They propose firstly that ideas people don't have the skills to market and that it is better to form a company with an entrepreneur to go to market, sharing risk and profit. Bad ideas which can't sell should be dropped rapidly and without punishment. Secondly, they suggest that organisations will better spot useful ideas when they have within them people (They call them Bees) who have deep curiosity in the way of polymaths, able to scan the literature of many fields (named Meadows) for best outcomes and methodologies. Bees don't seem to me like easy people, and they probably need careful handling and nurturing.

Professor Martin Elliott MD FRCS, *Professor Emeritus of Cardiothoracic Surgery UCL. Non-Executive Director at The Royal Marsden Hospital, NHS FT, London*

Watkins and May raise a big unspoken issue in this book - the very low rate of success in innovation. The impeller model proposed is unique in trying to change the very process of innovation itself. Swapping from technology driven innovation, or from attempts to rigidly analyse what the market need is, to a much more flexible and dynamic market impeller pull model. A must-read analysis and new model for all in the innovation game.

Dr Chris Winter, *Managing Partner Brightstar Partners*

If I'd known then what this book tells me now, I'd have been bolder and upped our innovation pace. Read it and change 'sucks' to invigorate'. This book is my new bible. If it doesn't change your organisation find another company.

Iain Sanderson, *CEO, Vanwall 1958 Ltd*

I hope this book acts as a wake-up call that engineers are the best and most inventive leaders, and provides greater understanding of the corrosive effect of so-called 'experts'. Engineers look at things differently, solve problems, and develop ideas through naivety and experimentation. Ours is a life of risk and of failure, when we first try things they fail, but we gradually improve them and persevere. I think that this, as an approach to life, should be celebrated, nurtured and encouraged.

Sir James Dyson

Innovation Sucks!

Businesses spend billions on innovation with very little to show for their investment or effort. This book challenges some of the 'ingrained truths' of innovation and suggests a different approach.

Innovation is not the creation of a novel idea. It is the successful commercialisation of that novel idea. Rather than starting with a costly, time-consuming problem assessment that seeks to push potential solutions through an innovation funnel, an 'impeller approach' starts with possible solutions and gets the market to pull the best ones forward so they can fail fast or flourish fast. This approach is made possible by the addition of a 'bee' – a new type of integrative thinker who can harvest the existing knowledge from the 'meadow of experts'. Completely reversing the innovation process means organisations are much better placed to win in the market rather than focusing on finding theoretical solutions or clearing innovation stage gates. In addition, this approach also recognises that the people who shepherd the solution through the ideation and testing stage are not the same people who must then take that solution to market for successful commercialisation.

Given the current innovation failure rate, coupled with the fact that society is beset with multiple wicked problems, it's time to think differently and innovate innovation itself. This book is essential reading for Heads of Innovation and Commercialisation, Directors of Marketing, Heads of New Product Development and New Service Development, Strategy Directors, Chief Technology Officers, Government advisers and policy makers.

Alan Watkins is Chief Executive Officer (CEO) and Founder of Complete – a consultancy that specialises in developing enlightened leadership through individual and team development. Alan is unusual in that he advises completely different businesses in totally different market sectors, in different geographies and works with many different types of businesses from innovative tech start-ups to FTSE 10 giants. He is the author of several successful books, including *HR (R)Evolution: Change the Workplace, Change the World* co-authored with Nick Dalton.

Simon May is Managing Director and Co-Founder of Impeller Ventures which was set up to pioneer this type of novel approach to innovation. Impeller Ventures is also dedicated to tackling the huge waste that poor approaches to innovation create. With over 30 years of experience at the intersection of design, technology and business, Simon has developed brands, products, services, processes and business models for a range of organisations from start-ups, technology transfers and small and medium enterprises (SMEs) to corporates and multinationals across a range of geographies and sectors.

Innovation Sucks!
Time to Think Differently

Alan Watkins and Simon May

 Routledge
Taylor & Francis Group

LONDON AND NEW YORK

First published 2021
by Routledge
2 Park Square, Milton Park, Abingdon, Oxon OX14 4RN

and by Routledge
52 Vanderbilt Avenue, New York, NY 10017

Routledge is an imprint of the Taylor & Francis Group, an informa business

© 2021 Alan Watkins and Simon May

British Library Cataloguing-in-Publication Data
A catalogue record for this book is available from the British Library

Library of Congress Cataloging-in-Publication Data
Names: Watkins, Alan, 1961– author. | May, Simon, 1965– author.
Title: Innovation sucks! : time to think differently / Alan Watkins and Simon May.
Description: Abingdon, Oxon ; New York, NY : Routledge, 2021. | Includes bibliographical references and index.
Identifiers: LCCN 2020044546 (print) | LCCN 2020044547 (ebook) | ISBN 9780367681913 (hardback) | ISBN 9780367681920 (paperback) | ISBN 9781003134596 (ebook)
Subjects: LCSH: Creative ability in business. | Technological innovations. | Research, Industrial. | New products.
Classification: LCC HD53 .W38 2021 (print) | LCC HD53 (ebook) | DDC 658.4/063—dc23
LC record available at https://lccn.loc.gov/2020044546
LC ebook record available at https://lccn.loc.gov/2020044547

ISBN: 978-0-367-68191-3 (hbk)
ISBN: 978-0-367-68192-0 (pbk)
ISBN: 978-1-003-13459-6 (ebk)

Typeset in Bembo
by Apex CoVantage, LLC

Contents

About the authors

Alan Watkins

Alan is CEO and Founder of Complete – a consultancy that specialises in developing enlightened leadership through individual and team development.

Alan is unusual in that he advises completely different businesses in totally different market sectors, in different geographies and works with many different types of businesses from innovative tech start-ups to FTSE 10 giants. He consults with them on how to grow their revenues, transform their strategy, step change their leadership capability and develop their culture. Alan is a disruptive thinker and a modern business innovator, perfectly positioned to write a book on how to innovate innovation. He can take complex global concepts from multiple market sectors, integrate his own ideas with the wisdom of the crowd and come up with novel answers that have proven extremely helpful to the 100 different companies that constitute his client base.

Alan has written several books including *HR (R)Evolution: Change the Workplace, Change the World* co-authored with Nick Dalton (Routledge, 2020).

Alan is based in the United Kingdom (UK) and has recently been appointed as Visiting Professor at Kingston Business School, London.

Simon May

Simon is Managing Director and Co-Founder of Impeller Ventures which was set up to pioneer a novel approach to innovation. Innovation is the successful commercialisation of a novel idea and both parts are equally important. Impeller Ventures is dedicated to tackling the huge waste that poor approaches to innovation create.

Based in the UK and with over 30 years of experience at the intersection of design, technology and business, Simon has developed brands, products, services, processes and business models for a range of organisations from start-ups, technology transfers and SMEs to corporates and multinationals across a range of geographies and sectors.

Putting his Master of Arts degree (MA) in Innovation into practice and teaching the subject at the master's level, Simon has co-authored this book with the vision of encouraging academia, businesses and governments to change the way they think, conceive, fund and execute innovation.

He has contributed to two books as well as presents at conferences and seminars on the topic of innovation.

Success for both authors would be a re-boot in the innovation conversation. A greater awareness about the ineffective thinking and approach that currently underpins innovation is needed. And, perhaps more importantly, a recognition that a better way may already exist.

Acknowledgements

The world is accelerating and humanity is creating an increasing number of problems, or wicked issues for itself. As we struggle to emerge from a global pandemic, we are having to change the way we think about our lives, how we work, how we relate to each other and how we individually show up. We all hope that, as a species, we will be smart enough to innovate our way out of the problems we have created. That is why I wanted to write a book on innovation. My desire was spurred on when I met Jim Dawton and Simon May.

Jim and Simon have been chewing on the issue of innovation most of their lives and they made perfect partners in this project. Jim is a disruptive thinker and we have had many stimulating conversations on how the mind of an innovator works and whether we are born this way or whether we can develop our abilities. Simon, his business partner, provided a wonderful pragmatic counterpoint to Jim's expansiveness and is a great writing partner. Thank you both for enriching my life and helping me to think differently about innovation. I am delighted by what we have created together and I really hope it will challenge people's assumptions and help companies step change their own innovative capabilities.

I would also like to acknowledge Karen McCreadie for her unrivalled editorial prowess. Karen has again been invaluable in bridging the minds of two diverse thinkers in Simon and I. She has been tireless in her efforts to work with us and marshal the manuscript into a readable format and chase down all the references, many of which we couldn't remember the details of.

I would like to acknowledge Rebecca at Routledge Press for her responsiveness and encouragement in the production of the manuscript and her willingness to support us in this, my second book with Routledge and eighth book overall.

Finally, I could do none of this without the unwavering support and love from my wife Sarah. She provides the space and encouragement that allows me to write well and provides the precise critique of my ideas during our daily early morning walks. Innovation doesn't happen without such unsung heroes in the background.

I truly believe that humanity can innovate and develop its way out of our current predicament, but the clock is ticking and we need to speed up our abilities to go further faster. I only hope that this book may provide everyone in innovation with some of the rock fuel and inspiration we will need to finally address these wicked issues.

Alan Watkins

Jim and I have both separately and now together at Impeller Ventures been driven by frustration, the frustration around the huge waste in poor innovation, the frustration that with all the incredible academics and scientists we have in the UK we are still running behind on getting brilliant solutions to market. The impeller approach is really an on-going conversation; as we learn, we add, change or modify what we think. This book begins a passing on of those conversations that will hopefully inspire, enthuse and ideally make you more than a little uncomfortable to get you to think differently about what innovation actually means to you, your organisation and what you can do about it. I really hope that this starts your conversation about innovating innovation.

Meeting Alan and subsequently partnering with him on the book has not only injected a sense of urgency in the project but also provided the ideal foil to test and debate some of the more contentious aspects of our thinking whilst still allowing for an element of disruption where needed.

Thanks also to Karen who managed not only Alan and me to deliver our content but the enormous task of bringing it all together in a way that creates a product from our thoughts.

Thanks to Jim, my business partner, who started it all many years ago with an idea that he floated when we worked together at an agency about an A Team. Not *the* A team as not everyone we employed then were old enough to remember them but similar in the way it had specialists with particular skills. We all hated it at the time, but it is now the Impeller Approach!

Along my journey to the book I have been challenged, helped, encouraged and supported by many to think differently. Particular mention must go to Naomi Gornick, who sadly is no longer with us, but remains a powerful influence in my thinking on innovation from her tutoring on my master's course and conversations for years afterwards and, more recently, James Barlow, Professor of Technology and Innovation Management at Imperial College Business School, who helped shape my thinking and writing approach to the book in its early life.

Finally, thanks to both my partner Lindsay, who generously gave me (and continues to) the time and room to read, think and write, and my parents, Jim and Sue, for their constant interest and encouragement in everything I have tried; your support has always been greatly appreciated.

Simon May

Introduction

Why is innovation important?

This may seem like a stupid question. The answer is thought to be so obvious that the question is barely worth asking. But if you push past the blank stare and insist on a reply, whether from a Chief Executive Officer (CEO), Chief Information Officer, Strategy Director, entrepreneur, someone in the innovation space or someone in government, the likely answer would be that innovation is considered an essential facilitator of growth and financial prosperity, whether for countries or organisations. According to PricewaterhouseCoopers (PwC), "Innovation is becoming a competitive necessity for companies and should be delivering significantly increased revenue growth. If it's not, then executives need to be asking themselves what they could do to improve their innovation process".[1]

But, if you probe still further and ask additional questions such as, "What is innovation?", "What are you innovating for?" or "How do you know if your innovation initiatives are working?", you will quickly establish that there is no mutually agreed upon definition of innovation that is universally accepted. According to PA Consulting's *Innovation as Unusual* Report, this confusion is identified as one of the five innovation killers. In their survey, over half of respondents (53 per cent) said they used the term 'innovation' to describe different things, while 42 per cent agreed innovation is something they talk about more than they do. This suggests many organisations lack a clear innovation strategy – which can lead to wasted energy and resources.[2]

We are therefore in the paradoxical position where everyone recognises how important innovation is, but no one agrees what it is or what successful innovation actually looks like.

Everyone is talking about it and most people think they are doing it.

Just about everyone thinks it's important. And everyone mentions innovation as one of the few answers to counter economic bad weather, create competitive advantage and drive growth.

Whilst some recognise that innovation may not be working particularly well, they often dismiss this as being due to ineffective processes or people. Rarely do they recognise that there is something wrong with their version of the innovation process itself. More often, there is an assumption that they *are* innovating successfully because their chosen definition of innovation allows them to draw that conclusion based on how much money they spend on innovation projects or how many projects are happening at any one time. If this is the case, then they falsely claim they are successfully innovating.

We would argue that innovation effort is not the same as innovation output. Huge sums of money are thrown at innovation from government departments or earmarked within corporate budgets or corporate venture capital (CVC) but what is the return on that investment? Does the innovation effort bear fruit or is it just innovation theatre?

The evidence is overwhelming; innovation is failing on a massive scale. In the United Kingdom (UK) for example, organisations are flushing £64.7 billion down the drain each year on innovation projects that go nowhere. To put this into context, £64.7 billion is over half of the European Union's (EUs) annual budget, equivalent to the global expenditure on cancer drugs and greater than the United States (US) Department of Education's budget.[3]

We were told by an industry insider during the course of writing this book that an FTSE 100 company had invested £800 million into their CVC fund over a period of 18 years. That investment failed to return the cost of capital. They never acquired any of the start-ups they invested in and never partnered with any start-up they invested in either. Basically, the £800 million delivered £0 value to shareholders and yet the company had just agreed on a new injection of £400 million into the CVC. Sadly, this is all too common in the corporate innovation space.

Businesses spend billions making better products or services only to find consumers roundly reject them. Studies show that new products fail at the stunning rate of between 40 and 90 per cent, depending on the category, and the odds haven't changed much in the past 25 years.[4] The late Clayton Christensen, a Harvard Business School professor, argued that the failure rate was even higher. He stated that 30,000 new consumer products are launched each year in the US and 95 per cent of them fail.[5] Most innovative products – those that create new product categories or revolutionise old ones – are also unsuccessful. According to one study, 47 per cent of first movers have failed, meaning that approximately half of the companies that pioneered new product categories later pulled out of those businesses.[6]

Mergers and acquisitions are another way that businesses seek to innovate. But 'buying innovation' is equally flawed for the same reason that most mergers and acquisitions fail. The 'bought-in' unit is either suffocated by the bigger business or is side-lined and rendered inert. Google's acquisition of Nest, a home automation company that designs and manufactures programmable thermostats and smoke detectors for $3.2 billion, is a classic example of this. Initially, Nest was a stand-alone subsidiary of Alphabet, Google's parent company, but was merged back into Google where it then failed to widen its smart-home ambitions, leading to the departure of the CEO, Tony Fadell.[7] Again, the statistics around buying in innovation are dire. Companies spend more than $2 trillion on acquisitions every year. Yet study after study puts the failure rate somewhere between 70 and 90 per cent.[8]

In addition, what's reported is likely to be the tip of the iceberg. Often if projects cost less than a designated amount, they won't even be reported on – despite the fact that the designated amount may run into millions.

What is innovation?

According to the Chambers Dictionary, innovation is:

> *Innovation* n. the act of innovating; a thing introduced as a novelty; revolution.

The word itself dates back to 1540 and stems from the Latin *innovatus*, 'to renew or change', from *in* 'into' and *novus* 'new'. Innovation is meant to change things; it's meant to improve outcomes and solve problems and yet all too often it does neither.

The best definition of innovation we've ever come across is from the UK Department of Trade and Industry (DTI), which states that:

> Innovation is the successful commercialisation of a novel idea.

It is the combination of these descriptors 'successful commercialisation' *and* 'novel idea' that matter – bringing something novel to market which makes money or is at least sustainable while meeting a need, solving a problem or delivering value.

Innovation is not just the commercialisation of an idea; the commercialisation has to be successful. 'Successful' in this context doesn't have to mean money but it usually does. It is the financial success of the idea that determines whether value has been delivered. If there is no value, if it's not sustainable, if it doesn't solve a problem, make a product or service faster or better or it isn't wanted or valued by the market then it won't be successful and shouldn't be considered an innovation.

Innovation is also more than just the successful commercialisation of any idea. Potentially that is simply copying what's already gone before. Innovation needs to be novel. That may mean an old idea modified and applied in a new market or sector or used for a new purpose or it may mean a completely new idea.

Traditionally, the UK has been relatively good at the 'novel idea' part of the innovation equation. The UK is home to some fantastic universities, world-class academics, researchers and the intellectual horsepower needed to lead the world in a number of fields. But the generation of novel ideas alone is invention *not* innovation. As Hanadi Jabado of Cambridge University points out, "The UK leads the world in terms of research but if you look at the commercialisation of innovation, the UK lags behind". Except for a handful of people, like James Dyson, we have not been able to convert our invention capability into financial success. Too often the invention goes overseas to be commercialised.

China on the other hand has excelled at the 'successful commercialisation' part, although the ideas being commercialised were usually not novel. For the most part, China profited from copying existing products and making them faster, better and cheaper.

It may be clear to everyone involved in government or business that innovation is important but we must also accept that, currently, efforts to innovate are falling far short of what is possible and needed. Too much time and money are being wasted on projects that never make it out of prototype testing never mind getting to market. We believe we can achieve far better results with the resources we have by completely rethinking how we innovate.

It's time to rethink innovation

The world is facing a number of super complex 'wicked' problems – multi-dimensional issues that involve multiple stakeholders, have multiple causes and display multiple symptoms. To have any chance of sustainable progress, we need innovation to deliver multiple solutions that can constantly evolve as the issues evolve.[9] Whether the wicked issue is a viral pandemic, a global political regression, a climate change–inspired extinction rebellion, a global economic depression fuelling a new wave of poverty and even greater inequity, a parochial healthcare system unable to care, a wasteful food supply system that exacerbates obesity and is unable to adequately feed a growing population, a stigmatising approach to mental health rather than a positive focus on emotional wellbeing or an educational system that focuses not on the innate curiosity and capability of its children but on the need to pass a test, the list of wicked issues is endless.

Set against this desperate and urgent need we see the vast amount of money, time and human resources currently squandered on failing innovation initiatives. This worsening list of issues is a testimony to the fact that the way we innovate is not working well enough. This is not to say that we should close all the innovation departments but rather that it may be time to rethink innovation. We need an approach that allows us to start with the solution and by-pass some of the more expensive and time-consuming problem analyses. We need an approach that allows us to fail fast, learn from those failures and direct our scarce resources and budgets into innovations that can deliver much more rapidly.[10]

This book explores one such approach.

Part one of the book looks at why innovation is not delivering the required results. Chapter 1 explores why. Chapter 2 explores the flawed assumption that we must start with the problem and better understand the problem. An excessive focus on describing the problem is where most of the time and money is wasted. Part two of the book presents a different way to innovate using an 'impeller' approach – which we will explain in detail. Developed by Jim Dawton of Impeller Ventures, an impeller approach offers a new way to think about and execute innovation to ensure we can all go further and faster without the usual costly detours.

Most approaches to innovation are designed to propel or push a possible solution or product into the market. If you have ever sat in an aircraft that has propeller engines rather than jet engines, you may have noticed that the blades of the propeller are tilted slightly. They are not flat at a 90-degree angle to the fuselage. They are facing very slightly front to back in line with the fuselage. As a result, they create propulsion by pushing the air backwards to create forward momentum.

An impeller is the rotating component of a pump that transfers the energy from the motor that is driving the pump to the solution passing through the pump by accelerating the solution outwards from the centre. In the context of innovation, that means you only need one pump to handle many solutions. Both a propeller and an impeller provide thrust, but they generate momentum in a different way.

When you attach a propeller to an object, such as a speedboat, it moves with that object. Thus, the propeller is fixed to a single object. In contrast, one impeller pump can support multiple objects and is still operational even if an object fails. This distinction is key and offers a new way of innovating. Innovation sucks is not only a statement of fact about the current level of dysfunction in innovation but also a hint to one type of solution – an impeller approach.

Traditional innovation processes are problem focused. The propulsion wastes a lot of time, money and resources identifying the need, challenge or the key question in order to invent the right answer. Each individual invention then needs its own propeller pushing it forward. The invention must clear the gates of an innovation process to get to the market. When that innovation fails, the propeller is destroyed along with all the resources.

An impeller approach avoids this because an impeller creates a vacuum that sucks new ideas or technology into a market. If the innovation fails along the way, it doesn't destroy the impeller in the process. The impeller simply continues to suck other solutions toward the market. This is a crucial distinction.

The impeller approach is solutions-focused not problem-focused. It suggests multiple potential answers which better define the question. This enables innovation to fail fast or flourish fast. The key is getting to market not just finding a theoretical solution, which then needs testing. As Reid Hoffman, the founder of LinkedIn, once said:

> Launch early. Unless you're Steve Jobs, you're most likely partially wrong about what your theory was. So, launch early and often. Launching early attracts customer engagement, and it's the customer who's going to tell you what's wrong so you can correct it.

Remember, true innovation is the successful commercialisation of a novel idea not simply invention or even successful invention. It has to work in the market and add value – everything else is failure.

So successful innovation really does suck and the traditional-approach innovation also sucks in the sense that more often than not it fails.

Part one of this book covers the theoretical aspects of the approach. If you find it heavy going at times, either bear with it because the content is important to appreciate or, if you are keen to get straight to the practical aspects of the book and how to improve your innovation output, feel free to jump straight to the second part of the book. Chapter 3 onwards unpacks the impeller process in detail so you can see the component parts and how they work as a whole. For the record, we are not suggesting such an approach is the best or the only way to innovate, but we need to consider that there is a different approach that can yield better results. Impeller is one such process and, although it is not suitable in all sectors, it definitely delivers faster innovation solutions with less up-front investment or costs.

Innovation paradigm shift

Given that innovation sucks and society is beset with multiple wicked problems, we need a paradigm shift but it will not come from tinkering at the edges.

According to innovation guru Clayton Christensen, too much time is spent tinkering with 'efficiency innovations'.[11] Such 'innovation' may lead to process improvements that save money, but there is insufficient investment in the 'empowering' market-creating innovations that lead to new technology or service breakthroughs that progress society.[12]

Making these efficiency innovations is an important first step and can elevate profitability and performance but they are inherently limited – there are only so many ways to improve efficiency. We need market-creating innovations that lead to new technology or service breakthroughs that progress society, and that is only going to be possible if we break out of established thinking around innovation and re-imagine a new, faster, lower cost and more successful way to innovate *and* get to market successfully.

A paradigm shift is required not only because the way we are doing it now isn't working and we need better solutions to a growing list of complex problems but because the world now faces some unique threats. The COVID-19 pandemic will live long in the memory as a game changing, unique threat. When seismic shifts like this occur politically or commercially on a national or global scale, they are normally seen as negative and rarely viewed as opportunities for a wide-scale resetting of the way a nation does business or interacts with its neighbours. In a few short months, COVID-19 up-ended the global economy but it also did more to advance remote working and facilitate a shift to digital technologies than all other efforts in the past decade. All too often, many organisations believe they must minimise the damage and the disruption caused by crisis. But effective resetting or recalibration needs innovative thinking, not damage limitation. Damage limitation is effectively just tinkering at the edges. At the time of writing, the jury is still out on whether COVID-19 will trigger a genuine and sustainable paradigm shift in humanity's approach to the global problems we face or whether we will simply continue to tinker at the edges.

According to PwC, humanity's ability to rise to the challenge of an increasing number of global problems is complicated by the current rise of economic nationalism. The flow of talent, investment and ideas that have boosted companies' global innovation efforts may soon be impeded by the escalation of protectionist and inward-looking politics that we are now seeing in Europe and the US. Regardless of the reasons, which are themselves extremely complex, a move away from globalisation to economic nationalism could create significant negative, unintended consequences for innovation. As politicians and policymakers in the world's major economic nations look inward, the world of innovation is at risk. The policies that will flow from economic nationalism may prove self-defeating, in part by disrupting R&D activities for the new products and services that are needed to generate the jobs, growth and wealth of the future.[13]

Brexit or the UK's departure from the European Union and the COVID-19 pandemic both exacerbated this economic nationalism. In fact, PwC's study highlights that the US, UK and China are most at risk from potential changes in policy that could impact R&D efforts. Canada, Germany and France are most likely to gain if protectionist policies became a long-term reality.[14]

Of course, when the UK exits from the EU, there may be a corresponding opportunity to correct the endemic British 'lag' in successful commercialisation and stop the continued waste of the UK's potential. If we don't do this, then outside the European Union that 'lag' could easily stifle the UK's economic progress and mark a drift into irrelevance on the world stage. Such a scenario is even more likely post-COVID. If the UK is to prosper internationally and take advantage of the opportunities that may exist post Brexit, UK plc must hone its innovation horsepower and combat the potentially destructive influences that economic nationalism could impose on innovation. Any replacement of today's integrated and interdependent network with more self-sufficient, fully-functioning R&D nodes could easily mean companies losing efficiency and taking on higher costs if it is not managed effectively.[15]

British enterprise must shake up innovation so that we successfully commercialise the brilliant inventions we already come up with. Margaret Thatcher once called Britain a nation of shopkeepers. To prosper in the new environment, Britain must become a nation of innovators.

But it's not just the UK. US innovation has taken a battering over the last few decades; although often more successful at the commercialisation part than the British, they have looked to the East for their goods. Consumer's flocked to better and cheaper from the East, so innovation took a back seat in US business as it struggled to complete. China too is changing. Around $77 of venture-capital investment poured into Chinese firms from 2014 to 2016, up from $12billion between 2011 and 2013. In 2016, China led the world in financial-technology investments and is closing rapidly on the US, the traditional global pacesetter, in many other sectors.[16] China, having utterly mastered the 'successful commercialisation' part of the innovation equation, is now turning its considerable attention to the 'novel idea'-generation part. And they are doing so at speed.

China has been accused of state-sponsored commercial espionage and cyber-attacks designed to steal US and UK Intellectual Property (IP) and trade secrets in order to fast track that outcome – something that the Chinese government denies.[17] But what is not up for debate is that China has developed plans to become an innovative nation and published a new design policy, "with a view to moving from 'Made in China' to 'Designed in China'".[18] Unless the rest of the world follows suit, everyone else could be left in China's wake. One of the obstacles to China's progress will be its own version of economic nationalism.[19]

Part of the problem in the West is that we have become uncomfortable in the face of change. All too often when things look difficult, we hear clarion calls for 'back to basics' approaches or some other types of regressive, retrograde manoeuvres rather than a desire to embrace change and innovate our way forward. When people achieve a certain level of economic prosperity, their focus can often switch to self-interest and protectionism. They want to defend what they have rather than push forward into uncharted territory. They lose interest in change, preferring to maintain the status quo. Whilst this is understandable, refusing to change is simply not possible in today's world and certainly not desirable. Change is what makes life interesting and enjoyable. In fact, we would go so far as to say that change is vital in everything from commerce to mental health! Cultivating an attitude of continual re-invention, embracing a growth and evolution mindset, is what is required in today's fast-paced world. We need to develop a much more positive attitude toward change. We need to study change, the different types of change, the factors that influence the speed of change and how to drive change. Forget coping with change; we need to see it as a revitalising force in our lives. Certainly, in the UK, the ability to become a nation of innovators depends on it.

Notes

1 Percival D and Shelton R (2013) Breakthrough Innovation and Growth PWC www.pwc.es/es/publicaciones/gestion-empresarial/assets/breakthrough-innovation-growth.pdf
2 Chandraker A, Houmas H, Hogg J, and Reilly C (2015) Innovation as Unusual PA Consulting.
3 Chandraker A, Houmas H, Hogg J, and Reilly C (2015) Innovation as Unusual PA Consulting.
4 Gourville JT (2006) Eager Sellers and Stony Buyers: Understanding the Psychology of New-Product Adoption *Harvard Business Review* https://hbr.org/2006/06/eager-sellers-and-stony-buyers-understanding-the-psychology-of-new-product-adoption
5 Nobel C (2011) Clay Christensen's Milkshake Marketing *Harvard Business School Working Knowledge* https://hbswk.hbs.edu/item/clay-christensens-milkshake-marketing
6 Gourville JT (2006) Eager Sellers and Stony Buyers: Understanding the Psychology of New-Product Adoption *Harvard Business Review* https://hbr.org/2006/06/eager-sellers-and-stony-buyers-understanding-the-psychology-of-new-product-adoption
7 Metz R (2016) Nest's Biggest Problem Wasn't Tony Fadell *MIT Technology Review* www.technologyreview.com/s/601639/nests-biggest-problem-wasnt-tony-fadell/
8 Christensen CM, Alton R, Rising C, and Waldeck A (2011) The Big Idea: The New M&A Playbook *Harvard Business Review* https://hbr.org/2011/03/the-big-idea-the-new-ma-playbook

9 Watkins A and Wilber K (2015) *Wicked & Wise: How to Solve the World's Toughest Problems*, Urbane Publications, London.

10 "Fail faster, succeed sooner" is a core axiom in the field of innovation attributed to David Kelley, founder if IDEO.

11 Christensen CM, Bartman T, and van Bever D (2016) The Hard Truth about Business Model Innovation, *MIT Sloan Management Review* https://sloanreview.mit.edu/article/the-hard-truth-about-business-model-innovation/#:~:text=The%20hard%20truth%20about%20business%20model%20innovation%20is, the%20priorities%20associated%20with%20each%20business%20model%20stage

12 Christensen CM and van Bever D (2014) The Capitalist's Dilemma *Harvard Business Review*, June.

13 PWC (2017) The 2017 Global Innovation 1000 Study *Will Stronger Borders Weaken Innovation?* www.strategyand.pwc.com/innovation1000

14 PWC (2017) The 2017 Global Innovation 1000 Study *Will Stronger Borders Weaken Innovation?* www.strategyand.pwc.com/innovation1000

15 PWC (2017) The 2017 Global Innovation 1000 Study *Will Stronger Borders Weaken Innovation?* www.strategyand.pwc.com/innovation1000

16 Print Edition Briefing (2017) The Next Wave: China's Audacious and Inventive New Generation of Entrepreneurs *The Economist* www.economist.com/news/briefing/21729429-industries-and-consumers-around-world-will-soon-feel-their-impact-chinas-audacious-and

17 White E, Woodhouse A, and Yang Y (2018) China Denies US Accusations of Mass Cyber Espionage *Financial Times* www.ft.com/content/52de1d10-04bc-11e9-99df-6183d3002ee1

18 Sharma Y (2011) CHINA: Design Education for Future Economic Growth *University World News* www.universityworldnews.com/article.php?story=20111118193754828

19 PWC (2017) The 2017 Global Innovation 1000 Study *Will Stronger Borders Weaken Innovation?* www.strategyand.pwc.com/innovation1000

Part I

The current approach to innovation

1 Traditional 'innovation' & why it fails

In large businesses or organisations, there is usually an in-house innovation team. It usually consists of a dedicated group of people who are charged with coming up with new ideas that could make or save the business money, explore new business models or innovate around the existing products or services. This group may be a collection of individuals scattered across many departments reporting up the line or a dedicated unit reporting to the strategy or marketing director. The innovation group considers various problems or opportunities and tries to come up with novel ideas that could solve those problems or exploit opportunities. There are usually a lot of whiteboards and mountains of multi-coloured Post-Its in these innovation units. In smaller businesses, there may not always be a dedicated in-house innovation team. Smaller organisations more frequently borrow people from several departments to help with specific challenges or bring in innovation expertise from outside the business. The assembled innovation team may therefore include some employees and some consultants. Alternatively, a business, large or small may choose to outsource the innovation entirely to external innovation experts.

The composition of the innovation team may change depending on the business but what rarely changes is the way the group then thinks about and embarks upon innovation.

The innovation funnel and its origins

The way most businesses currently conduct 'innovation' is through some iteration of the innovation funnel. When people talk about the process of innovation, they are usually referring to this funnel. Typically, the funnel is a definition of 'need'. That need can be anything from an answer to a particular problem that aims to increase revenue, increase market share or deliver more value to customers. Without this need or challenge, the funnel wouldn't be relevant. The imagery of a funnel has been in use for several decades as a visual depiction of the new product development (NPD) process.

Thanks to the effort of the Executive Vice President of Applied Marketing Science, Gerry Katz, we have a better understanding of where the funnel came from.[1] One of the earliest attempts to create a flowchart within the innovation process appeared in *Design and Marketing of New Products*, a textbook written in 1980 by Glen Urban and John R Hauser.[2] Most of the real-world examples used as evidence for the efficacy of the flowchart came from the world of Fast-Moving-Consumer-Goods (FMCG). In this market, ideas may be plentiful and usually don't require any particular insight to imagine – a new biscuit variety, different toothpaste or washing powder with a new fragrance.

There is no problem to solve per se other than increasing revenue through new products. Their success is largely dependent on marketing, product positioning, advertising, etc. Sample products could usually be made alongside existing products with existing materials and resources and were therefore not prohibitively expensive or technically challenging. Small geographic launches could test customer interest relatively inexpensively before major investment. This environment is a world away from the environment we operate in today; even those in the FMCG space usually face stiffer regulation and testing protocols than in the 1980s.

In 1986, Robert Cooper published *Winning at New Products*.[3] In it, the author presented a diagram of the product development process broken down into five stages *preceded* by a process he called 'discovery', which included idea screening. Two years later, Cooper gave his process the name of *Stage Gates* – another term that has entered the innovation vernacular. Cooper's approach advocated a formal management review process in which innovation teams were required to come before high-level management committees to present their project so that the management could then make an informed decision about whether to green light the next stage or kill it.

The earliest use of the term 'innovation funnel' appeared in Steven C Wheelwright and Kim B Clark's 1992 textbook *Revolutionizing Product Development*.[4] Their diagram consists of three major stages, which they label 'Investigations', 'Development' and 'Shipping Products' which illustrates that the innovation process business usually follows to identify ideas for assessment, development and getting the successful ideas to market (Figure 1.1).

It's highly likely that the take up of the name 'innovation funnel' is largely down to the subsequent reputation of Kim B Clark. Clark was the dean of Harvard Business School from 1995–2005. Before he passed away in January 2020 innovation authority Clayton Christensen was Kim B Clark Professor at Harvard Business School.

In 1996, consultant Michael McGrath published his book *Setting the PACE in Product Development*.[5] Similar to the work of Cooper, McGrath's process advocated a periodic management review but also included the development of a formal 'business case' as a major phase before the project moves onto formal development. A similar diagram was put forward in 2005 by the Massachusetts Institute of Technology's (MIT's) Center for Innovation in Product Development (CIPD).[6] It has many of the characteristics of all of the preceding diagrams. It is a funnel which assumes multiple projects proceeding in parallel. As with all the others, the 'discovery' process falls *outside* the funnel in a stage called 'Opportunity Identification and Idea Generation'. What's particularly

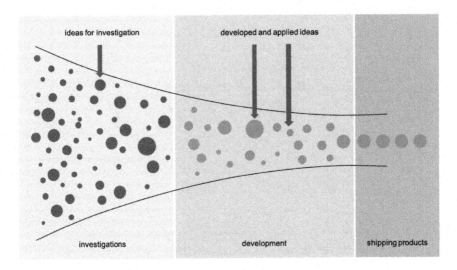

Figure 1.1 Wheelwright & Clark's Early Funnel

Adapted from Source: Wheelwright & Clark "Revolutionizing Product Development" (1992)

interesting is that none of the models or theories that have so completely shaped our thinking about innovation offer any advice about how to go about that ideation process. There are, of course, countless books, journal articles and seminar hours dedicated to it but the models themselves say little.

What seems to have happened is the widespread adoption of the term 'innovation funnel' along with an amalgamation of the various 'stage gates' within that funnel. Tweaks have been made along the way by various high-profile individuals in high-profile institutions, therefore cementing the validity of this approach. And, this approach is almost always the same regardless of the source of the model (see Figure 1.2).

The innovation funnel itself starts at Gate 0 – *after* idea generation. The idea generation usually comes from traditional R&D, but R&D is *not* innovation. R&D is the invention, the ideas, the science and experimentation to see what's possible. An idea or invention that looks promising is therefore pushed out of R&D into the innovation funnel for greater scrutiny.

Gate 0 marks the start of some sort of 'discovery' or insight gathering. The innovation team goes off and talks or workshops with various stakeholder groups from suppliers to customers to industry experts – whoever they believe will be able to shed some light on whatever issue they are looking at. Insight gathering might take three months, maybe longer. Once the insights have been gathered, the innovation team comes back together and uses those insights to scope out a potential solution. That will take a few more months. A business case is then created for the most promising ideas, which will help decision makers determine which to take forwards and which to ignore.

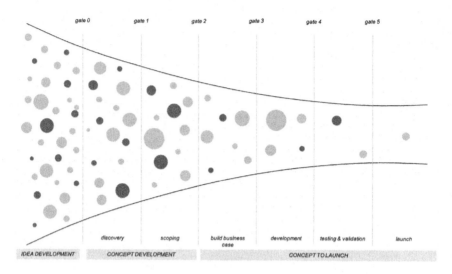

Figure 1.2 The Innovation Funnel

Concepts will be developed and their respective business cases are then re-presented to the decision makers who send the team back to test the viability of the best concepts. That might take another six months, often longer. At this point, at least ten months have lapsed. Money has already been spent, often a substantial amount of money, and yet there is nothing much to show for the effort.

The concepts considered most interesting are then sent off for testing and validation. This may involve the creation of prototyping or system changes. They are then put to the market to get some test feedback. By this time, the process is probably 12 to 15 months down the line. More time, more money with no concrete results and the market has already moved on. Based on the response to the tests, the business might then decide to roll out one or two 'innovations' or reject them and go back to the drawing board.

What's ironic is that for all the attachment to the visual of a funnel, the innovation funnel is not a funnel; it's a filter. If it were a funnel, everything that we put in at the start would come out the other end, but that doesn't happen. Instead, ideas are systematically filtered out so that maybe one or two of the ideas that went in come out . . . eventually. This may seem like unimportant semantics but it's not because it alters our thinking and behaviour around innovation.

By calling it a 'funnel', we try to keep ideas and projects *in* the funnel far longer than they should be. If it were called the innovation filter, we'd probably try to get things out as soon as possible. The world is littered with examples of 'innovation' that limped through the innovation funnel or stuttered into the marketplace when it should have been cancelled years earlier.

One such innovation was Motorola's Iridium – a constellation of 66 low earth-orbiting satellites that would allow subscribers to make phone calls from anywhere on the planet (see break out box). Knowing when to stop innovation is every bit as important as knowing when to start. Failing fast and cutting your losses so you can divert scarce recourses to the projects that show real promise, as opposed to stubbornly backing doomed projects, is crucial to successful innovation.

Motorola's Iridium

Communication satellites, in use since the 1960s, were typically geostationary satellites that orbited at altitudes of more than 22,000 miles. That meant chunky phones and an irritating voice delay while making calls. Iridium's innovation was to use a large constellation of satellites orbiting at approximately 400–450 miles. The result would be a phone similar in size to any other mobile phone at the time with imperceptible voice delay. The engineer who came up with the idea shared his idea with his manager who wasn't enthusiastic. But then Chairman Robert Galvin and later his son Chris Galvin were convinced that Iridium was going to transform Motorola's fortunes and gave the project the green light.

The problem was need – it solved a problem very few people actually had. To access the solution subscribers would need to buy a $3000 handset and pay up to $8 a minute to make a call. Despite this Iridium was launched in 1998, with then Vice President Al Gore making the first phone call. To reach that launch stage, Motorola had invested over $5 billion, $180 million of which was spent on an advertising campaign to attract the 52,000 subscribers it needed just to cover the interest on its project debt. Only 10,000 people subscribed.

Iridium was pushed through the innovation funnel out to market even though all the evidence suggested it should have been killed off years earlier. The idea behind Iridium was that there were still large parts of the world that did not offer mobile coverage – making those areas accessible was the perceived opportunity. But, in the 11 years it took from concept to development, cellular networks had spanned the globe, effectively solving the problem and eradicating the apparent opportunity. What's almost unfathomable, is that Iridium was developed in two stages: 1987–96 (development of the technology) and 1996–99 (construction and launch of the satellites). This later stage was, by far, the most expensive and yet by the time it was initiated in 1996 Motorola executives knew that the cellular network had effectively destroyed their market. On top of which they also knew they had still not solved design, cost and operational problems, and yet they continued anyway.[7]

Innovation corrupted!

We believe that our pre-occupation with 'innovation funnel-type thinking has had a detrimental impact on innovation. For the most part, the consequences of this thinking have been unintentional but they have converged to muddy the innovation waters and obfuscate results.

It's not working. Or, at the very least, it's not working as well as we need it to if we are to lift productivity and embrace a rapidly changing commercial environment. If you already agree with that sentiment and don't need convincing further then feel free to jump to Chapter 2 or even part two where we dive into the new approach.

There are six big problems caused by this old-fashioned type of innovation thinking that prevent us from making real progress. They are:

1   The 'why' is missing
2   Poor support for innovation within the organisation

   • From the top
   • By the system

3   A pre-occupation with process over outcome
4   Defensive thinking bias
5   Thinking/doing is out of balance
6   Insufficient focus on the 'valley of death'

The 'why' is missing

The funnel approach to innovation fails to consider the 'why'. It may propose a systematic 'how' but it ignores the 'why'.

In truth, it's not just, "Why is innovation important"? that is typically met with a blank stare. "Why do we innovate"? or "Why do we spend all that money on innovation"? usually elicits the same confusion and bewilderment. Eventually, we might hear responses such as, "we innovate because that's what we do" (it's one of our values) or "we innovate because it is important". Often what people want to say but rarely do is, "we innovate because everyone around us is doing it and we don't want to look out of step or be left behind". This may not seem important but we believe that this lack of 'why' or lack of clarity around the motivation driving innovation is instrumental in its eventual failure.

Traditionally in business, there are plans – business plans, marketing plans and even financial plans but rarely innovation plans (or its older brother the Innovation Strategy). Planning for the future based on certain existing assumptions is relatively straight forward but planning for the new is difficult. Once we have identified what that new is, a project plan can then be easily created. However, there is a gap in the thinking about how to translate what a business needs for the future into reality. In nearly all the books available on innovation, the main focus is on the 'how' as the why is assumed to be too obvious to mention. We all need to innovate; here's how to do it. The bit that is repeatedly ignored is why, as a business, we are choosing to innovate and what we want to achieve through the activity.

In their seminal *Harvard Business Review* article on managing uncertainty, *Strategy Under Uncertainty*, the authors, Courtney, Kirkland and Viguerie, suggested that even in the most unpredictable environments there is a lot of strategically relevant information that can be used to reduce the uncertainty. For example, in most markets it is possible to identify clear trends, such as market demographics, that define the potential demand for future products or services (something Motorola either didn't do or ignored). There is also usually a number of factors that whilst currently unknown are knowable – with the right analysis. The uncertainty that remains after trends and analysis have been considered is known as residual uncertainty. Residual uncertainty is supremely important to innovation strategy.

Four levels of residual uncertainty

According to the authors, there are four levels of residual uncertainty:

* A clear enough future (level 1)
* A second viable alternative future (level 2)
* A range of futures (level 3)
* True ambiguity (level 4)

With innovation, too many decision makers seek to reduce residual uncertainty using the standard strategy tool kit – market research, competitor analysis, value chain analysis, Michael Porter's five-forces framework, etc. But these tools are insufficient to reduce residual uncertainty. In addition to underestimating residual uncertainty, strategy decision makers also underappreciate the *strategic postures* a company can take in relation to the uncertainty or the *portfolio of actions* that can be used to implement that strategy.

Strategic postures

There are three strategic postures that a company can take, depending on their ambition, courage and confidence:

1   Shaping – shapers aim to drive their industry toward a new future of *their* making
2   Adapting – adapters take the current reality and evolve or react to opportunities as they arise
3   Reserving the right to play – this is a specific form of adapting where decision makers are seeking to make incremental investments today to put the company in a privileged position should a possible future reality play out

Depending on which posture an organisation wants to take, they can engage in three actions. They can make big bets which require major capital investments or an acquisition. Big bets can result in a large payoff if they work or redundancy if they don't.[8] Alternatively, the strategic decision makers can hedge their bets by trying to secure a big payoff from the best-case scenario while minimising losses in the worst-case scenario, Finally, there are usually a number of no-brainer moves or quick wins that will probably pay off regardless of the level of uncertainty.

Where the future is clear enough (level 1), the why of the innovation is usually clear and the decision is often relatively straightforward. But as the uncertainty increases, which is the world in which we are increasingly in, the tendency is to throw up our hands in confusion and work on pure instinct.

Decision makers believe the unknown is unknowable even with the right tools. So most vacillate between survival and all-out growth – both require a business to do something differently.

Innovation is almost always the answer suggested to both challenges. But innovation is only the approach and not the potential solution to the problem. A business can address the survival and growth problem by trying to do more of the same, do things better, more efficiently or at a lower cost (adapting) but unless there is significant change in the approach to innovation, then such strategies are only really sustainable in the short to medium term.

The world is changing and changing fast and unless actionable opportunities are identified on a regular basis and we change the way we innovate, then the ability to move a business forward will always be limited.

A greater appreciation of uncertainty is needed along with a better understanding and application of the tools we can use to reduce residual uncertainty. These tools will facilitate a much clearer 'why' (and why not). A clear why or reason to proceed or not proceed is needed if the opportunities are to be adequately grasped and a better future designed.

Organisations are generally very good at identifying their internal problems and identifying incremental improvements to those problems (adapting and no-regret plays). Such incrementalism is useful; but once we've optimised all the identified internal areas for improvements, adapting the 'no regret' mindset can become a hinderance.

Looking inside the business is easy; looking outside the business is not. Once the bulk of the internal process improvements have been delivered. one of two things can happen: the person in the role that has successfully optimised internal processes feels that their job is done and moves on to a new role (either leaving to do more of the same externally or repeating the process in a different division) or a more senior executive sets a new direction and kicks off a further round of incrementalism.

But we need much more than this to succeed now and into the future.

Overall, way too much innovation is started without a clear strategy and strong strategic 'why'. Instead, innovation is started so that someone can tick the innovation box.

Poor support for innovation within the organisation

The innovation funnel is a stand-alone model designed to provide a road map that can make the innovation process successful. But such a funnel says nothing about the why of innovation or the support that is required to make innovation work. Both clarity about the purpose of innovation and appropriate support for innovation are crucial ingredients for its success. Motivation and support are both ignored by the funnel model.

Two different types of support can be differentiated as necessary to drive innovation: support from the top and support by the system itself. Sufficient senior sponsorship is often lacking. How many Chief Innovation Officers are there at the board level with the full responsibility for innovation activity? Typically, someone on the board will have this responsibility as part of their remit and therefore it will only have part of their focus.

When a Chief Operating Officer (CEO) or other senior executive says, "I want this, we are going to do it", it changes the conversation and focus in the business. Up until that moment, everybody is often invested in finding reasons not to innovate. They want to be creative and 'do' creative things. But individually, they don't want to be the person who made the decision to green light an innovation project that then fails. They don't want to be the one that is asked awkward questions on cost or overspending. They don't want to be the one that has to stand up and justify a choice if that choice fails. It's too risky for them personally.

Most staff still conform to the widely held belief that taking unnecessary risks is career limiting. This is a very real quandary for executives and businesses. We heard a story from a reliable source that one of the luxury car brands is still spending millions on R&D for combustion engines. Everyone knows that the future is not combustion but when asked why the company chose to continue to spend so much money on R&D in a dying area, the response was, "We don't have a choice". The logic was simple, if they halved the R&D budget, it would need to be reported to shareholders. If something then happened to the cars, say a recall on brakes, even if it had absolutely nothing to do with R&D or the reduction in budget, it would be reported alongside the R&D budget cut to make it appear causal and the share price would tank and heads would roll. Everyone knew the company was throwing away millions unnecessarily but that was better than the alternative. And the fear kept the charade in place.

This was born out in the PA consulting report into why innovation fails, where the number one 'innovation killer' was 'fear'. Around 58 per cent of respondents stated that they are unlikely to back high-potential but risky innovations, while overzealous risk management ranks as the top reason why brilliant ideas fail. A significant minority (47 per cent) of respondents stated that they are not striving to be pioneers, suggesting that almost one in two organisations today do not even aspire to radical new thinking.[9] Hardly surprising when radical new thinking can get your fired!

This can be changed but only if the CEO or person of a similar seniority commits to the innovation so that everyone else can breathe a sigh of relief.

This commitment and support from the top gives implicit permission for everyone to stop finding all the reasons *not* to do something and think instead about how to make it happen.

Unless innovation is given the green light at the top, it's very difficult to pull it off in business and it's almost impossible to shift a culture of caution. Very often, innovation is seen as risky, but the smart, forward-thinking CEOs know that it's actually much riskier not to innovate. The speed with which the world is now changing means that a competitive advantage, even one that has been enjoyed for decades, can disappear in an alarmingly short space of time. According to Professor Richard Foster from Yale University, the average lifespan of a company listed in the S&P 500 index has decreased from 67 years in the 1920s to just 15 years by 2012.[10] Fifty-two per cent of companies listed in the S&P 500 have disappeared since 1960. Considering the similarity in markets, the longevity of companies on the FTSE is likely to be similar. New entrants can move quicker and leapfrog existing innovation in record time, unencumbered by a large global business structure.

Far from being a threat, if handled properly, innovation can be a significant opportunity for renewal and growth but it will almost certainly require a shift in mindset and culture within a business. And that shift usually comes from the recognition, right at the top, that innovation as we know it is not working and there has to be a better way.

Without that recognition, innovation will continue to be viewed as a risk where everyone in the business is constantly applying the brake instead of the accelerator or using established processes to protect themselves going forward.

The second area of poor support is the system itself.

Even if the leaders of a business support the innovation, it can still fail if the desired approach to innovation is not supported by the system. A leader may look at innovation and say, "Yes, we need this, let's do it", but they may recognise that the business is not capable of creating the desired breakthrough or converting the idea into a commercial success. Drawing on a survey of 246 CEOs from around the world, PwC found that while the eyes of the CEO are fixed on innovation the body of the organisation is not always following it.[11]

CEOs may support the invention or new idea, but if the system and business infrastructure – the budget, people and skills – is not in place, then the innovation may still fail. In the PA consulting report, the fifth 'innovation killer' was 'reluctance to invest'. When ideas fail for avoidable reasons, the cause most frequently cited by respondents is a lack of budget, people or skills (29.9 per cent). Simply, the resources required for innovation are not made available.[12]

This isn't always down to a lack of will or support from the top; it's simply the nature of the business at that time. There is often a whole raft of legitimate business reasons that can prevent an invested leader from pressing the innovation 'Go' button. Increasingly, businesses are having to respond to the accelerating world and leaders are accepting that they have to get leaner and faster; and as the world gets more complicated, they don't always have the internal resources to make certain things happen. According to the PWC 20th CEO

Survey, 77 per cent of the CEOs are concerned that key skills shortages could impair their company's growth. And it's the soft skills they value most that are hardest to find. "Creative, innovative leaders with emotional intelligence are in very short supply. If anything, they're even thinner on the ground than they were in 2008, when we asked a similar question".[13]

Innovation is just one area that is at the sharp end of this resource problem and it is flagging up the need to outsource innovation capability. This need is likely to increase – especially for the large global brands that are not necessarily attracting the type of people they need, compounding the risk of poor innovation success. Generation Y and the digital natives behind them are looking to work for the Google's of the world not Proctor and Gamble. They want work that is meaningful and makes a positive difference to the world as well as a better work/life balance than their parents achieved.

When there is insufficient support from the top or in the system, innovation initiatives are likely to fail. It's too easy for them to disappear or fall through the cracks if no one is really driving them or the system doesn't support them.

A pre-occupation with process over outcome

The innovation funnel model is a road map for the process of innovation but the map is not the territory. And, the focus on process has had a detrimental impact on outcome.

Ask most people in business and they would say they want greater growth and prosperity. Frequently, innovation is seen as one way to achieve that. As a result, business leaders, government officials and senior executives want to find people to help them deliver that outcome. Unfortunately, the lack of a clear why and a definable target have conspired to switch the focus from the outcome to the process. Everyone has stopped looking forward to what can be achieved, instead they are looking in the rear-view mirror seeking to de-risk the decision and justify or validate their choice so they won't be blamed if things don't work out. This backside-covering from both the commissioner of the innovation and the provider of the innovation means that too many barriers are erected toward the outcome and everyone misses the opportunity innovation can deliver. They are no longer looking at why the innovation is being sought in the first place, what problem needs a solution or how something can be improved.

They just follow the process.

The destination becomes secondary to the journey. And whilst that approach may work in philosophy (enjoy the journey, instead of being too focused on the destination), it absolutely doesn't work in innovation. The whole point of innovation is to create something new, better or different that will make or save money or otherwise add value. If that outcome is never reached, then what's the point? Too often what happens is that the innovation team busies themselves building endless roads to nowhere.

Focusing on building an innovation process means effort is invested in laying out a series of steps to follow, defining what activity is required and the expected output for each step. A process focus defines the amount of time and money that should be spent on each activity and allows staff to follow it in the same way that they might assemble flat-packed furniture. There may be training courses or access to in-house experts, but this will be to ensure a level of compliance to the process and techniques recommended rather than the delivery of the outcome.

The reduction of innovation to a process has occurred for many reasons. Firstly, since most innovations fail, when a project works the process used is often adopted – particularly if the project team recorded what activity led to their success. The business then decides this process should be used for all innovation efforts. Repeatability is mistakenly thought to be the key. While the business rightly wants more innovation, it fails to understand that the conditions and environment that the initial project team worked under are unique and may be difficult to replicate. There is no innovation crank shaft that simply needs to be rotated to spit out the innovation – the need, environment, team, budget and timeline will all insert multiple variables that make consistent replication very challenging. Even as a starting point to learn from, such a process is tricky as the learnings are rarely fed back into the process. Sadly, a process that may have worked only once just becomes the norm. That said, having an approach, even if it is built on a one-time process, is better than not having any approach.

The second reason for mistakenly relying on a process is that if all innovation projects follow the same path, it makes it easy to measure and report progress. If the terminology for the process is the same, then the audience for the reporting will be able to understand what is happening and hopefully identify when something is not working. This is critical as there may well be multiple projects running at the same time, managed by different teams across the business and taking time to understand the nuances of each project will cost the senior management team time. It will also help when the time comes to select projects to invest further in and projects to kill off. If we can evaluate them all as 'oranges', then we can separate the good from the not so good. Evaluating a fruit basket is just too daunting to the uninitiated.

Finally, the process itself acts as its own success measure. The challenge with innovation is that the new thing that we have come up with is probably still a few years away from contributing to the company. This means that any remuneration directly tied to performance is also in the future. So, the process acts as a way of measuring its own performance, partly based on the traditional project measures of delivering on time and on budget as well as other potential measures such as user feedback (not to be confused with sales) and what the press or other influential bodies might say at the time of launch.

The only thing that businesses really pay attention to is how an innovation is tracking through the process and whether they are sticking to budgets and meeting timelines. As a result, innovation is becoming a tick box exercise, rather than a serious quest for new, better or different. The driver is never, "Is this a great idea, will it deliver value"? Instead it becomes, "Can I demonstrate I tried to innovate and justify the cost without losing my job or creating a disappointment or a miss, leading to market embarrassment or a fall in share price"?

Only when leaders wake up to this futile pretence of innovation does it become possible for a company to start to genuinely innovate. Only when leaders say, "keep trying new things, I support you", will people in the business be liberated to focus on the challenge with less fear about the repercussions and less reliance on the process.

Outsourcing innovation

Having a process coupled with a lack of internal resources often creates the opportunity to supplement innovation teams with consultants or agency staff. This is often the preferred approach rather than hiring or developing existing internal staff. Insourcing innovation is preferred partly because it avoids any increase in head count and budget and partly because of the inability to recruit suitable hires.

If the decision is to insource innovation, this might involve hiring innovation consultants to acquihiring (a combination of 'acquisition' and 'hiring') where an innovative business is bought or brought into the parent business to recruit its employees, without necessarily showing an interest in its current products or services. The potential benefit of acquihiring is that the new employees might trigger a new innovative and creative culture which then permeates the whole company.

If a company decides to insource disruptive capability, such a move is most often taken in the early stages of innovation when the external expertise can complement existing efforts rather than add to the confusion or work against existing efforts.

Ironically, many new innovation consultants and some established providers seek to differentiate themselves by drawing business leaders' attention to this futile preoccupation with process over outcome. However, such warnings usually fall on deaf ears. In the end, nearly all providers are forced into the game of building roads to nowhere, rather than delivering a solution.

A preoccupation with process over outcome has become endemic in most organisations, partly because such a focus often works in a sales environment. A buyer or procurement department needs to be certain about what they are buying and buying a process is easier than buying an answer. So, a consultant that comes in to sell an answer is normally dismissed as ill-informed. Why? Because there is a widespread belief that delivering a solution at this early stage is impossible if insufficient time has been spent on looking at the client company, the market and the potential going forward. Selling an approach and a process is much easier. This is especially true if the seller's process bears some sort of resemblance to the company's own process. Such an offer seems to resonate and buyers feel 'aligned'. Alternatively, the buyer might feel that their approach is not working and will set out to buy a process or approach that is deliberately different from their own.

Either way, the external supplier is forced to quote and invoice for a process, not an outcome. Instead of proposing something that might just break the deadlock, innovators are often trapped by process; so they seek to come up with some funky new terms to mask the pointless charade they are participating in. They obfuscate the problem by adding in a few more steps or stages to the road to nowhere. Building such a 'new' process creates the pretence of *looking* different. All of this is just noise – the end result is still a process and not an outcome. This is akin to saying to corporations "don't worry that this road won't take you anywhere, our road-building expertise is second to none and we have added neon lights to our road since we last spoke to you".

Another common ploy to distract purchasers from the truth is that sellers may over-emphasise parts of the road-building process. A classic example of this faulty thinking is the idea that research should start with the customers. Consultancies selling their innovation capability will ask to be paid to research what customers want. This idea that innovation should be based on what customers want is so deeply engrained that it has almost become an innovation mantra. The position being that when it fails, there is someone new to blame. It's the customers fault because they told us what they wanted and then didn't buy it.

There are, however, many examples of extremely innovative and bold companies who chose to shape their industries and never asked the customer what they want, including Apple, Cirque du Soleil and IKEA. Distinct process steps often simply present an opportunity to justify costs or blur where the costs actually occur but do little for the eventual outcome.

In addition to the process outcome confusion, there are four reasons why buying in innovation expertise from outside the business can be especially challenging:

1   Businesses don't know how to evaluate what they are buying
2   Businesses usually have an innovation budget that needs to be justified
3   Businesses struggle to focus on outcome – even if they wanted to
4   Attitude to risk

BUSINESSES DON'T KNOW HOW TO EVALUATE WHAT THEY ARE BUYING

Innovation starts with good thinking. The thinking may focus on a new way to open up an existing market, the creation of a new market, the design of a new product or a new way of using and marketing an existing product. The list of possible outcomes is endless.

But how do we put a price on thinking?

How can we if we don't even understand the nature of thought? Very few leaders think about thinking; even fewer have any technical training in the construction of cognition. So, it is hardly surprising that purchasers are unable to put a price on thinking and are unable to evaluate what they are buying. The problem is exacerbated by the fact that until the innovative thinking starts, it is impossible to know what the outcome of that thinking is likely to be. So, if the purchaser doesn't understand thought, doesn't really know what is likely to emerge from innovative thinking and they have no way of quantifying the quality of that thinking, all they can do is fall back on a process and simply choose the innovator who is offering the 'right process' or the 'right price' that fits their budget.

Say a company has a budget of £100,000 for innovation; if the potential suppliers know that budget, they will invariably say the innovation project will cost £100,000. The company then needs a way of understanding what they perceive they are getting out of the innovation supplier. The easiest way to do that is to describe a process, not an outcome. The process is quantifiable and concrete – there are steps to take, people to meet, interviews to conduct; all of which can be broken down to arrive at a price.

There may be an implicit assumption (usually wrong) that the more expensive a supplier is the better they are, but this is usually just an attempt by the supplier to differentiate themselves when perhaps no differentiation exists. Besides, if the client isn't even clear about what it is they expect the supplier to deliver – just that they will come up with some good ideas – then who is to really say if they failed or not. This means there are a lot of people in the innovation space pitching their process and making good money for delivering absolutely nothing – over and over again. Whilst this may be a good business model for those selling nothing, it is pointless for everyone else.

Rainmaking Ventures is a notable exception of external specialists in the innovation space. With offices in London, Berlin, Copenhagen and Singapore, they don't consult or charge fees; they assess markets and come up with possible opportunities with a company. If, based on their extensive start-up experience, they identify an opportunity both parties believe in and want to pursue, they partner with the company to create a NewCo. That business is then driven by a team of specialists who grow the business toward successful exit (sold back to the company). Both parties financially invest in the business and they either win together or lose together.

But for the most part, buyers purchase a process where the seller wins and the buyer loses. Often the buyer of innovation doesn't know if the person pitching will deliver or whether they just talk a good talk. As a result, it's often viewed as safer to buy a process from an established name. This is incredibly ironic given that anyone who has studied the history of innovation will realise that the best breakthroughs rarely come from established consultancy brands. The greatest breakthroughs usually come from mavericks working outside the system, unconstrained from mainstream assumptions.[14] Nevertheless, time and again, purchasers return to what they consider to be 'safe sources' even though those sources are often unable to deliver any breakthroughs.

If a company needs to innovate and they don't have the expertise in-house, they have two options. They can hire an unknown quantity or they can recruit a big-name consultancy. If a company hires a smaller innovation consultancy or finds a company that creates quantifiable results, albeit intermittently, the reputational risk is significant. Often, hiring a big name established consultancy such as McKinsey's or BCG is a safe bet because they will be able to cover costs in court if something goes wrong and the person who authorised the innovation isn't going to lose their job.

The last thing a global business really wants to do is try a new option, or new business model or new product under their brand. If it works, it might be okay. However, if it doesn't work, they will be slated in the press and their share price could nose dive. It's just not worth the risk.

Modern business is not just about results, it's about managing expectation and managing the narrative. Even if the innovation fails and it costs millions, if that innovation project was conducted by a big-name consultancy, the failure is unlikely to affect the share price significantly or have a long-lasting effect on the consultancy.

It's a little like fund managers. The behaviour of fund managers is pretty consistent despite claims about differentiated value adds. They are following the crowd, safe in the knowledge that if it doesn't work, they can justify the loss. If they step outside the norm and follow a different path, they will struggle to justify that loss. Both options result in loss, but one is considered recoverable and the other isn't. The same is true in medical practice. Doctors that go the extra mile in the interests of their patients could struggle to defend such actions in court if their intervention is outside the norm in the treatment of the patient's condition – especially if the treatment doesn't work.

Current innovation practice follows the same herd mentality. Everyone knows it's not working. But, as long as it can be explained or justified, the risk is too great and the reward too unpredictable to change. So, everyone keeps focusing on the process and not the outcome – even though it's wasteful and ineffective.

BUSINESSES USUALLY HAVE AN INNOVATION BUDGET THAT NEEDS TO BE JUSTIFIED

Right from the start, innovation is viewed as a cost, a gamble, rather than a value-add, and that cost or budget needs to be justified.

A company may allocate a certain amount of money to innovation. They may have to do so for a number of reasons, from the genuine need to innovate through to managing the narrative in the city. Whatever the intention of the exercise, the task of purchasing the innovation often involves or ends up in the procurement department. The procurement department's task is to select the 'best' innovation supplier to deliver the project. But as we've already said, many don't know how to evaluate what they are buying.

Plus, their primary job is to meet the brief for the lowest cost. Often, a procurement professional's remuneration is linked to cost savings, so they are incentivised to secure the cheapest supplier. To be fair, they may well know the innovation is likely to fail anyway because it usually does, so buying the lowest cost option makes some sense when viewed in that context.

Price alone is a poor way to assess suppliers. Hiring the most expensive supplier on some assumption that they 'must be good' is as ill-informed as hiring the cheapest to save money or assuming they offer an inferior service. Surely the only thing that matters is whether that supplier can actually deliver what was promised and the investment makes a positive contribution to the business.

Instead it's a race to the bottom to find the cheapest, regardless of quality. Not only does this not deliver the best outcome but it just leads to gamification.

If faced with the option of a supplier who is charging £100,000 for the project and another who is charging £60,000 for the project, the procurement person is probably going to believe they did a good job hiring the cheaper supplier. If there is no focus on output, then it doesn't even matter that the £100,000 option could have come up with an idea that would make the company millions and the £60,000 fails.

BUSINESSES STRUGGLE TO FOCUS ON OUTCOME – EVEN IF THEY WANTED TO

Say, for a moment, that a business wakes up to the colossal waste of time and money in their innovation area and decides to do something about it. What do they do? If they decide to outsource their innovation needs to a consultancy, that consultancy will need to invoice the business at some point. But right now, the business is set up to accommodate process. These transactions must take place within a fiscal year and 'fit' accepted accounting norms.

The most obvious way to solve the innovation problem is to shift the focus from the process to the outcome. Pay external innovators or reward internal teams based on the quality of their ideas, not on their ability to nurse nonsense through an innovation funnel or build a road to nowhere. But even if innovation professionals would be willing to work on a retainer and/or a 'no-outcome no fee' basis (and few are), how would the finance department manage the investment? Charging an initial fee with a performance element or success fee is very hard to accommodate or police in most businesses. Accounting systems can't account for it and they don't know how to manage it; so, again, it's just easier to fall back on pricing the process and submitting an invoice.

The financial management of a business can easily get in the way of the leverage and growth and disruption of that business, purely because a more outcome-focused pricing structure won't neatly fit into some set financial boxes.

Certainly, many industries, such as advertising, have tried to institute a performance-related pay structure. Making it happen proved almost impossible partly because the accounting systems just couldn't handle it and neither the buyer nor the seller were experienced enough in having different types of conversations about payment and couldn't differentiate between the options.

There is no real reason why more people couldn't operate like this – especially in the innovation and creative space. One of the big stumbling blocks however is the financial accounting and management of it. Another is the risk that the commissioner of the innovation doesn't execute properly or doesn't deliver their end of the bargain. Remember, there are two discrete stages in innovation: idea creation and commercialisation. How does the inventor know that the business will successfully take that idea to market?

Such an approach also requires that the consultant has a great deal of faith in their own ability to come up with the goods time and time again. For those that do, the upside is significant, not just for the innovator but for the buyer of the innovation through the removal of a great deal of the risk. They only pay for what works. There are now a couple of innovation companies, including Impeller Ventures and Rainmaking Ventures, that take an equity stake in businesses that they create thereby bypassing these accounting stumbling blocks. Both buyer and seller are in it together as financially invested partners.

ATTITUDE TO RISK

The challenge with innovation is that, by definition, it is focused on coming up with something new, different or better and translating that into a beneficial commercial or organisational reality. However, no one knows at the start of the project what that new, different or better something will be. This creates risk. Obviously, that risk exists whether a business buys in the innovation expertise or seeks to innovate internally, but the market is more likely to know about that activity if the expertise is bought-in. Markets are somewhat schizophrenic about risk. On the one hand, analysts want to see that companies have reduced their risks, even though that's boring. On the other hand, they want companies to take certain risks because they know that there is no growth in boring and therefore no likelihood of larger returns.

What they are ideally looking for is a balanced risk. A well-managed innovation approach with an injection of excitement is what generates income, business value or moves share prices. Getting that balance right is tricky. Get it wrong and share prices as well as heads tend to tumble. It's a little wonder that innovation is viewed as such a poisoned chalice.

Given the considerable downsides for getting it wrong, it's easy to see why those involved in innovation plump for what they believe is a sensible approach. Cover off the basics and point to the safe, well-managed aspect of an innovation process while vaguely signalling an exciting potential future contained within the disruptively clever innovation. No need to spook the analysts.

Of course, innovation is never just about the project. It's never simply about the idea and how much that idea is worth. It's about what that innovation can do to change perception and therefore the effect it will have on a company's performance, income, value or share price.

In an attempt to manage the risk, corporations fill the void with a process. Companies looking to innovate usually don't know where the innovation journey will lead them; they don't even know if it will lead them anywhere. At best, they may have an area of investigation that they direct the innovation team toward but they don't know what will emerge from the project or the quality or value of that output. But whilst the output is vague, the process – the innovation funnel – is not. There are clear stages, with actions, budgets and deliverables. What's interesting is that businesses seem prepared to pay for the steps of a process even if it delivers nothing. At least we can justify a process. We can point to a process and explain the time and money spent on it. What we are very resistant to paying for is an 'outcome', even if that outcome could transform business fortunes. Granted, outcome definition is difficult but this shift of attention away from the outcome or the results of innovation has had a profound impact on the effectiveness and success of innovation across the board.

Defensive thinking bias

Thinking about innovation as a funnel fosters defensive thinking because the desire to protect the solution in some way immediately distorts the sort of answers that we create. If innovation is tasked with the creation of some IP that can be protected, then what goes into the funnel will be thought of as 'small IP'. It's just fledgling 'small IP' because it has yet to become fully fledged IP that can be fully protected or patented.

There are four ways to protect any IP we create:

- Patent – this protects technical features and processes and allows the patent holder the right to make, use or sell the invention that the patent refers to; a patent typically lasts up to 20 years and must be paid for and renewed if required
- Copyright – this gives automatic protection to original written, dramatic, musical or artistic works; it usually lasts 70 years after the originators death unless steps are taken to protect it further
- Design right – this protects the physical appearance and visual appeal of an object; registered designs can be maintained up to 25 years, subject to payment and renewal every five years; registration can often notify competitors about what someone is doing and make their IP more attackable or by-passable; design rights don't have to be registered to be protected in court; defence can be made based on the fact that a design has been first to market and used by the public
- Trademark – this protects any sign that distinguishes goods and services from competitors; it can be maintained indefinitely, subject to renewal every 10 years[15]

As a business or innovation team decides what to put into the innovation funnel, the idea probably doesn't have much shape, there is usually no product yet so we can't put a design right into the funnel, we haven't said anything yet so we can't copyright it and nothing actually exists yet so we can't trademark it. Patent is the only possibility and yet patents protect technical features of something tangible – either a product or a process. If, when assessing what enters the innovation process funnel, the aim is to create something that can be defended in court, then the answer is likely to be biased towards a product or process that can be protected. But a better answer might be something else entirely, such as a business model change or a paradigm shift in thinking about an issue. For example, Airbnb didn't usurp the Hilton Hotel group by building better hotels or providing fluffier towels; they up-ended the market by matching people who had spare accommodation to people who wanted accommodation without owning a single property themselves.

Innovation that is constrained by a desire to create something that can be protected will constrain the depth and breadth of thinking around what the answer may be. Seeing innovation from a strictly proprietary standpoint can immediately diminish its relevance.

It is becoming increasingly difficult to protect IP anyway. The world is moving on. We live in the share economy; many more companies and entrepreneurs take an open-source approach. By the time one company sues another over breach of copyright or patent infringement, the market has already jumped to the next newer, faster, better model that leaves both companies in the dust. This often means that the things that have been innovated may be nowhere near as important as the development of innovation capability. The ability to continuously take new ideas to market faster, fail faster and evolve faster is where the real competitive advantage lies.

The key is to test the viability of the idea quickly and *create* the market rather than necessarily being the first to market or the only one in the market. Remember the statistics from the opening chapter. Most innovative products that created new product categories or revolutionised old ones were unsuccessful. According to one study, 47 per cent of first movers have failed, meaning that approximately half the companies that pioneered new product categories later pulled out of those categories.[16]

First mover advantage is not what it used to be. Very often the pioneer in the space wastes too much time and effort educating the market first. In a new space, customers don't know if the product is good or bad until they experience the next entrant. It's the classic restaurant scenario where we eat Turkish food for the first time. We have no idea if it's good or bad. We may know if we like it or not but we have no way to gauge quality until we can compare the experience to another Turkish restaurant.

Entrepreneurs should never become disheartened when someone enters the market doing something similar because the market needs to experience something *similar* to be able to decide which is best. Instead of protectionism, if business sought to continually improve and innovate, they would stay ahead of the pack anyway. The creation of a monopoly may sound attractive to a CEO or senior business leader but customers hate monopolies – they demand choice. Focusing on 'best' not 'only' is the more realistic and constructive on-going strategy. Other players are what help to make the market.

We have become so used to the idea that we must crush the competition that we have missed the opportunity that competition can create. The old way of thinking would suggest that the best place to open a new shoe shop is where there are no other shoe shops. But actually, the smart play is to open a shoe shop next to three other shoe shops – just have better shoes. With three other shoe shops on that street, consumers know where to come if they need shoes, they won't necessarily know that if we choose an out of town location.

In business, the natural instinct is to hold on to ideas and attempt to seek a competitive advantage from them or to expand into a new, un-tapped market. This is understandable but outdated thinking.

Thinking/doing is out of balance

Invention is, at least initially, a cognitive activity. It's a thinking pursuit. And yet the innovation funnel is a doing process. What do we need to do at each stage to produce innovation? The innovation funnel doesn't even acknowledge the ideation stage – it happily skips past that. This focus on action is hardly surprising. We live in a world dominated by action. In our professional lives, we are almost exclusively judged and rewarded for what we do as opposed to what we think.

Back in 1975, writing in the *Harvard Business Review*, management guru Henry Mintzberg stated, "Study after study has shown that managers work at an unrelenting pace, that their activities are characterised by brevity, variety, and discontinuity and that they are strongly orientated to action and dislike reflective activities".[17]

Thinking is a reflective activity.

And yet our space for that reflective thought and idea generation has shrunk considerably since Mintzberg wrote his article over 40 years ago. That statement was made before the Internet, before mobile phones, smart technology, constant connectivity and the tsunami of information that crosses our desks on a daily basis across multiple channels. If it were true then, it's exponentially true now.

Innovation requires staring into space. It requires thought experiments, doodling and the willingness to ask a lot of questions as well as the dedicated accumulation of new or different knowledge to fuel it. In a world that is much more interested in action, it becomes extremely challenging to price the activity required for genuine innovation to emerge.

We are just not prepared to pay people to sit around and think. One of the reasons is we don't really understand the nature of thinking. So, if we don't understand thought, how can we know who our best thinkers are, or whether they are doing it 'properly'. Most people just think. Very few people reflect on *how* they think, which is often even more important than *what* they think. Improving the *quality* or the *how* of our thinking can add massive value on top of improving the *content* of our consciousness or *what* we think about.

Most people have noticed that some days they can come up with good ideas while on other days they draw a blank. But they never take the next step to discover why the content and quality varies. At best, they may attribute the variability between their 'good thinking' days and their 'bad thinking' days to some random external condition like the weather or the office environment. Such false attribution leads many companies to waste an enormous amount of money building 'creative spaces' or running off sites in a desperate attempt to increase the quality of the thinking of their workforce.

Such manoeuvres are really a testimony to the profound lack of understanding that corporations have about the nature of thinking. It has become a cliché to see creative agencies in advertising, media or tech sectors that are awash with grass carpets, brightly coloured walls, festooned with massive whiteboards or forests of Post-Its. In their desperation, companies will throw in a climbing wall, table tennis equipment or even a children's slide! And all this expense occurs even though thinking is an internal phenomenon, not an external process.

Ironically, if you study some of the greatest breakthroughs in science and technology thinking in the last 100 years, they often occur in pretty ugly spaces. Some of today's tech giants including Google, Amazon and Hewlett Packard were all started in a garage – hardly an inspiring external space! Desperate not to miss a trick, some companies have even tried to ape the grungy nature of the environment that many innovators work in, giving rise to urban 'industrial chic' architecture full of hipsters. Now trendy or beautiful spaces are all well and good but they have very little to do with thinking.

Often the idea itself, the flash of genius, doesn't actually come out of left field. It emerges from convolving two distinct tangents of conversation that merge in a split second.[18] One moment, there is nothing as the innovator chews over the challenge, doodles on their notebook and allows their mind to turn over the situation; the next moment, a killer idea emerges that might save or make millions, may solve a crucial problem or improve lives. But such phenomena are not random flukes.

For most, including many inventors, invention can appear somewhat mercurial. But this is only because most people have not studied thought, so they suffer with unconscious competence. People with a talent undervalue their talent and therefore think it is natural (which it is) or that everyone can do it (which they can't). We see this phenomenon play out with singers or comedians when they don't' really know how they are achieving greatness and will institute all sorts of rituals in order to maintain access to their ability to write great songs or come up with new jokes.

What is clear is that quality thinking is not the inevitable outcome of systematically following a step-by-step 'innovation process'. It may show up in three seconds or it may never show up at all, particularly for the unconsciously competent. The ideas that emerge may be terrible or they may be utterly brilliant. If we understand the nature of thought, we can definitely increase the probability of emerging great ideas consistently and on demand, as we shall explain later.

The generation of brilliant ideas is not necessarily time-constrained. And this itself creates a commercial problem. Imagine that the brilliant idea arrives three seconds after the innovator has been briefed on the challenge. If a business had outsourced their innovation challenge to a consultancy, how would they feel if they were then told three seconds later that they had an answer already and the idea would cost £50,000? Even if the business agrees that the idea is phenomenal, we are so deeply entrenched in a time-based remuneration system that it would almost certainly meet with resistance. £50,000 for three seconds work is hard for most people to stomach. And, interestingly, it would remain challenging even if that £50,000 idea could generate millions in additional revenue. All that will matter is the time it will take to come up with the idea and the inability to quantify that within an established time-based, process-addicted model.

Faced with this reality, and the stubborn refusal to even entertain the true purpose and end point of innovation those involved in coming up with the new ideas often don't have a choice and are forced to comply with the road-building paradigm and its emphasis on process. They bundle up their thinking time, staring into space time and doodling time with concrete steps and processes so that the commissioner of the innovation feels more comfortable about what they are getting for their innovation dollar so they can, in turn, justify the cost.

The commissioner of the innovation, whether internal or external, rarely takes the experience of the innovator into consideration and instead falls back to time-based rates or rates based on process because the alternative is too vague and confusing. And it's incredibly difficult to justify if the thinking doesn't produce much. Unsurprisingly, those seeking innovation are much more willing to budget for it based on agreed time and process inputs than unclear or unknown quality outputs.

Insufficient focus on the 'valley of death'

Finally, and perhaps most importantly, our pre-occupation with the innovation funnel and therefore the current way we think about innovation completely disregards or at least diminishes the importance of commercialisation and getting to market successfully. Innovation is about results. At least, it should be. We believe that the only meaningful real-world definition of innovation is, 'the successful commercialisation of a novel idea'.

Of course, getting an invention out of the innovation funnel to successful product or service and then getting that new offering to market is not easy. It's also traditionally not that fast.

The funnel itself can get congested. There is a clamour for scarce resources as multiple innovation projects compete for funding, expertise or time. In an effort to remove some of the congestion, the innovation industry has collectively redefined the 'finish line' or endgame. Logically, the finish line should be demonstrated success in the market through the delivery of value to the business, department, customer or user. Instead, the finish line has often been brought forward to 'Gate 5' (see Figure 1.3) – the end of the testing and validation stage.

This has, in effect, created a premature stop or false finish line. On the up-side, this fabricated finish line allows those involved in the innovation space to point to good ideas and working prototypes as evidence of success. On the down-side, nothing much ever changes. No new revenue is generated, no customers are delighted, no value is derived.

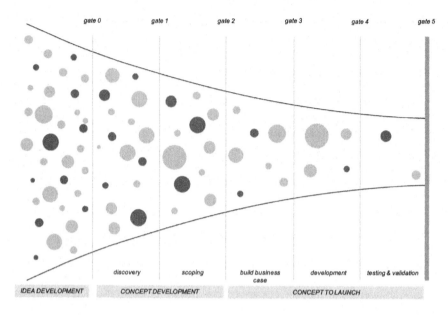

Figure 1.3 New Innovation Funnel Finish Line

In addition, this shift in what business considers 'success' means there's now a valley – often known as the 'valley of death' – that needs to be crossed between test and validation of the invention or concept and the launch and subsequent success of that solution in the market (Figure 1.4).

At this point, the research resources have been scaled back because a working prototype has been successfully created. But that is just part of the journey and pretending otherwise is ridiculous. At the same time, the commercialisation resources have not yet scaled up. The gulf this intersection creates is the valley of death and its relevance and importance is seriously downplayed in the current thinking about innovation.

Often the people involved in the invention are so passionate and excited at having successfully tested and validated the invention that they simply assume that the world will beat a path to their door. Successful launch and commercialisation are inevitable. They are not.

Launch and successful commercialisation are not a progression or tinkering of the solution, it's a completely new process aimed at getting that innovation to market. The role of the innovator in coming up with a new idea and validating its usefulness *is* effectively over. To take an idea and make money from it or ensure that it delivers value requires different people, different departments and different skill sets. It is this disconnect or transition between testing and validation and successful commercialisation that creates the valley of death and leads to so much 'failure' – even though it is often not viewed in those terms.

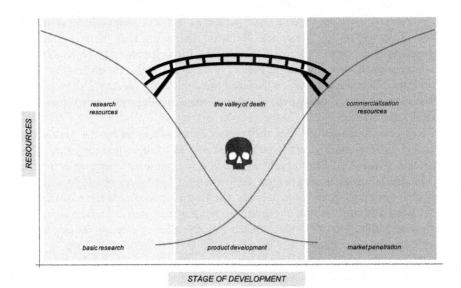

Figure 1.4 The Valley of Death

Meet 'The Boffin'

What happens in the traditional innovation funnel model is that someone in a laboratory, let's call them 'The Boffin', comes up with a great idea. It shows promise and sounds exciting, and so the Boffin is given the responsibility of taking that idea to the next stage. The Boffin is given a budget and encouraged to bring together a team to explore the idea further. The Boffin has never done this before but is excited to get their work recognised by a wider audience. The idea seems to have legs and management is keen to see what can be done next.

As the Boffin develops a new product or service idea that has not been offered by the company before, they move into the next phase of development. Now, they need to promote the idea within the business, get additional funding, get the development working and get to market. But the Boffin is an R&D person. By now they are out of their depth and have moved away from what they are really good at. The idea eventually becomes a product and moves into the next phase: sales. The Boffin knows all about the product so they become Head of Sales – because they are the only person that can explain and demonstrate the idea in order to sell it. Only the Boffin isn't a natural sales person. They are an inventor. As hard as they try, the product fails to reach its full sales potential and the resulting decline is blamed on the Boffin. Eventually the Boffin is asked to leave the business rather than return them to the place where they operate best: R&D.

This is unrealistic and unfair on everyone – not just the Boffin. The bit that the Boffin is really good at was invention. They should have stayed in R&D

where they could use their skill set most effectively. Instead, it's automatically assumed that they are the best person to lead the project because it was their idea and they are passionate about it. Again, the logic here is relatively sound. Thomas More, author of *Utopia* said, "It is naturally given to all men to esteem their own inventions best".[19] People are highly motivated by their own ideas. Behavioural science has since proven More's assertion. It's called the 'Endowment Effect', where we overvalue our own ideas and over value what we already own.

It is therefore assumed that the person most motivated by the idea is the creator and they will naturally be the best person to drive it through to commercialisation. This rarely ends well and is a significant contributor to the inevitable failure that occurs. The endowment effect is a double-edged sword when it comes to innovation. Initially, the Boffin's passion for the idea may be infectious and inspiring for the team but getting that idea to market requires a broad and diverse set of skills which the Boffin doesn't possess. What's more, the Boffin usually knows that they don't have the necessary business or sales skills, but they learn to live with it in the hope that they will be able to muddle through and see their idea come to life. Plus, ironically, having someone who is so invested in the idea lead the project can also mean that it is allowed to live on long after it should have been killed off.

One of the most unhelpful consequences of the valley of death is that it creates two completely separate worlds (Figure 1.5).

Those involved at the discovery stage to the testing and validating stage are measured on how well they *spend* money against the project plan and are often

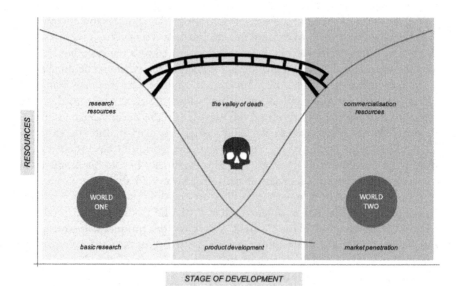

Figure 1.5 The Two Worlds of Innovation

incentivised to spend the entire budget. In contrast, those involved in the commercialisation of the idea *after* testing and validation are measured on how much money they *earn* and/or how successful they are in the market.

This means that the people involved in the invention should be a completely different set of people to the people required for the commercialisation. Only they rarely are. The Boffin is expected to be a jack of all trades and master of none as they navigate a commercialisation process they have no experience or interest in. The skill set and mindset of invention are completely different from the skill set and mindset of commercialisation. Both are incredibly valuable. Both are necessary. But, usually, they are mutually exclusive and the two worlds don't tend to talk to each other about how difficult, albeit different, their respective tasks are. The inventors of the world, the scientists, technicians, engineers and R&D people, are fully focused on invention and they will spend *all* of their budget and more if they can get it to pursue those novel ideas. Contrary to popular myth, none of these individuals want to be entrepreneurs or want to run businesses or take the invention to market. It's not what interests them and it's not their skill set.

They, quite rightly, want to hand it over to someone else and go back to spending money on invention – pushing the envelope in their labs or innovation units. This outlook is totally understandable and it is also a sensible use of their knowledge and resources. But their lack of ability to communicate the work to date exacerbates the hand over to the next stage and someone needs to take it to market or implement it; otherwise what's the point?

At a corporate level, this is costly and inefficient. The world is littered with examples of corporate invention ignored or not actioned at the eventual expense of the business. Kodak's invention of a digital camera is a classic case in point. Although Kodak created the digital camera, they were understandably reluctant to cannibalise their film business; so instead of following a bold strategy to shape their industry, they reserved the right to play by investing in the technology. They even understood trends in the online sharing of photos. Where they failed and what ultimately led to their bankruptcy was that Kodak didn't realise that online photo sharing *was* the new business, not just a way to expand their photo printing business.[20]

In government, the issue is perhaps even more pressing. If the innovation is government funded with industry's co-investment, the companies that may take the innovation to market need to be domiciled in the country of that government; otherwise, the tax payers of one country are subsidising the profits of another country. But once the innovation is out of the innovation funnel, companies from all over the world can buy up the IP, which has been de-risked with the aid of significant government funding. Under the existing innovation funnel model, this effectively means that in the UK, for example, millions of pounds in UK government funding is being spent to make overseas companies wealthier. For example, a US or European company can pick up what comes out of the innovation funnel and cash in on the invention. Sir James Dewar invented the Thermos flask but forgot to patent it, allowing the

German Thermos Company to do so; hence why we enjoy a hot drink from a Thermos not a Dewar. Richard Trevithick built his Puffing Devil (the father of all steam trains) but he died penniless.[21] Today when we think of an MP3 player, we think of an iPod; but Apple didn't invent the MP3 player. Serial British inventor Kane Kramer did in 1979 when he was just 23 years old! Unfortunately for him and his co-inventor James Campbell, they let the patent lapse and the rest as they say is history.[22]

Remember, innovation is the successful commercialisation of a novel idea, not just the invention of that novel idea. The UK may excel at generating novel ideas. but if the inventors can't or won't convert those ideas into commercial success then the UK will remain a nation of inventers, often government-funded inventors, helping the world to profit at their expense.

Of course, there are always exceptions, and some innovations do successfully cross the valley of death and make it to market but they are far rarer than we might like to think.

This shift of focus from outcome (the successful commercialisation of a novel idea) to process (the creation of a validated novel idea) means business continues to spend a huge amount of time and money to come up with novel ideas that are then shelved or shoved in a cupboard. Even if those novel ideas and successful prototypes are pushed out the door at market launch, there is insufficient appreciation of product life cycles and the journey that the product is likely to make from launch to successfully commercialisation.

Adoption curve

In his business bestseller *Crossing the Chasm*, author Geoffrey Moore shed more light on the valley of death by introducing the technology adoption life cycle (Figure 1.6) to represent how new products (technology and otherwise) are assumed to proliferate the market. Figure 1.6 also includes the percentage of any market that adopts a new product or service at different stages in that life cycle as outlined by Everett Rogers. According to Rogers, people tend to adopt new technology at varying rates and the relative speed of adoption can be plotted as a normal distribution with the primary differentiator being an individual's psychological disposition to new ideas.[23]

Bizarrely, whilst this life cycle model has become central to our understanding of how a product or service gains market share and prominence in its sector, the original research that gave rise to the model examined potatoes! Specifically, how a new strain of seed potato was adopted by American farmers. The model essentially describes the market penetration of any new product in terms of the psychographic profile of various customer groups who are attracted to the product at different times in the product life cycle.[24] It is also worth pointing out that the numbers attributed to each customer cohort are at best indicative as they rest on the assumption that the rate of innovation remains constant with time, which is manifestly not true.[25] That said, they still provide a useful insight into the potential size and type of customers at each stage.

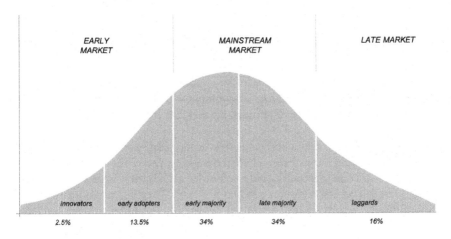

Figure 1.6 The Technology Adoption Life Cycle

First, there are the innovators who account for about 2.5 per cent of the market. Innovators in this context are the customers who are actively and aggressively seeking out new products, especially in the tech space. These customers are intrigued by what's new and what's possible. Their endorsement reassures other customers in the market that the product could be worth buying.

Early adopters, as the name suggests, are also keen to buy-into new product concepts very early in their life cycle. They find it easy to imagine and appreciate the benefits of the new product and are willing to put up with a few glitches to reap that benefit.

Those people who queue outside an Apple shop in the pouring rain to get their hands on the latest iPhone are almost always innovators or early adopters – they love getting their hands-on stuff first when hardly anyone else has it. They make up the early market, which accounts for about 16 per cent of the entire market.

The early majority and late majority make up the mainstream market and represent 68 per cent of the entire market. While the early majority shares the early adopter's ability to see value in the new product or service, they are more driven by practicality. They want to wait until the product is more proven and the glitches have been ironed out. The late majority are similar but they are keen to wait even longer before buying the product; they want the new product to be cheaper through market competition and choice and they want to make sure the product has established a high enough standard before they will purchase it. Needless to say, penetrating these markets is critical for long-term commercial success.

What's especially interesting is the impact that technological advance and global connectivity is having on the speed of adoption. For example, in December 2005 smartphones had penetrated just 2 per cent of the US mobile phone market. By December 2016, 81 per cent of the US mobile phone market owned a smartphone.[26] Figure 1.7 shows the time to reach 50 million users in a variety of products or innovations.

Finally, the laggards are those who may eventually make the purchase. They represent the late market and account for about 16 per cent of the entire market. Their reluctance may be driven by money or, in the case of technology products, a fear of technology or unwillingness to learn how to use it. From a marketing and market-development perspective, it's not worth targeting the laggards.

In theory, as is so often the case, this model makes sense. It's logical. We know these people in our lives. The friend who is always the first to get everything (they still have a Betamax video recorder in the attic) and the friends who wouldn't even accept a certain product as a gift. They are just not interested. So intuitively, it feels right. The model assumes that in order to commercialise a product or service invention, the innovation team simply needs to work the curve from left to right focusing on the early market and then the mainstream market, while letting the late market look after itself. Success in each market creates momentum, which automatically launches that product or service into the next market. Except, in real life, it doesn't work like that.

What Moore found was that there were cracks or chasms in the bell curve life cycle (Figure 1.8)

When a new product or service goes to market, its success is not an automatic, simple or linear march to market penetration. There are gaps between the different customer groups that, if not accounted for and managed, can see a product or service slip into oblivion.

The first crack is between innovators and early adopters; too often the innovation team will secure the interest and attention of the innovator group who

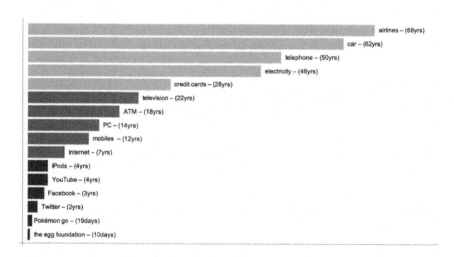

Figure 1.7 Time to Reach 50 Million Users[27]

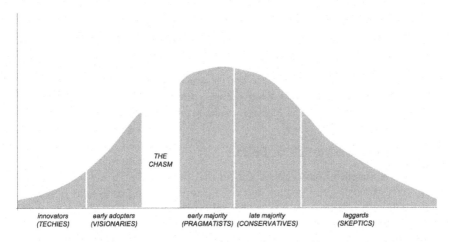

| innovators
(TECHIES) | early adopters
(VISIONARIES) | early majority
(PRAGMATISTS) | late majority
(CONSERVATIVES) | laggards
(SKEPTICS) |

Figure 1.8 Moore's Revised Adoption Life Cycle

will buy the product or service. This is encouraging but it's often nowhere near as encouraging as the business assumes it is. The market size of innovators is relatively small. Even if they successfully straddle that crack and attract the early adopters, the new concept needs to reach the mainstream market to be considered successful.

A similar-sized crack can be found between the early majority and the late majority and between the late majority and the laggards; but the gap between the early adopters and the early majority is not a crack at all, it's a chasm. There is a huge gulf between getting the early adopters to buy your new product or service and getting the early majority to follow suit. Virtual Reality (VR) is a great example of this. Initially, only the geeks bought VR. Customers had to be serious enthusiasts because it was expensive and not very good. The processing power wasn't sufficient to make the experience seamless and appealing. VR has attracted early adopters but it is years, possibly decades, away from attracting the early majority who are looking for bug-free, accessible products that improve their lives.[28]

The gulf between enthusiastic early adopters and the practical early majority is significant. And yet Moore suggests that most businesses don't even realise the chasm is there. They are so excited to have attracted innovators and early adopters that they assume their work is done and the product will be an inevitable success. What they don't always appreciate is that even if they have managed to secure interest from those customer groups, they only account for 16 per cent of the market, and 16 per cent of the market is unlikely to deliver sustainable long-term results.

It is this lack of capability to understand how a product is adopted in the market and therefore how to successfully navigate the valley of death that serial entrepreneur, former CEO and Angel Investor Sherry Coutu CBE picked up on in her *Scale Up Report*.[29] Coutu identified that a great deal of investment in innovation never returns value on that investment. She therefore argued that governments would actually be better served investing in scaling up businesses that are already successful and taking them to greater success rather than endlessly investing in the process or stages before market success. Coutu believes such an approach would deliver a better return on their investment and she's probably right. If innovation never delivers the results it was set out to deliver in the market, then there is zero return on investment, time and time again.

But our innovation is not failing

There are currently two types of stances that people take on innovation: those who recognise that the money and time poured into innovation is not delivering enough or could deliver more real-world value and those who are still convinced that their innovation is working.

The first group is likely to believe that the shortfall in results is caused by poor people in the wrong roles or poor process, and those factors will definitely play their part. But the statistics on the failure of innovation remain relatively unchanged over several decades; tinkering with roles and processes is not the answer.

As for the other group, we fully accept that there are people working in the innovation space who don't believe their innovation is failing. The way we currently think about innovation makes sense on so many levels; investors or funders need to be reassured about what they are going to invest in. The innovation team therefore outlines what they are going to do based on a predetermined stage-gate process. The team then moves through the innovation funnel and reports progress against the project plan. Once an innovation project is authorised, whether in government or industry, as long as the innovation team do what they said they were going to do in the project plan, following the deliverables outlined at various stages, everybody's happy.

The team may reach the end of the funnel and, as long as they've done everything on time and on budget, the project is considered a success. So much so that those involved in these 'successful' projects are congratulated, often given more money and encouraged to go back to the start of the funnel and start the whole process again. As a result, people are being habitually rewarded for what is effectively a cycle of activity, not results. Those people and their managers and reports believe they are doing innovation whereas actually what they are doing is invention, which is a necessary first step but a very long way from successful commercialisation of that invention. Even if they manage to successfully reach the test and validation stage, there is the valley of death to contend with.

This is the way that government and industry perceive innovation. Currently, everyone is utilising some form of the innovation funnel because they believe that they can 'do' innovation. But innovation is a noun, not a verb. Technically we can't 'do' innovation, we achieve it. Again, it would be easy to think this semantic distinction doesn't matter but it does. It's distracting us from the real outcome of innovation which is not the successful development of a novel idea but the successful commercialisation of that novel idea.

The idea of an innovation funnel is therefore profoundly unhelpful because it shifts the focus to what we're doing, not what we're achieving. Consequently, we can do the various stages outlined in the innovation funnel ending with a successful test and validation or even a relatively successful launch and be deemed successful, regardless of whether that invention goes on to market success – where it makes money, saves money, changes lives or delivers any other outcome measure we might have identified.

The innovation funnel and the current innovation thinking this model facilitates doesn't always work. All it does is waste resources, building endless roads to nowhere. We believe there is another way.

Notes

1 Katz G (2011) Rethinking the Product Development Funnel https://ams-insights.com/wp-content/uploads/2016/06/Rethinking_Product_Development_Funnel_VisionsJuly11Katzl.pdf

2 Urban G and Hauser JR (1980) *Design and Marketing of New Products*, Prentice-Hall, Englewood Cliffs, NJ.

3 Cooper RG (1986) *Winning at New Products*, Perseus Publishing, Cambridge, MA.

4 Wheelwright SC and Clark KB (1992) *Revolutionizing Product Development*, The Free Press, New York.

5 McGrath ME (1996) *Setting the PACE® in Product Development*, Butterworth-Heinemann, Boston, MA.

6 Hauser JR (2008) *Note on Product Development*, MIT Sloan Courseware, Cambridge, MA.

7 Finkelstein S (2003) *Why Smart Executives Fail and What You Can Learn from Their Mistakes*, Penguin, New York.

8 Courtney H, Kirkland J, and Viguerie P (1997) Strategy under Uncertainty *Harvard Business Review* https://hbr.org/1997/11/strategy-under-uncertainty

9 Chandraker A, Houmas H, Hogg J, and Reilly C (2015) Innovation as Unusual PA Consulting.

10 Gittleson K (2012) Can a Company Live Forever *BBC News* www.bbc.co.uk/news/business-16611040

11 Percival D, Shelton RD, and Andrews H (2013) Unleashing the Power of Innovation PWC www.pwc.com/gx/en/innovationsurvey/files/innovation_full_report.pdf

12 Chandraker A, Houmas H, Hogg J, and Reilly C (2015) Innovation as Unusual PA Consulting.

13 PWC 20th CEO Survey (2017) 20 Years Inside the Mind of the CEO . . . What's Next? www.pwc.com/gx/en/ceo-survey/2017/pwc-ceo-20th-survey-report-2017.pdf

14 Le Fanu J (1999) *The Rise and Fall of Modern Medicine Little*, Brown and Company, London.

15 Phadke U and Vyakarnam S (2018) *Camels, Tigers & Unicorns: Re-Thinking Science and Technology-Enabled Innovation*, World Scientific Publishing, London.

16 Gourville JT (2006) Eager Sellers and Stony Buyers: Understanding the Psychology of New-Product Adoption *Harvard Business Review* https://hbr.org/2006/06/eager-sellers-and-stony-buyers-understanding-the-psychology-of-new-product-adoption

17 Mintzberg H (1975) The Manager's Job: Folklore and Fact *Harvard Business Review* 53(4) 49–61.

18 Thagard P and Stewart TC (2011) The AHA! Experience: Creativity through Emergent Binding in Neural Networks *Cognitive Science* 35 1–33.

19 More T. (1516), Utopia
20 Anthony SD (2016) Kodak's Downfall Wasn't about Technology *Harvard Business Review* https://hbr.org/2016/07/kodaks-downfall-wasnt-about-technology
21 Wright B (2015) Have Brits Stopped Inventing Things? Or Are We Just Bad at Turning Ideas into Companies? *The Telegraph* www.telegraph.co.uk/finance/comment/11631787/Our-nations-splendid-yet-isolated-inventors-seem-to-lead-the-world-in-modesty.html
22 Nicholson S (2008) Briton Invented iPod, DRM and On-Line Music in 1979 *Wired* www.wired.com/2008/09/briton-invented/
23 Rogers EM (1962) *Diffusion of Innovation*, Simon & Schuster, New York.
24 Moore GA (2014) *Crossing the Chasm: Marketing and Selling Disruptive Products to Mainstream Customers* (3rd Edition), Harper Business, New York.
25 Phadke U and Vyakarnam S (2018) *Camels, Tigers & Unicorns: Re-Thinking Science and Technology-Enabled Innovation*, World Scientific Publishing, London.
26 Lella A (2017) U.S. Smartphone Penetration Surpassed 80 Percent in 2016 www.comscore.com/Insights/Blog/US-Smartphone-Penetration-Surpassed-80-Percent-in-2016
27 https://steemitimages.com/0x0/https://steemitimages.com/DQmZpkndvrY7pT3beU45XZJ4wveqbV2VgFscfbhnapGDSEo/brilliant.png
28 Rosenberg A (2018) A Major Annual Survey of Game Developers Brings Troubling News for Virtual Reality *Mashable* https://mashable.com/2018/01/24/virtual-reality-gaming-loser-gdc-2018-survey/?europe=true#dGTaBymec5qZ
29 Coutu S (2014) The Scale-Up Report on UK *Economic Growth* www.scaleupreport.org/scaleup-report.pdf

2 Focusing on the problem may be the problem

Before we explain what the 'other way' might be, it's worth exploring why the current innovation approach, using the innovation funnel and focusing on the problem, can be misleading. Again, if you are already convinced that the way innovation is currently done is not working and you are eager to get to one possible solution, then jump ahead to part two.

When we turn on the news, open a newspaper or scroll through our social media feeds, we are presented with a mind-numbing array of local, national and global problems. The scale, number and jurisdictional complexity of these problems can feel overwhelming; it's almost impossible to know where to start. Problems exist from the relatively small to the systemic. As such there is no shortage of problems for the innovation industry to focus on.

In the UK for example, the government regularly publishes problems in need of a solution, via Innovate UK, such as how to create more ventilators to deal with the COVID-19 pandemic. They also hold innovation competitions. Innovation competitions occur all over the world and run all the way up to the Oscar's of innovation – the X Prize with millions of dollars up for grabs across multiple categories, such as turning CO2 into products or how to use Artificial Intelligence (AI) to solve global issues (2020).

Whether at a local council level or as a small business or even a large government or corporate department, most people involved will explain passionately what the problem is. Currently, we have no problem identifying problems. As a result, there is never going to be a shortage in the need for diagnosis, but it's our ability to do that and get it right which is the key challenge.

Logic tells us that if we have a problem, we must first understand that problem thoroughly so that we can diagnose it with a high degree of accuracy. If someone is ill, we need to diagnose their condition. This enables us to assess the severity of their condition and provide the right treatment or solution. And whist that works in health care and many other fields, we don't believe it works in innovation. For innovation to gather speed and momentum so that the proposed solution can fail or flourish fast, we need to reverse our thinking again and start with the solution, *not* the problem.

There are many reasons why we spend more time on the explanation or the diagnosis of the problem. Some of those reasons are practical. Currently, the vast majority of money spent in innovation is spent in the discovery, scoping and business case stages of the innovation process. Even the imagery of the innovation funnel encourages us to put as many new ideas, projects and inventions into the funnel for assessment as possible. As a result, a company or government department may have multiple innovation projects running concurrently – all requiring time, money and human resources to progress. But if we were to skip straight to proposed solutions, discarding those that are flawed, followed by testing and validation of an *informed* solution, we would immediately cut out a great deal of the cost and time.

But if we focused more on the solution, we would be better at understanding the problem. Have you ever struggled with a cryptic crossword all day without success and then when you see the solutions in the next day's paper you can't understand why you didn't get the answer? If you have, you will know that the solution always allows you to understand the clues better. The solution suddenly seems obvious. The same thing happens when we focus on the solution in innovation. Focusing on the solution and not the problem actually helps us to better diagnose the problem we are dealing with. Thus, if we implement the solution and it doesn't actually solve the problem then that means we have almost certainly misdiagnosed the problem in the first place.

What few of us appreciate is that our individual and collective ability to start with the solution and use this to better diagnose the problem and subsequently hone the solution is dependent on the quality and sophistication of our thinking. And this is itself dependent on how mature we are as human beings or what is called our level of adult development.

Quality of our minds

When a person thinks about a particular problem and its potential solution, they will always be constrained by the limits of their own mind. We can't think of any answer beyond the limitations of our own understanding. Put another way, our level of understanding determines the quality of our answers.

Therefore, the more awareness we have of our own mental limitations the better because only then will we be able to know when we are out of our depth.

Unfortunately, most people lack this awareness. As a result, when people think about a problem, they do just that – think about the problem, as an object or issue in their awareness. They never consider the sophistication of their thinking and how fundamental this is to solving the problem.

A couple of years ago, Alan attended a conference called "Thinking the Unthinkable", which was a prelude to a book of the same title.[1] A whole range of luminary business leaders, CEOs and Chairmen gathered to explore the perilous state of the world and what needs to be done. When asked to share his thoughts on the topic as a neuroscientist, Alan suggested that the conference may have been called "Thinking the Unthinkable" but the one thing the attendees were not thinking about was "thinking". What they were actually engaged in was a conversation about how they might be able to "do the undo-able". Ironically, this observation beautifully encapsulates the problem. If our model of the world does not contain the idea of our own mind, then it will not even occur to us to include that dimension.

The people in the room couldn't quite grasp the idea that their mind might be limited by their ability to think about their own mind. In fairness, most people are not aware of the constraints of their thinking because, typically, they have no map for quantifying their own level of sophistication. In the absence of this map, they mistakenly conclude that their minds are as sophisticated as possible. If they are successful business people, they are even more likely to conclude this even if it is not true.

People are often stuck in this loop, constrained by their mind, which doesn't allow them to realise there is a constraint! But it is possible to break free from such constraints when we discover that there are in fact 'developmental maps' that identify the levels of sophistication that exist beyond the level that any one of us may currently be operating from. Such maps, which have been around for over 50 years, can be an absolute game changer for innovation.[2]

These maps detail the key 'lines of development' that adults can work on to step change their innovative capability. For example, someone who is exhausted rarely comes up with great ideas; the ability to manage our own energy levels successfully can alter our ability to consistently generate ideas. Likewise, some-one blessed with very advanced levels of emotional and social intelligence is much more likely to be able to engage stakeholders and drive their solutions to commercial success. Cognitive sophistication will clearly alter the ability to innovate, as will ego maturity (Figure 2.1).

While there are multiple potential lines of adult development over the last 20 years, Alan has identified what are probably the eight most important *lines of development*, capable of making the biggest impact in the shortest time in most businesses, government departments or institutions.[3]

Most of us don't appreciate how much our own development across these lines influences our ability to assess a problem accurately or come up with solutions that address the multi-dimensional nature of the problem.

If we want to step change our innovative capability, we will often make much more progress by studying and understanding the quality of our own thinking than we would by spending all the time focused on the problem itself.

The realisation that our ability to innovate may be constrained by the lack of sophistication of our own minds has been referred to as 'waking up'. It really is a 'wake-up call' the day we realise that we may be the source of our own failure to come up with better answers. Putting the effort into improving the sophistication of our own minds has been referred to as 'growing up'.[4]

Let's look at how 'waking up' and 'growing up' impact our ability to address a problem, like poverty which is in desperate need of more innovative solutions. Someone may take the view that poverty is due to laziness. Then one day that person 'wakes up' to the realisation that such an opinion is a massive over-simplification and poverty is actually a considerably more complex problem

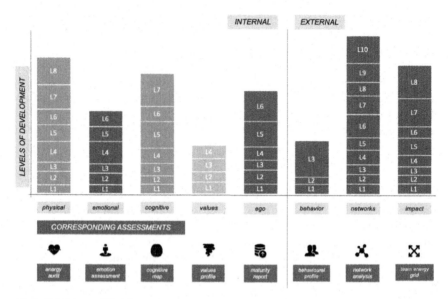

Figure 2.1 Lines of Development

that cannot be attributed to a simple lack of effort. They have woken up to the fact that their own mind had settled on a very simple answer and, until they woke up, they did not even realise that they were over simplifying the problem.

If that same person then became curious about what else could be causing poverty, they might start 'growing up' and developing a much more sophisticated understanding of the causes of poverty. Someone who recognises the many complex contributing factors to poverty is more likely to propose multiple solutions that address different aspects of the challenge. Such an analysis of poverty has been done by Foundation Paraguay, which has been consistently voted as one of the top two or three organisations in the world for ending poverty most effectively.[5]

Too many attempts to innovate are flawed from the start by a lack of sophistication or insufficient 'adult development' on the part of the very people we turn to for the solutions. They haven't woken up or grown up, so they can't appreciate the interdependencies of the issue and they don't anticipate the unintended consequences that an overly simplistic solution might create, or worse they don't care. As a result, they rush to simple solutions that are almost certainly doomed to fail. In such an environment, problem assessment is utterly futile.

When we wake up, we appreciate that the world may not be as black and white as we first thought. With this simple insight, we create a platform for us to 'grow up'. Growing up is like unlocking several new levels on a computer game, and in those new levels we are able to conceive of things and do things that we couldn't do at previous levels. With these new-found abilities, we can create more nuanced solutions because we have deeper, subtler insights that can transform results and unlock new potential. Growing up thus unlocks our 'superpowers' that can transform the outcome. A leader's maturity can also change their sponsorship and the language they use to position the problem. This in turn can change how the problem is perceived by others and expand everyone's ability to see new, more innovative solutions.

Most of us are completely unaware that we are living with a sort of disability called 'arrested development'. Our failure to continue developing creates in us a view of the world that is fixed, most of the time, at a relatively unsophisticated level and certainly below what we are capable of. As a result, we see the world through an adolescent lens which, in turn, influences how we assess and diagnose any problem and inhibits our ability to generate a solution. Until we 'wake up' to this fact, we are likely to remain part of the problem and will continue to misinterpret the issues resulting in a waste of time and money as we go around in circles generating over simplified answers created by the constraints of our own mind.

The need to wake up and grow up is urgent given the fact that barely half of all leaders (55 per cent) are operating at a level sufficient to solve the problems we collectively face.[6]

But, our lack of development is not the only challenge we face when assessing problems and seeking innovative solutions. We are also blind to the fact that we have become one-dimensional in our approach to our problems, which severely limits our ability to correctly diagnose the real causes let alone solve the problem.

4D leadership

The truth is that all the problems we try to solve with our innovations are multi-dimensional. Understanding what 'multi-dimensional' really means is absolutely key to being able to solve the plethora of problems we face.

Thus, every aspect of human experience and every second of that experience is occurring in one or more of four critical dimensions.[7] If we only consider one dimension of the problem, namely what we do, and we do not consider the need for a wider system change, a change in human attitudes and a change in the way people relate to each other, then whatever solution we come up with won't be sustainable. This is part of the reason why so many 'solutions' show early promise but fail – because they don't adequately address the whole problem, just part of it. Any effective solution must address all four dimensions, not just one dimension, otherwise it just won't work.

Once you appreciate the existence of these dimensions, it changes the way you approach every problem in the future. Right now, as you read the words on this page, thoughts may bubble up. Thus, you might be thinking, "What have these dimensions got to do with innovation"? Whatever thoughts and feelings you are having right now, they are your own personal invisible inner response.

No one else knows what you are thinking or feeling at this moment. You are having a subjective experience to what is written on this page. This is your interior dimension of 'I' or 'being'.

In addition to this inner subjective experience, you are simultaneously doing something. For example, you may be reading this book on the train to work. As you approach your stop, you will probably put the book or e-reader away and make your way toward the exit ready to disembark. You can be seen leaving the train. This is your observable behaviour and that is happening while you are still thinking. As you get off the train, your experience is both individual interior 'I' and individual exterior 'IT'. This 'IT' dimension is what you are personally 'doing'.

When you exit the train, you might bump into two of your colleagues and you start talking to them. This conversation is observable, so there is an 'ITS' or social convention that you are all following. This 'ITS' dimension speaks to the exterior visible systems and conventions but can also be simplified to 'doing' and can, therefore, be observed. But while you are chatting, what cannot be observed are the unwritten social rules that exist between you and your colleagues. The norms of social interaction, the acceptable level of banter that exists in your group and the degree of trust between you are the interior of your relationships. None of this can be seen. This is the 'WE' dimension of 'relating'.

Of course, each individual experiences the cultural norms or 'WE' in the group slightly differently through their own subjective 'I' experience. But we all know exactly who our colleagues are; we know who belongs and who doesn't belong. We can't see this 'WE' connection 'out there' in the exterior world, just as our interior 'I' experience can't be seen 'out there' in the objective world. But none of our colleagues doubt the existence of this shared knowledge. No one doubts the existence of the shared dimension that makes up the relationship. Each 'I' being in that 'WE' group feels connected, strongly or weakly, to every other 'I' in the group through the 'relating' dimension.

Every single moment of our lives occurs simultaneously in all dimensions – 'I', 'WE', 'IT' and 'ITS' – although we don't appreciate the distinctions. Or if we do, we certainly don't see the relevance or importance of this insight. This deceptively simple frame allows us to understand a good deal of the complexity of the modern world, and explains why some of the most intractable problems, often those innovation is focused on solving, have become so intractable.

The reason this is extremely important is that all problems, and particularly complex problems, have an 'I', 'WE' and an 'IT/ITS' dimension. The 'I' dimension or 'being' dimension includes all unobservable phenomena of the human experience, such as values, ego, morality, identity, etc. The 'IT/ITS' or 'doing' dimensions includes all observable interactions plus all objective systems and processes. The 'WE' or 'relating' dimension embraces the unseen interpersonal dynamics, degrees of trust, depths of understanding and quality of rapport that exist on the inside of our relationships rather than the fact that there is a relationship.

When we search for solutions to the challenges we face, the common tendency is to focus almost exclusively on the exterior objective dimensions. In other words, we only consider behaviour ('IT') or systems and processes ('ITS') in the world of 'doing'. What are people doing about the problem? What systems and structures do we need to put in place to make this situation better? Changing what is being done is important, but the objective solution will not be sustainable without people's individual commitment in the 'I' dimension ('being') and the collective will to sustain the effort in the 'WE' dimension ('relating'). Innovative solutions must also address these other, less obvious dimensions.

Currently, innovation almost always starts at the need or problem and everyone involved gets busy 'doing' some analysis of the issue. People's natural addiction to tasks and 'doing' means that the solutions will be focused on behavioural or system changes while completely ignoring the dimensions of 'being' ('I') and 'relating' ('WE'). This is despite the fact that whatever that problem or need was, it will almost certainly be deeply rooted in the 'I' and 'WE' dimensions. Everything from terrorism to global warming to corruption to poverty to the dysfunction of the world's political systems or the inadequacy of the world's food production and distribution systems all require individuals to change what they are 'doing' in significant numbers.[8] But this only happens if we change our inner beliefs and evolve our values. We also need to connect much more effectively with others, whether they are like-minded or have diverse opinions from ours. In the end, it is individuals who start to think differently about a problem, because they feel differently, and this allows them to connect differently and causes them to push through the change that alters what we all end up 'doing' in the world. For example, the undergraduates at Oxford University have been trying to remove the statue of Cecil Rhodes for years, but it was not until the 'town' joined forces with the 'gown' following the death of George Floyd and the subsequent Black Lives Matter protest of 2020 that there became a realistic possibility that this would happen.

Solution over problem

This lack of awareness of the multi-dimensional nature of the challenges and our own and other people's level of human development means that many of the people charged with finding solutions to the problems or needs that exist are not equipped to accurately assess the problem in the first place.

If we continue to take a one-dimensional, partial approach to multi-dimensional issues, then we should not be surprised by our corresponding lack of progress. If we compound our one-dimensional approach because we see the world from the unsophisticated, immature and undeveloped level, then we clearly won't come up with a very innovative breakthrough. What is worse, our view about our own answers or those generated by others can also be pretty unsophisticated and one-dimensional.

For example, many people currently operate from an "I'm right, you're wrong" mindset. This makes it difficult for us to connect successfully with others as those 'others' also think the exact same thought (i.e. that they are right and it is you that is wrong). The result is an argument about who is right rather than seeing the value of each person's perspective.

Unfortunately, such a binary approach fails to recognise that no one is smart enough to be right 100 per cent of the time. Which equally means no one is wrong 100 per cent of the time either. It's much more likely that both parties bring important considerations to the table – thus illuminating more of the complexity of the problem, which invariably gets us all closer to a wiser solution.

When considering how to effectively innovate with others, it is important to remember that preservation is an important part of innovation. This means that the perspective that someone else brings may be slightly out of date; but, in order to innovate, we need to understand what worked about the previous answers we had and preserve that while discarding the bit that no longer works. So, paradoxically, innovation requires preservation. If we don't embrace and preserve the good of the past, if we are locked into a binary right/wrong mind-set, then we are likely to throw the baby out with the bathwater. Being able to engage with the problem with some humility and preparedness to open up to other people's views is vital for success. Preserve the good and build; don't scrap everything and start again.

Such openness is especially important because there are no clear simple or obvious answers to the problems innovation is designed to solve. There are layers of complexity and interdependencies. No one person's solution is going to be 100 per cent correct or 100 per cent incorrect. No one solution is going to be enough; we need multiple solutions.

As a result, we need to get to solutions faster, remain open to ideas from others, be able to seek out the value in diverse views and effectively integrate multiple perspectives to define a wise way forward. And the diverse views we must integrate have to address all dimensions of the problem – the 'I', 'WE' and 'IT'/'ITS' – or they will continue to fail.

Take obesity as an example. We could, literally, spend decades figuring out what causes obesity. There are research studies that look at nothing else, each pursuing different hypotheses, each influenced by the level of development and natural bias of the people conducting those studies. Two groups could come together and argue for months over what causes obesity and each would believe they are correct and the other is wrong. Some of the research may look at genetics or personal behaviour. Others may look at internal flora and fauna in the gut. Some might look at what the individual is doing in terms of exercise. Another study might look at their friends and family, known as the 'obesogenic environment' to see who an obese person spends time with and how likely it is that their friends and family are also obese. Yet another group may look at beliefs, values and perhaps past trauma that may influence the person's emotional regulation.

What we are saying is that it doesn't matter. All of these possible causes and a hundred more besides them are probably true or at least play a role in the development of obesity. Obesity is not a binary, simple problem that manifests the same way for everyone because of the same reasons and triggers; it's a highly complex problem with many interdependent factors that will never be solved by a magic pill or potion. We need multiple, smart, multi-dimensional solutions running along-side each other to really tackle the issue constructively. They must also address all three dimensions of 'I', 'WE' and 'IT/ITS'. In other words, the solution must help people feel differently about themselves and alter their identity to a more constructive self-image, provide intrinsic motivation to change behaviour as well as connect them to other people who are seeking to make change within a system that supports them.

We believe that there is never, or at least very rarely, only one answer to any problem or need. The solution we start with is therefore just part of the resolution of that problem – only we get to it much faster and spend significantly less money than we would using the traditional innovation funnel approach.

In that old model the innovator is told to provide only one answer. As mentioned earlier, if the Boffin provides more than one solution then this is often seen as a failure, an inability to choose the 'best' solution. But there is rarely a best solution that will tackle every dimension of the problem or need simultaneously. What is much more likely is that there will be several best solutions that will address the 'I' 'being' dimension of the problem, several best solutions that will address the 'IT/ITS' 'doing' dimensions of the problem and several best solutions that will address the 'WE' 'relating' dimensions of the problem – all stitched together to deliver the required overall solution.

Starting with the solution therefore pre-supposes that we should explore multiple different solutions and must embrace those multiple solutions across all dimensions if we stand any real chance of solving the problem at all.

Of course, this is not to say that an impeller approach simply plucks solutions out of thin air. People using this approach are as susceptible to the same one-dimensional blind-spots and the same developmental biases as everyone else. Instead, an impeller approach demonstrates that there are enough educated and informed people involved who constitute an existing knowledge base that can be tapped into. This short-circuits much of the research toil and saves a huge amount of time and money.

We don't need to re-invent the wheel; we can instead go to the existing range of experts who already have years, sometimes decades of knowledge and experience in that area. Bring enough of those perspectives together and solutions start to emerge. For example, going back to the question of obesity, a lot of the necessary research has already been done. Having spoken to the right experts an integrator (more on this shortly) can very quickly come up with working versions of the constellation of answers needed. Thus, years of academic research shows that reducing an individual's calorie consumption requires people to see very clearly the connection between their behaviour and their personalised health data (i.e. the link between what they 'do' in the 'IT' dimension and the measurable outcome of those actions, such as waistline or blood pressure).

General platitudes from health services about obesity in the general population simply don't change an individual's behaviour or impact their weight. So, making the connection between calorie consumption and calorie burn on a daily basis and using ambulatory and personalised data to predict the short-term impact of excessive calorie consumption is a critical part of the answer (connecting personalised 'I' and system 'ITS'). If we then add predictive imagery of the person involved using 360-degree cameras and augmented reality (impacting how people feel about their future selves in the 'I' dimension), we are much more likely to drive behavioural change, as people can see immediately the consequences of their daily choices. Add an online or in person meeting group for support or collective exercise (to reinforce the power through 'social proof' or 'social sanction' in the 'WE' dimension) then the multi-dimensional solution has much more chance of being successful.

An impeller approach is not advocating zero research. It is suggesting that we focus on honing possible solutions rather than seeking to simply describe the problem in more and more detail. Starting with a solution can be achieved by going straight to the leading edge of research across multiple dimensions and integrating the insights to define a starting point for the answer. This can then be swiftly verified, if it has merit for continued development, or rejected.

These early solutions are not fully formed but they are formed enough to provide a 'direction of travel' for further testing without wasting resources understanding a problem that many people in many areas or existing fields of expertise already fully understand. It doesn't matter that many of those experts may have a different opinion about the solution; the more diverse the input, the more likely an integrator is to come up with genuinely insightful solutions (this will be fully unpacked and explained in Chapter 3). And, access to these experts can trigger the emergence of two or three solutions in minutes, not months or years.

The power of this solutions-focused approach is amplified when more of the people involved in innovation have woken up and grown up. The power of the answer is further multiplied when we become aware of the complex, multi-dimensional nature of the problems we face; when we become more aware of our own natural biases; when we become more aware of other people's biases and different cultural contexts; when we are more consciously competent about our own level of thinking. The power of our ability to innovate with such amplification and multiplication is accelerated to an incredible degree when we then do the developmental work necessary for vertical development. If we develop vertically, we unlock completely new levels of cognitive ability, increase our ego maturity, access deeper degrees of emotional intelligence and expand our ability to take broader often multiple perspectives to create more inclusive, collaborative and sophisticated answers to the many problems we face. All of this constitutes a genuine game changing capability, not just the incremental improvements that are claimed to be game changing or transformational but legitimate breakthroughs and paradigm shifts that complex problems require.

Ironically, the type of people who think differently about innovation are normally already in the innovation space. In the course of our work, we often meet senior executives who are confused and struggling with the innovators in their own businesses. Too often, these individuals are marginalised, seen as mavericks or just 'weird'. But actually, innovation needs these mavericks. Often these are the people who have woken up and grown up to the complexity of the world around them and can harness huge amounts of information and draw creative, viable solutions from an ocean of data. We need to start identifying these people and developing a way to harness their potential and encourage them to get to the solution faster rather than wasting time dissecting the problem.

This speed to solution and therefore speed to success in the market has profound implications for innovation and offers a truly different way to innovate.

Notes

1 Gowing N and Langdon C (2018) *Thinking the Unthinkable: A New Imperative for Leadership in the Digital Age*, John Catt Educational Ltd, Woodbridge www.thinkunthink.org/
2 Wilber K (2000) *Integral Psychology: Consciousness, Spirit, Psychology, Therapy*, Shambhala, Boulder, CO.
3 Watkins A (2015) *4D Leadership*, Kogan Page, London.
4 Wilber K (2017) *The Religion of Tomorrow: A Vision for the Future of the Great Traditions: More Inclusive, More Comprehensive, More Complete*, Shambhala, Boulder, CO.
5 www.fundacionparaguaya.org.py/?lang=en
6 Rooke D and Torbert WR (2005) Seven Transformations of Leadership *Harvard Business Review* 66–76.
7 Wilber K (2007) *The Integral Vision: A Very Short Introduction to the Revolutionary Integral Approach to Life, God, the Universe, and Everything*, Shambhala Publications, Boulder, CO. Watkins A (2015) *4D Leadership: Competitive Advantage through Vertical Leadership Development*, Kogan Page, London.
8 Watkins A and Wilber K (2015) *Wicked & Wise: How to Solve the World's Toughest Problems*, Urbane Publications, London.

Part II

The impeller approach unpacked

3 Start with the solution

With the innovation funnel approach, you have to travel through the funnel in a largely linear way to get to the answer. It is, therefore, the stage gate *process* itself that is typically funded or attracts an internal budget and is monitored to determine 'success'. Most people are unwilling to put their neck on the line to define a solution from the outset and therefore it is hard to know what success will eventually look like – other than a well-run project. This addiction to a stage-gate process is the 'propeller' approach to innovation.

Being ideas-centric, a funnel confuses the creation of novel ideas, typically derived through R&D, with innovation itself. Idea creation is invention; innovation is the successful commercialisation of that invention. This is only achieved having performed in the market for a period of time; 1–0 in a football match after five minutes is not success if you eventually lose 1–2.

Getting to the end of the funnel successfully is not enough. It is still not innovation because it is the next few years *in the market* that will really determine whether the invention has successfully crossed the chasm between the early adopters and the early majority and, therefore, successfully navigated the valley of death. Has the invention solved a problem, achieved a desired outcome or delivered value? That is the only real measure of successful innovation.

Part of the appeal of the innovation funnel is that it suits the analytical world. The various stage gates deliver evidence all the way along the process. We put a whole bunch of ideas into the funnel in the hope that one or two good ones will drop out the end – therefore presenting itself/themselves as the best solution(s). But this is an incredibly expensive and inefficient approach which rarely delivers the required results, as we discussed in Chapter 1.

So how do we change all that? How do we rethink the innovation process? What would happen if we did the opposite and reversed the funnel? What if we started with the solution?

An impeller approach

An impeller approach uses some of the same principles from the old innovation funnel (albeit reversed) but adds some new concepts and players. Let's start with the new, unique elements:

- Starting at the solution
- The impeller 'bee' (explained in more detail in Chapters 4 and 5)
- A 'meadow of experts'
- An entrepreneur (explained in more detail in Chapter 7)
- A stand-alone delivery/commercialisation vehicle (explained in more detail in Chapter 7)

Starting at the solution

In the traditional innovation funnel, there is a wide inlet to encourage as many ideas into the process as possible but a small outlet to allow only a few inventions or ideas to escape the stage-gate assessment process. It's more of a filter than a funnel as we discussed in Chapter 1. An impeller approach is the exact opposite. In the old innovation funnel model someone says, "What's the problem? Let's go investigate that and after some analysis and assessment we'll come up with the answer". With an impeller approach, the 'bee' (more on this role in a moment) identifies early on what the solution could be based on discussions with experts already in the problem area (see the meadow of experts section). Or the person accountable for the solution may know immediately that they don't actually know what the answer is or if there is one. This is a radically different way of doing things.

This never happens in the current approach to innovation. In the current approach, if the innovation team gets the funding or the go-head then they will provide an answer after an agreed upon period of time. The answer might be terrible or it might be great but they will come up with an answer that meets the agreed upon deliverable based on the problem they have set out to resolve. There is almost no occasion where a project doesn't end with a conclusion. In an impeller approach, the innovators can often come up with a number of potential solutions much faster.

Again, the traditional funnel process would never come up with multiple potential solutions – to do so would be considered a sign of failure or weakness, not a sign of strength. But if all three of those solutions are good solutions that could be effective in the market in meeting a need or solving a problem, a business might want to pursue all three.

Starting with a solution forces everyone involved to look again at the problem and determine whether the right questions are being asked and answered in the first place. The solution helps to clarify or confirm the question in the same way that an answer to a crossword puzzle helps make the clue seem obvious.

This 'obviousness' can manifest itself in the realisation that 80 per cent of the solution may already be available. It may be that it is not something that is commonly used in the sector or that it involves a combination of elements or technologies to make it work. But the fact that these are all available means that the route to market is suddenly shorter.

Perhaps the most famous example of what can be achieved when we start from the solution is the moon landing. John F. Kennedy (J.F.K.) had a problem: the Russians were winning the space race and he felt that the US needed to do something about that. To solve the problem, he would need funding; so he went to congress to secure that funding. He didn't suggest that money was made available to fund a few clever people and hopefully they would collectively come up with something that might solve that problem. He didn't say, "Look I think I know what the answer is. Can we fund a prototype? Can we do a minimal viable product and see what happens? Can we test it"? What he said was, "I know what the problem is and I know what the solution is. I want you to invest in the solution".

Putting a man on the moon was not actually the hard bit. In the worst-case scenario, a few rolls of gaffer tape and some long-range ballistic missiles might have done the trick. Of course the man would be dead in five seconds but so long as the missile was positioned properly the US could boast the first man on the moon, albeit a dead one.

The Russians would probably have laughed. Any test would have quite clearly shown that putting a man on the moon was not the answer to the space race problem. Often prototypes and tests simply confirm what we already know. The solution was therefore to put a man on the moon before the end of the decade and bring him home safely. It wasn't a technological problem, it was actually a political problem, and he needed coverage on the front page of the newspaper.

When J.F.K. came out of congress and turned to the guy that would become the head of NASA, he probably said, "Look I'm sorry about that. It was just an intuitive answer to the problem. I should have told you I was going to do that". The story goes that the guy said something like, "Oh it's absolutely fine. I know where the earth is, I know where the moon is, I know what you want and I know by when. I will do everything I can to deliver that".

On 20 July 1969, the United States' Apollo 11 touched down on the moon; Neil Armstrong and Buzz Aldrin arrived back on earth safely on 24 July 1969.

J.F.K. thought differently. He was clear about the problem and arrived at a solution that would solve that problem, bringing the full weight of the US government behind its execution. That single act of innovation established the US as a world leader. We need to re-engage that type of alternative thinking about innovation.

We need to look at innovation in much the same way, not just in starting with the solution and moving forward from there but also in terms of what we are actually trying to achieve. The goal is not to create new ideas. The real end game is to create great ideas and successfully bring them to market to deliver value in whatever way we wish to measure it.

The bee

This approach can sound unnerving, it may even sound arrogant, but it's made possible because an impeller approach uses a very different type of person to generate solutions. It doesn't just engage analytical people; it also utilises a specific type of person who thinks very differently. When everyone else is looking right, they are looking left. When everyone else is considering one set of factors or one option, they are thinking about very different things, different data and different outcomes. An impeller approach starts at the solution because it is driven by a specific type of person, we call a 'bee'. This bee is known by many other terms, such as polymath,[1] integrator,[2] maverick,[3] nexialist[4] or neogeneralists[5] (and the role of the bee is thoroughly explored in Chapters 4 and 5). It is worth pointing out that, from an accuracy point of view, the bee is actually a honey bee because honey bees are the only bees that actually make something: honey. And a bee is the one that makes or comes up with the solutions. But constantly referring to honey bees throughout the book would become irritating, so we are using bee as a shorthand for honey bee.

The bee has an extraordinary ability to make connections between snippets of knowledge gleaned from multiple expert sources. Those insights and conversations are stored away in the bee's 'hive' (their mind). But this connective ability has to be balanced with the ability to bring all this information together to imagine potential solutions. This solution is not just a collection of thoughts brought together and verbalised. It is a packaged solution so that when it is being discussed, the solution makes sense, both from a story-telling point of view and a desirability and usability point of view.

But bees don't just make up solutions or pull them out of thin air, they do so by buzzing around a 'meadow of experts'.

The meadow of experts

An innovation funnel is full of experts. As we were writing this book, Simon's colleague and impeller creator, Jim Dawton, started wondering what the collective noun is for a group of experts? There isn't one. So, he decided to coin the term a 'meadow' of experts. Partly because it fits perfectly with the metaphor of the bee, as the bee visits each expert in the 'meadow' in order to come up with solutions. And this 'meadow' is vital to the success of the impeller approach. Access to this 'meadow' is central to the bee's ability to generate solutions, fast.

What better way to learn about anything than to speak to experts in the area? Leonardo da Vinci used this approach. He would relentlessly seek out people whose brains he could pick. We know this because thankfully many of his notebooks survived and are now preserved. In those notebooks, he would write endless lists of things he wanted to investigate. Those lists were littered with notes such as, "Get the masters of arithmetic to show you how to square a triangle", "Ask Giannino the Bombardier about how the tower of Ferrara is walled" and "Ask Benedetto Protinari by what means they walk on ice in Flanders".[6]

Da Vinci recognised that the fastest way to learn anything is to ask someone who already knows.

More recently, Hollywood producer Brian Grazer has used a similar approach. In fact, he attributes much of his success to what he calls 'curiosity conversations'. For decades, Grazer scheduled a curiosity conversation where he would seek out anyone who was renowned or an expert in any area other than entertainment. Every two weeks he would speak to someone in science, medicine, politics, religion, the arts, technology, etc. to better understand that area. What he found was that these informal discussions often sparked the creative inspiration behind many of his most successful movies and TV shows.[7] In many ways, both da Vinci and Grazer were consulting their 'meadow of experts'.

These experts can be as varied and diverse as the wild flowers in a meadow.

In the old model of innovation, huge amounts of time and money are effectively wasted as a designated unit within the innovation team investigates and assesses the problem. They are seeking to get up to speed on issues from multiple perspectives but there are already people, experts out there in the world, who are already up to speed in relation to the problem. Those experts in the meadow cover a wide range of topics and disciplines and provide faster access to necessary insight and information.

The bee and meadow relationship

Both the bee and the meadow of experts are critical in the new innovation model. Think of the bee like a honey bee. The honey bee visits the meadow every day. It touches lots of different flowers, extracting small amounts of nectar, pollinating the plants and then storing it away in its honeycomb in its hive. The bee continually visits the meadow of experts to hoover up knowledge. The nectar or knowledge it extracts from the experts on a regular basis is stored in its head so that when a problem or need is presented to it the solution might already be in its mind. In addition, they know that a specific expert knows about a particular branch of science and another might know about the law or have expertise in health or micro payments. When someone comes along and says, "I've got a problem that needs solving", it is possible that the solution has already been discussed or solved, individually or collectively, within the meadow.

Using bees and the knowledge from the meadow of experts, it is possible to quickly define the future or what could be possible in the next two, three or 10 years. Individually and collectively the experts in the meadow know what is possible on a specific dimension of the problem, although none have a complete view. Every single expert has a partial view; their expertise means that often they can only see the problem from their unique vantage point. This is the challenge with experts; but if we get enough experts together in, say, a hypothetical meadow, the bee is able to gather the perspectives and see more of the problem or issue.

Left to their own devices, experts often end up at loggerheads with each other. Academic medicine, for instance, is awash with such egoic turf battles with each expert advocating their own analytical, siloed knowledge base and their single perspective as the answer. They continually demand evidence if they are to accept progress. But the evidence they seek is only the type of evidence that they can recognise from their own vantage point. As a result, a great deal of effort is wasted in this fight between expert 'flowers' and solving the problem often seems a secondary concern. To make matters worse, the system of academic research only seems interested in the size of its flowers. Thus, the primary academic measure of success is how many papers the expert publishes in the best journals and whether they get their funding from the best sources. Both measures are elitist and seek to quantify the size of the flower.

Nowhere in this rating algorithm is there how many people the insights have helped or how many problems the expert has solved. Such a notion is not even part of the assessment of academic prowess. Surely the whole point of academic research is to improve people's lives? It is shocking to realise that improving lives is not even considered as a legitimate part of the algorithm that determines the value of academia. That is not to say that such an idea does not form part of an academic's motivation; it nearly always does but it is absent from the assessment rating of their performance.

In contrast, bees are not concerned with the size of a flower. They are only interested in collecting the nectar, integrating the nectar from the diverse flowers in the meadow and creating a useful honeycomb. Their start point is often the commercial solution. Something that might help solve the problem before the problem owner even realises they need help.

Since each flower only sees a partial answer, their authority is very limited; as a consequence, they are perpetually in search of more evidence. In contrast, a bee has natural authority because it has buzzed around the entire meadow and collected all manner of insights in the field where the problem exists and in many other fields as well. The bees' need for evidence is much smaller and they can jump to the solution faster. Bees carry implied authority because the source of their insights is from the very people we believe have the authority we are looking for.

We are all familiar with the idea of collecting multiple bits of data from multiple sources and integrating those sources into a much bigger picture in different areas of our life, but we are not yet familiar or comfortable with this sort of activity in the field of innovation.

Bees break the restraint that analytical and linear thinking imposes on innovation. Breaking the constraints releases the bee to think differently and then use its own integrator capability to create novel commercial answers and make the future tangible. The greater the integrator capability of the bee, the larger the number of solutions that can be analysed and the more precise the power and authority a bee can have to design or pick the right investment idea for maximum return.

Putting the bee at the heart of the innovation approach makes it possible to come up with more than one way to solve the problem. It may be that the problem is so big that it will actually require a range of solutions to resolve. If we consider obesity, there is currently no one way to resolve this on a national level. It has different audiences with different causes that need to be considered and a wide group of interested parties all trying to deliver their own solution to a very generically stated problem.

Entrepreneur

We typically think of entrepreneurs as people like Sir Richard Branson – dynamic, larger-than-life figures that see opportunities everywhere and are constantly seeking to disrupt industries or create new businesses. However, in the context of an impeller approach the entrepreneur is more a role and a mindset than a title. An entrepreneur, whether brought in from outside or sourced from inside, is the person who has the business and management skills and problem-solving attitude to drive the solution to market. Remember, successful commercialisation will almost certainly require a different person or team to those involved in the generation, test, build and verification of the novel idea. The entrepreneur is that *different* type of person who has the expertise to drive the invention to market and commercial success. These individuals are adept at getting stuff done, turning ideas into commercial reality, developing strategy and, more importantly, executing that strategy with enough flexibility to make alterations to the approach as things evolve.

This is not a project management role; they may well need to have a project manager in the team but the entrepreneur's role is all about decision making, authority and responsibility. The entrepreneur typically has had very little exposure to the solution before agreeing to take it to market. This lack of involvement in the early stages is often vital to ensuring that effective decision making can be carried out.

One of the biggest reasons innovation fails to deliver is that the new product or service fails to traverse the various cracks and chasms in the market and never makes it across the valley of death after the point of validation. The entrepreneur is the person charged with crossing that valley. They will have done it before, probably many times. Clearly, successful commercialisation requires a successful outcome but the role of the entrepreneur is to take an invention through to market.

In the FMCG industry, the entrepreneur could be the brand manager who has experience of half a dozen product launches and was brought in to get this new product to market as fast as possible. Even if all the evidence points to success, the only real measure of success is whether it delivers value in the marketplace. These individuals know how to bring together all the resources to make it work and are incentivised to do so. Their mission is either to make it a success as fast as possible or to shut it down as fast as possible if it's not working.

Too often, especially when the person taking the invention to market is the same person that came up with the invention, they become too attached to the solution. It's very hard for that person to close it down, especially if they have already spent a significant amount of capital. But the entrepreneur is agnostic. Their job is to get to market or kill the project, even if it has already cost more than £100,000. Closing it down is better than ignoring the signals and spending a further £5 million before someone else steps in and pulls the plug. The entrepreneur is not wedded to the solution or the business that is created around it and doesn't own that solution, so they are not fighting for or justifying it. They are fighting for its success and validation in the market.

As we pointed out in Chapter 1, the responsibility of everyone up until this point has been to spend money, to utilise their budget. When the solution is passed over to the entrepreneur, that changes. Their responsibility is to earn money as soon as possible or to stop any further haemorrhaging of capital. Often in the drive to market, the solution may only be 80 per cent complete. But, if that partial solution is earning money, then the market is further validating the solution. The product or service is being improved by customer feedback while also generating revenue.

A stand-alone delivery/commercialisation vehicle

The creation of a stand-alone delivery or commercialisation vehicle is also critical to the success of an impeller approach. Often, a new product or service is run alongside existing operations or run inside an existing business. Small innovation pods can easily get lost in a large business and end up going nowhere. Plus, this type of approach tends to poach resources from other departments on an ad hoc basis, which makes accurate reporting, costing and assessment extremely difficult.

It is therefore important that the solution is housed in a stand-alone, autonomous entity that is distinct from the parent business and that this semi-independent unit includes the right people for the commercialisation task ahead. The exact structure of that entity will depend on the business and the solution being commercialised. It doesn't really matter whether the vehicle is called an innovation division, a special or small Business Unit (BU), a department or a skunkworks. Whatever the terminology, the speed to market is key; creating a stand-alone, autonomous unit facilitates fast decision making where the entrepreneur is given a budget, freedom and decision-making control to get on with the job. That said, this license to operate will not be without constraints and the entrepreneur will only be able to operate within a tightly agreed upon governance framework.

Getting the governance framework right is itself a vital part of building a commercialisation vehicle. The polarity that needs to be managed here is speed or wisdom. Having a single decision maker clearly provides speed but risks wisdom, unless the entrepreneur is a genius who always makes the right calls. Allowing one person to make all the big decisions is always a risk; a parent company will often impose all sorts of checks and balances to prevent poor decisions being made. This is an attempt to inject a little more wisdom into the system but it often slows the process down and embroils people in endless report writing rather than what they are actually meant to be doing which is commercialising the product or service. Repeated rounds of bureaucracy or compliance can quickly kill the morale inside a commercialisation vehicle and cause a failure of what was a very promising product or service.

What is required is both speed *and* wisdom. This is a polarity, not a problem, and as such we need both, not one or the other.[8] In order to achieve both, we need to be able to see the benefits and the risks of both speed and wisdom. If the unit tries to move too fast, it loses wisdom. If it spends too much time trying to unlock the wisdom, it loses speed.

Often the optimal way to achieve both speed and wisdom is to build a team of mature operators, capable of working very well together under pressure and at pace while also implementing governance processes that can unlock the wisdom of the crowd without taking an age to do so. This approach is also gathering momentum and is used by companies like Impeller Ventures, Rainmaking and Accenture.

There are various ways to ensure that the commercialisation vehicle succeeds. It could be set up as a new department with a level of autonomy away from the day-to-day operations of the existing business or it could be a new stand-alone BU. Depending on the need to bring together external partners, it could also be a joint venture or a Special Purpose Vehicle (SPV) insulating the new entity from the parent business and allowing for full visibility whilst balancing the risk associated with any new venture. This SPV approach has significant benefits and will be unpacked in more detail in Chapter 8.

Clayton Christensen proposed something similar when he suggested setting up a separate corporate structure to foster new ideas so that they don't compete with the core business for resources. Cisco does this with its emerging markets technology group. The group is responsible for a fledgling technology until it is a $50 million to $100 million business. At that point, it becomes attractive for the established corporation to absorb.[9] The impeller point of difference is that there is a separate entity for each invention as it makes its way to market. Plus, as mentioned in Chapter 1, corporate venture funds have their own challenges and are in many ways too big to be successful.

It is also worth pointing out that when an impeller process is operating smoothly and efficiently, the bee is likely to offer up multiple potential solutions to a myriad of challenges that he or she is focused on. It will be down to the individual business to choose which of those potential solutions to action first and which will trigger the creation of stand-alone BUs. Few businesses, with the possible exception of CVC, have a limitless innovation budget; the ideas presented will need to be prioritised based on need and/or potential upside.

Build a saleable entity from the start

If the invention is brought to market successfully and delivers value and makes money, this creates a number of commercial options that need to be explored.

The parent business may decide to sell the stand-alone business or simply re-absorb it back into the larger existing business. Whatever option is chosen, it's always wise to design the commercialisation vehicle to become a saleable entity right from the start. There are several growth models in the marketplace employed by private equity houses, Mergers & Acquisitions (M&A) brokers, venturing funds or companies with deep domain expertise in the consulting sector that broker the sale of SMEs. Most of these companies are focused on creating higher valuations and better deal outcomes; so they have their own growth model.

There are countless additional resources on growth models, but to give a flavor, we have included a little information on one particular approach that might prove useful.[10] In this approach, there are eight levers that drive value in the commercialisation vehicle of a service-based consultancy. These levers are encapsulated in the Growth Wheel shown (Figure 3.1). By pulling the various levers, a business can increase the speed and equity growth of their business.

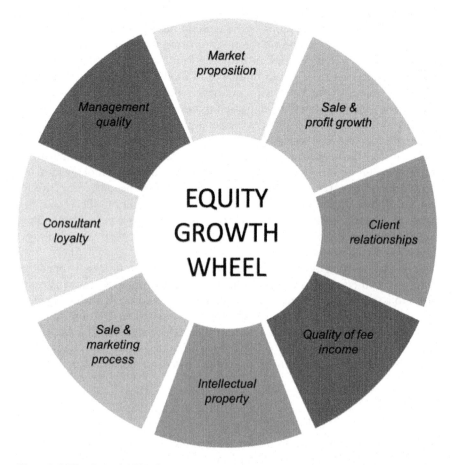

Figure 3.1 The Growth Wheel

Using this Equity Growth Wheel as a benchmark as well as a strategic planning tool, it can help the entrepreneur to plan for equity growth right from the outset. The levers give greater appreciation and control over the ability to ratchet up the value of the firm to maximise the return at the point of sale.[11]

Typically, businesses are valued as a multiple of the last 12 months profit, occasionally turnover or some combination of the two. When someone is looking to purchase that business, or the owner/parent company is looking to spin it off, there has to be evidence that profits will continue or grow over time. If that evidence is not sufficiently robust, the business is viewed as a greater risk and the sale price or value will drop. The eight levers in the Equity Growth Wheel are used to assess the risk, allowing the entrepreneur or parent company to manage that risk in real time to ensure the highest possible multiple.

Each lever represents an opportunity to minimise risk and increase the probability of the stand-alone BU delivering predictable and robust profit growth.

Lever 1: Sales and profit growth

Can you show a consistent growth in revenue and profits?

Sales and profit growth are the primary drivers of equity value. Erratic revenue and profit send a troubling message to would-be buyers. Obviously, this is likely in the early stages of commercialisation as the entrepreneur and the team seeks to get the innovation to market and gain traction beyond the early adopter market. Once the chasm between early enthusiasts and the mainstream market has been successfully crossed, then the BU is more likely to be able to demonstrate sustainable revenue and profit growth – ideally with healthy margins. If so, this will increase the equity value of the BU. Ideally, the business should be able to demonstrate consistent growth over the last three years.

Any business seeking to find a buyer should aim for 20 per cent organic growth year on year, manage cash so growth isn't constrained and achieve predictability, which is so crucial to investors.

Lever 2: Sales and marketing process

Can you predict top-line sales revenue with accuracy?

The sales and marketing process of any business is the most important factor in determining the outcome of sales and profit growth because it allows the entrepreneur to forecast profits. Robust and effective marketing delivers a healthy business pipeline and de-risks the traditional feast and famine issues often found in business. If the entrepreneur leaves all their sales and marketing activity to a small number of rainmakers, or serendipitous sales opportunities, then they are hostage to a group of very mobile assets and the sales pipeline will be vulnerable and unpredictable.

Investors want lead generation to be independent of any individual, with automation embedded into the sales and marketing process. A marketing-led

BU, where prospects are attracted through a balance of 'pull marketing' and 'push sales', is more likely to deliver a robust sales pipeline. Overall, they want a culture where sales and marketing are seen as an investment, and not as a cost, and by 'cranking the marketing handle faster' it is possible to drive more sales and cash into the business.

In order to drive growth, brand building and reputation is key, especially now in the digital age with extensive social networking. Strong brands take market share in difficult times. Businesses or SPV that focus their marketing efforts on where their business can win while proactively driving sales and measure and manage sales performance will do better than their competitors.

Lever 3: Go To Market (GTM) proposition

Does the GTM proposition provoke a 'wow' or a 'so what'?

The more unique, compelling and targeted the GTM proposition is, the better the entrepreneur can demonstrate that the BU can command market attention with greater ease than its competitors and increase the price of the product or service without a dip in demand. A business that has little to distinguish it is much more vulnerable because competition risks are higher. Defining a brilliant GTM even when there is a unique value proposition is far from straight-forward. Many have written about how to create 'clear blue water' between your offer and your competitors.[12] In practice, establishing a competitive advantage requires a considerable amount of high-quality thinking to get it right. That said, what the BU has invented will need to be sufficiently new or creative and will have been verified through a market testing stage; but this should be less of an issue for the entrepreneur. A clear GTM value proposition helps the invention stand out in the crowd. This will increase its equity value and attract attention from would-be buyers.

To optimise its potential, a good GTM strategy should focus on the financial benefits and return on investment (ROI) it can deliver for its customers and its parent business. Such clarity will also help the relationship between the new idea and the parent business. A BU embedded within a parent company that delivers something integral to a customer and is even part of its client's business plan rather than just a cost line in their Profit & Loss (P&L) is extremely attractive to the parent company. Such embedding of a start-up within another company's plan is the holy grail of all innovative start-ups.

Lever 4: Management quality

Does your leadership team work 'on' or 'in' the business?

Perhaps the single biggest determinant of success in a start-up, innovation engine, skunkworks or BU is the quality of the leadership team. A great idea needs careful cultivation by a high-quality team with a range of skills to enable the invention to be successfully commercialised. This is why if the BU is incubated inside a parent company, it needs to become a dedicated resource with some of the best people available, rather than being seen as a 'special project', which is often a euphemism for one small step from being exited from the company. When private equity or venture capital firms look at start-ups, they want to see a balanced, experienced leadership team with a track record of delivering results. That team has to spend more time working 'on' the business than 'in' it.[13]

If the BU is embedded in the parent company once it reaches a certain size or revenue threshold, then a range of options become possible. Firstly, if the new idea is sufficiently compatible with the parent, the unit can become fully re-integrated back into the parent. The leadership team is then probably best broken up or reassigned to the next entrepreneurial idea. The skills in building the business are different from the skills now required to develop the business. If the new business is not compatible with the parent, then it can be divested to generate capital for the parent or spun off as a stand-alone business and be managed independently as part of a portfolio. When divested, the entrepreneur or any of their team may go with the sale or they may cycle back to commercialise the next potential solution in the parent company.

All start-ups should be crystal clear on their strategy for growth as well as their exit strategy. The leadership team should make explicit how all profits are going to be handled (reinvested, distributed or retained) and how performance should be managed throughout the growth phase. They need a clear plan for how to internally and externally communicate results and empower staff.

Lever 5: Client relationships

Do you have a well-managed contact base and low client attrition?

All businesses live and die based on the quality of their client relationships. This is also true for start-ups, whether they are stand-alone or a skunkworks/ new delivery entity within a parent company. Such stakeholder management extends from your account planning methods to the way you nurture influencers, decision makers, dormant clients and old contacts. Good firms employ methodologies like Miller Heiman's Large Account Management Process to protect and grow strategic accounts; they use a customer relationship management (CRM) such as Infusionsoft or contact management system to assist in relationship development with individual contacts. Quality processes such as these enhance your ability to acquire, retain and build your client base, increase your revenue per client and improve the quality of your fee income.

All start-ups are keen to develop long-term relationships with their client base so they can build equity. Sustainable relationships are more commercially valuable because loyal customers deliver predictable revenue. All relationships must be matured, even in difficult times. A flexible CRM and account management process is critical with the aim to grow client's year on year.

Lever 6: Quality of income

Do you have long-term contracts and no bad debt?

The source of revenue for all start-ups is always crucial, whether they are standalone BUs or incubator divisions inside a parent company. If a sizeable percentage of future revenue is locked in through long-term contracts (12 months or more) with a number of customers, then the business will be viewed as strong. Investors like to see a diverse customer base (not too many eggs in one basket) with income growth balanced across existing customers and new business. Add to that a quality approach to billing and debt collection, resulting in minimal bad debt and low to zero working capital requirement, then you have a very strong card to play with investors.

It is always important to create ways to increase the predictability of leads, sales, profits and capital generation. There should be a focused investment, of time and attention, on strategic clients and, if possible, a link of revenue to customer results. The other key move to secure income for start-ups is to minimise dependency on any single customer and manage capital collection tightly.

Lever 7: Intellectual property (IP)

How much IP is transferable or locked up in key people?

A systematic approach to innovation, knowledge management and IP building will make any business more valuable because it de-risks the acquisition from the buyer's perspective. If the IP is well managed and baked into the system or processes of a BU or start-up, then it is less vulnerable to the loss of key people, either post-acquisition or after re-integration. This will make the idea at the centre of the BU more scalable. Also, effective IP development and management improves any company's market position by raising the bar for competitors.

The goal is to develop IP that drives sustainable profitable client relationships. It is vital to make sure IP is secure in uncertain times. It can help to create two types of IP: business-related (internal) and customer-related (external).

Lever 8: 'Key person' loyalty

Can you stop your equity assets from walking out the door?

There's no point in winning market share if the new start-up can't provide the skills and manpower to deliver. Ideally, it needs to create an environment people want to work in, where they get recognition, reward, personal development and have fun. By focusing on creating this environment, the business will be more likely to attract the best people and reduce their desire to take the next head-hunter call. Also, if you've locked your key staff into the future of your firm through profit-sharing and share options, then you'll have a team where people are much more focused on the equity growth of the business and its future acquisition. For parent companies, incubating start-ups and creating share options or loyalty bonus schemes is a pretty standard commercial move.

The goal here is to attract, develop and motivate the best quality staff; link compensation to profit growth and reduce the risk of key people attrition through the use of contract professionals.

As entrepreneurs and their teams embark on the commercialisation and growth journey, the Equity Growth Wheel can remind everyone of the opportunities to increase the value of the stand-alone business entity. That way, if the business is successful it is ready for sale or re-integration and there will be less work to do when the entrepreneur needs to hand back or hand over.

How it all comes together

An impeller approach may include players and roles that are not part of the current innovation approach, but more familiar roles will include:

- R&D
- Government
- Private Sector Organisations
- Analysts
- Designers

These roles will be explored in more detail in Chapter 6, but for now let's just take a moment to review how they all come together.

There is no shortage of problems that need innovative answers; they are everywhere. We can see the huge need for innovation in everything from the numerous books and journal articles to government-sponsored competitions and funding rounds. All such activity is seeking to solve something.

A bee, through their interactions with the meadow of experts, also identifies potential problems as well as identifies the people that have insights and the people that need the solution. Deciding which problem(s) to solve will either be based on a functional opportunity review or the bee generating a solution and then testing its hypothesis through a series of conversations with other stakeholders. The review, whether created by the opportunity analysis or the bees' intuitive response to the problem, focuses on what will be delivered and whether it is fit for the business.

But because the bee is always in the meadow, every day is an opportunity to talk about the solution and add or modify the approach depending on who the bee is in conversation with. The bee will use the solution to identify more experts to have conversations with, now that they know who they need. But even in these conversations, the solution is only part of the conversation with time spent in continuing to acquire more knowledge about that and even other issues.

Once the solution is confirmed, the bee passes it on to the delivery team to move it forward. At this point, the bee may or may not also pass on any insights they have regarding the implementation and commercialisation of the solution. But, primarily, the bee needs to keep moving in the meadow, accumulating knowledge. They are not normally part of the delivery team. The delivery team will package the solution (or solutions) to a point where it (or they) can be given to the analyst for review. At the point of hand over, the likelihood is that the solution will only really exist in the mind of the bee. They may have something documented, but not much.

The role of the innovation team is to develop more detail around the solution so that it can be accurately measured against the problem. The team will need to draft a business plan for each potential solution. The team will therefore need an understanding of research, business modelling and financial modelling. A researcher may be required to support the information needs of the model depending on the complexity or type of data required. The designer will work with the planner to create a visualisation of the solution. This is not the final design, it is only a way of illustrating the solution so that each audience that sees the proposed solution is able to quickly understand what is being suggested and perhaps, more importantly, all take away the same understanding.

This information can then be passed to an analyst for review. In some cases, it may be that external analysts are sought to review the opportunity so that the decision process is reviewed by an independent third party. The role of analysis, especially in cases where there is more than one potential solution, is to confirm that the solution or solutions will solve the problem. If there is more than one proposed answer, analysis should recommend which one represents the best opportunity.

Whilst the analyst is carrying out its review, the innovation team looks to see what is immediately possible based on the solution(s) being proposed. As previously discussed, it may be that there is already a combination of things in the market that can deliver up to 80 per cent of the solution.

This process of identification of resources will help inform likely partners and suggest potential market entry strategies. It may be possible to license technology or purchase outright the rights to what is required in the solution. Identifying who might be best placed to supply or sell early will improve the speed to market. It may be that there is another company that has a major component of the solution required but they are not interested in licensing or selling. This will require a longer timeframe to allow for developing a way of working together and ultimately the legal challenges in setting up a vehicle that would facilitate all interests. This is a traditional make or buy dilemma in most manufacturing businesses and is now increasingly seen within service-based businesses.

It is more likely that once the solution has been identified there will be an initial market launch and sometime later a final answer that will require new products or technologies to enable it. These technologies which act as accelerators to the novel idea may be known already. They may have been identified by the bees in conversation with academics or start-ups, where the technology is already under development but not yet market ready.

The bees' honeycomb – the output

The final output is to create a document that looks more like an investment 'prospectus', where all of the work that has been carried out to date resides. This will include everything from stating the problem and the solution and why to detailing the experts consulted to the business plan and modelling plus the analyst's response. It will include the work of the designer illustrating what the solution could look like as well as identifying what is possible now with whom and finally what is needed to deliver the final solution. Lastly, it should, where possible, identify the 'entrepreneur' who will have the responsibility to take it to market. It will be one of the entrepreneur's early tasks to start to identify their team based on the agreed upon delivery plan.

In summary, the outputs from the solution-focused, bee-driven innovation approach are:

- A recommended solution or solutions – flowing from the integration of experts' nectar by the bee
- A visualisation of what the solution might look like to help with further development
- Communication supported by analysis of the solution(s)
- Early identification of what is needed to deliver the solution in the market
- A business plan to take the solution to market

Advantages and benefits of impeller innovation

While the valley of death between successful test and validation and successful commercialisation still needs to be navigated, with the impeller approach only three to four months will have elapsed with the corresponding lower level of spend to get to a 'go'/'no go' decision point. The impact on an organisations ability to drive new solutions to market faster should now be clear. The traditional process acts like a brake, slowing down an innovation team's ability to deliver, increasing the total spending on innovation in the process and therefore requiring a much bigger return to cover the investment. In fact, the return on investment needs to cover the investment of the solution taken to market and needs to cover the failed project spending as well. The scale of this return has a direct impact on the decision process, as the organisation will be looking for bigger and bigger returns to cover their investment.

Under an impeller approach, speed to market is crucial. The approach will have identified what is possible immediately based on the knowledge of the solution. It will also know when the missing elements of the solution will be available based on an understanding of their development paths. At this point, an '80 per cent solution' can be taken to market.

Market entry with an 80 per cent answer allows the new delivery vehicle to not only get started fast but to test the market in advance of the 100 per cent solution. This will include developing the brand and route to market as well as the supporting resource and infrastructure. In most cases, a business will already have this in place. A new brand will be required but this is relatively low cost in the scheme of things.

Crossing the valley of death, the big barrier to market entry for new products and services is now being done at the lowest possible cost. At this point, one of two things could happen in a short period of time: the solution is well received and the need for it increases or it fails.

Success means that customers are already being acquired for the new solution even though it is only the 80 per cent version. Acquiring customers also means that income is already being generated and will allow data to be generated to feedback into any future development. This does set up a potential decision, albeit a positive decision. If the 80 per cent solution works and is solving a problem for the target customers, do you actually need the 100 per cent version? Time in the market will tell. But at this point, further unnecessary investment could be avoided if customers are happy. Alternatively, if feedback suggests that more customers would take up the 100 per cent solution (or pay more for it perhaps) then you have a very clear brief for the further development required. The costs for this development are then reduced as the solution is already generating sales and making a positive contribution to investment.

If the solution fails, far less money has been committed up to the point of failure than in the traditional innovation funnel approach. The failure has happened quickly, less money has been spent and lessons have been learnt fast. The options based on what now looks more like a test phase is to either shutdown or shelve the delivery vehicle, depending on the feedback and review. If the 80 per cent solution was not right and it really does require the 100 per cent solution, then confidence should be gained from the experience and a timeframe and development plan put in place to accelerate the 100 per cent solution to market, secure in the knowledge that the investment is justified.

The key here is to work out how best to position 'failure' and how the business deals with it both internally and externally. We know that 'innovation' fails but perhaps not that publicly. However, if organisations want to be seen as innovative then there is real value in promoting the idea that they are trying new things rather than just conducting research.

An impeller approach enhances and supports the rapid adoption and diffusion of novel solutions, whether new products or new services. This solution-pull rather than a technology-push saves time and money. It also shifts the focus to the early stages of adoption, as there is now a solution available. This enables more attention to be paid to channel preparation in the overall delivery of the innovation.

Notes

1 Ahmed W (2019) *The Polymath: Unlocking the Power of Human Versatility*, John Wiley & Sons, London.
2 Wilber K (2007) *Integral Vision*, Shambhala Publications, Colorado.
3 Semler R (1993) *Maverick! The Success Story Behind the World's Most Unusual Workplace*, Grand Central Publishing, New York.

4 Shenoy G (2017) The Nexialist Approach: Van Vogt and the Idea That 'Specialisation Is for Insects' *Factor Daily* https://factordaily.com/new-worlds-weekly-van-vogt-nexialism/

5 Martin R and Mikkelsen K (2016) *The Neo-Generalist: Where You Go Is Who You Are*, LID Publishing.
   Pilkington G (2017) The Rise of the Neo-Generalist Medium https://medium.com/startup-grind/the-rise-of-the-neo-generalist-5da52116b743
   Pontefract D (2017) Don't Be Afraid to Call Yourself a Neo-Generalist *Forbes* www.forbes.com/sites/danpontefract/2017/02/15/dont-be-afraid-to-call-yourself-a-neo-generalist/#76e6b8a33b08

6 Isaacson W (2017) *Leonardo Da Vinci*, Simon & Schuster, New York.

7 Grazer B and Fishman C (2015) *A Curious Mind: The Secret to a Bigger Life*, Simon & Schuster, New York.

8 Johnson B (1996) *Polarity Management: Identifying and Managing Unsolvable Problems*, HDR Press, Amherst, MA.

9 Clarke H (2016) Innovation: A Waste of Money? *Forbes Magazine* www.forbes.com/2006/08/23/leadership-innovation-requiredreading-cx_hc_0823moore.html#7546f25f4783

10 Collins P (2017) The 8 Levers of Equity Value www.equiteq.com/equiteq-edge/prepare-your-business-for-sale/the-8-levers-of-equity-value/

11 Equiteq.com [Accessed 2018] The 8 Levers of Equity Value www.equiteq.com/equiteq-edge/prepare-your-business-for-sale/the-8-levers-of-equity-value/

12 Chan Kim W and Mauborgne R (2015) *Blue Ocean Strategy, Expanded Edition: How to Create Uncontested Market Space and Make the Competition Irrelevant*, Harvard Business Review Press, Boston.

13 Gerber M (2001) *The E-Myth Revisited: Why Most Small Businesses Don't Work and What to Do about It*, Harper Business, New York.

4   The role of the bee

When we initially explain the impeller approach, it's often met with a little confusion. "If you already have a solution in mind, surely there is no innovation? Besides, how is it even possible to start with the solution"?

Current thinking suggests that we need an R&D phase to better define the problem and then come up with options as a way forward. This is true but only if we choose to follow conventional thinking and build an innovation system that depends on research and investigation of the problem. If the innovation system puts a different kind of individual – a bee – at the centre of the system, we can transform the entire process.

At the moment, the world recognises two types of thinkers: experts and generalists. In fact, our entire educational system (whether at school or university) trains us to be one of these two types of thinkers. When we are stuck for an answer, we most commonly turn to experts for their insight. There is no doubt that we need experts and that they play a vital role in all walks of life, as we shall discuss next. But there are other ways of thinking that can add value. Similarly, generalists are also helpful, not least because they can often provide a useful overview without diving into the detail that many experts get stuck in.

If we take the medical profession, for example, the entire system is built around these two types of thinkers – experts and generalists. Thus, we have expert consultants and primary care general practitioners (GPs). The experts may be surgeons or physicians who specialise in one bodily system. The generalist GPs often manage the volume of issues to filter out those that need to be referred to a specialist. Similarly, we have general nurses and specialist nurses, such as those we see in neonatal intensive care or midwives on the labour ward. All this health care activity is supported by medical research, which itself is super specialised with academics publishing their views in journals dedicated to their area of interest. Academics often invent their own language and research methods that often only a handful of colleagues in their own speciality can understand. Journalists, or more accurately specialist 'medical journalists', who are tasked with translating this cleverness for the public can, if they themselves are not sufficiently specialised, misunderstand the implications of such research or widely exaggerate its implications in search of an attractive headline.

But such micro-specialisation is not restricted to the medical field; it is endemic in virtually every human system or organisation. Take banking for example. It has been argued that the global financial crisis of 2008 was, in part, due to specialists inventing complicated 'consolidated debt obligations (CDOs)' and selling them on to others who did not have the expert knowledge to understand what they were buying.[1] The technology sector is also awash with experts who generate algorithms that are increasingly controlling our lives, determining what we pay attention to, what we buy and even which way we vote.[2] The 2018 furore over Cambridge Analytica's use of data scraped from over 50 million Facebook profiles to create targeted adverts to influence voters in the Brexit Referendum and 2016 US presidential race is a case in point.[3,4]

But as the world becomes increasingly complicated and the number of 'wicked' problems[5] we create continues to increase, we need a third type of thinker. We need people who can understand many different disciplines and see the connections between them. Not at the general superficial level but at a much deeper level. We are not the first to make this observation. Anders Sandberg from the Oxford Future of Humanity Institute said,

> At least for the next few decades, until machines become smarter than humans, the human polymath will be very important to society. Futurist Ray Kurzweil has said, Increasingly, the solutions to problems are found at the intersection of multiple fields . . . experts in highly specialised fields can be part of the team, but the team leader needs to bridge multiple fields.

And Peter Thiel has suggested, "A lot of the world-class entrepreneurs . . . they're not specialists, they're something close to polymaths".[6]

The good news is that such thinkers already exist. At first glance, this individual may sound rare or unusual but they may not be as rare as we think. Most human systems have been built on expertise and managed by generalists; as a result, this third type of thinker has often been rejected or been perceived as weird or quirky. Most systems have rejected these individuals because they don't fit the mould of expert or generalist. They are neither; they are bees. And they function in a profoundly different way from either experts or generalists.

We have reached a point in our evolution where the increased complexity of societies, nation states and organisations require us to go beyond expertise and turn to people who can better handle the complexity. At our current level of evolution, experts alone simply won't cut it anymore. We still need experts and generalists, but we need this new type of thinker too. We need to take that next evolutionary step toward greater integration. What's interesting is that the evolution of anything always follows the same three-step process.

The evolution of anything

Development psychologist and US intellectual Ken Wilber states that there are three stages within the evolution of anything – from ideology to biology to business. Let's take business as an example; it is, after all, businesses (along with governments) who are desperately seeking breakthrough innovations.

There are three stages of evolution, namely:

1   Emergence (generalist)
2   Differentiation (expert)
3   Integration (polymath integrator or bee)

Emergence (generalist)

First a business emerges. It may emerge in a garage like so many of the Silicon Valley giants of today – a couple of university friends with a good idea. Or it may be the result of a thorough business case analysis and years of planning. But one day it's up and running. The business is real; it's emerged into reality, it has been incorporated and has a bank account, revenue and a cost base.

This is the domain of the first type of operator, the generalist. Anyone who has ever started a business will tell you that despite being drawn to the creation of a business because of a specific skill set or idea, inevitably they become a 'jack of all trades and a master of none'. They can't afford an accountant so do the books on a spreadsheet. They can't afford to hire a marketer so they read some books or articles online and place some ads. They don't have the resources to hire an information technology person so they get a couple of second-hand laptops and ask their cousin who 'knows a bit about computers'. They learn on the fly, making mistakes and trying new approaches. The generalist must learn a little about a lot in order to prosper and grow the business they have created.

Generalists are important in the progression of any business because they often understand the conditions needed to grow the business. They can filter out unnecessary details. Generalists tend to have a little knowledge about multiple areas and can anticipate issues before they arise.

This is not to say that business founders are always generalists. They are actually more likely to be experts or bees. It's just that in the first phase of a business what is mainly required is generalist capability. The role of the generalists is well known in business and well understood. Their contribution is accepted, albeit sometimes reluctantly. However, as the business evolves and grows, knowing a little about a lot is not sufficient. Specialists are needed who know a lot about a little! The generalist steps back to give experts the opportunity to accelerate the growth of the business. Generalists must recruit a whole range of experts to do specialist functions such as accounting, marketing, sales, operations, administration human resources and so on.

Differentiation (expert)

After the emergence of generalists, the next major developmental stage of anything is differentiation. The thing, in this example the business, must differentiate itself. It must know what makes it different from other businesses in the sector in order to become competitive. It must define its Unique Selling Point (USP). A little ad hoc marketing is no longer enough to grow the business. What's needed is a more thorough understanding of the market and what customers want and value. The business now needs an expert marketer who understands that market and can reach prospective customers. The same applies across all the areas of the business. This evolution is triggered by growth and complexity. As the business becomes bigger, it becomes more complex and a spreadsheet for the accounts is no longer viable; an expert accountant and tax specialist needs to take over.

The emergence of differentiation is a crucial evolutionary step in anything and we can see this stage in the world today, perhaps nowhere more clearly, as we alluded to earlier, than in modern scientific medicine.

In the early days of medicine, doctors were generalists and largely observers of illness. They didn't have a deep understanding of what caused illness and disease. They didn't know enough, and so illness was attributed to some imbalance in the 'humours', seen as "God's will" or due to some other cultural superstition. As human understanding evolved and we developed a more differentiated approach, doctors investigated the causation of disease. Pioneers in medicine made ground-breaking discoveries that changed the course of human history.[7] These 'experts' broke down what was happening in the human body to understand its component parts. As a result, our physiological understanding has advanced significantly, especially over the last 150 years. For most of that time, scientists and physicians have been unravelling the complexity of the human condition by systematically reducing every disease and every bodily system into ever smaller parts. This *systematic reductionism* has been the overriding approach to investigating human beings and it has been incredibly successful. Reductionism has shed new light on how the human body works. It has generated an enormous amount of new information, spawned whole new areas of medical research and created new languages to capture the myriad of discoveries being made. So much so that it became impossible to keep pace with all of the new data and discoveries. Each part of the human body now has its own experts. To paraphrase comedienne Maureen Lipman, everyone became an 'Ologist'.

These 'ologists' now publish their new insights in their own journals, speak in their own unique language and attend specialist conferences to share increasingly finer details about their specialism or area of differentiation.

These 'ologists' are not better than the generalists (although many experts like to think they are). We still need GPs in medicine; otherwise the whole system would grind to a halt. They are simply two solutions to a myriad of challenges that we face medically – both necessary, both needed.

In many ways, differentiation's hey-day was the industrial revolution.

In *the Wealth of Nations*, famous Scottish economist Adam Smith wrote about the 'division of labour' or the specialisation of the workforce. He believed that economic growth came from breaking down large tasks or processes into multiple specialised tasks. Each worker would focus only on one isolated area of the production process, thus increasing their efficiency. This made perfect sense in the Victorian factories of the nineteenth century. What's perhaps less well known or at least more readily ignored is that Smith also recognised the potential problems or unintended consequences of this approach: that the workforce would become ignorant of all but that tiny task and they would become bored and dissatisfied. As a result, he advanced the notion that governments had an obligation to provide education to workers to combat the negative impact of such differentiation, a revolutionary idea at the time. More recently, Yuval Noah Harari has majored on this point in *Homo Deus*.[8]

Of course, compulsory schooling emerged too and it followed the same path as everything else – emergence followed by differentiation. Even today we are taught subjects separately, as if physics had nothing to do with chemistry and neither impinged on biology in any way. In primary school, we are taught by generalists – one teacher teaching a little of everything. But even then, the subjects are soon split up. We progress into high school and the subjects are taught by 'experts' with a greater depth and understanding in that subject. We are taught maths in one lesson and English in another; biology, physics and chemistry are distinct entities with no obvious point of contact.

Whilst the breaking down of information into subject areas is important in order to understand things properly, the school and university systems we have today have become stuck at this evolutionary stage and the quality of education has suffered because of it. Topic areas have become fragmented and disconnected from each other, which undermines the relevance and inhibits a greater more integrated understanding. When forced to separate these subjects, it's drilled into children's heads, from an early age, that knowledge is fragmented into separate curriculum areas. This regimented approach crushes any natural polymathic capability. The International Baccalaureate (IB) was designed, in part, to counter balance this trend. The IB offers four programmes, through 5,000 schools in over 150 countries around the world. Their education programmes focus on teaching students to think critically and independently and how to inquire with care and logic, seeking to prepare students to succeed in a world where facts and fiction merge in the news and where asking the right questions is a crucial skill that allows students to flourish long term.

Britain, whilst having a generally good reputation for education, is also known to promote greater specialisation than most other nations' educational systems and at an earlier age. Children grow up and go to university with siloed knowledge and then specialise even further around their chosen topic. They leave, get work in that field and stay in that echo chamber or commercial silo, often for their entire working lives.

In an increasingly volatile world, corporations realise this siloed approach is not working and is actively holding them back from growth and genuine innovation. They know they need to break down their silos but are unsure how to do it effectively. Some are moving back to general manager roles but, alone, a generalist is profoundly under horse powered against the rising number and complexity of issues we face in business. Although some more enlightened businesses have spotted the critical importance of breaking down their silos and are working more collaboratively and cross functionally, most are still in the early stages of learning how to do this.

Many organisations, in an attempt to manage the complexity and diffuse the siloed nature of their businesses, created complex 'matrix management' practices. These are, in truth, often a labyrinth of hierarchical relationships and power battles with people reporting to two bosses with 'dotted lines' to one boss and a 'hard line' to another. The more mature matrix structures are really an attempt to crystallise the differentiation rather than actually integrate properly. Many Millennials have seen the inflexibility of such a highly differentiated and specialised approach and are actively seeking to develop multiple capabilities or are much more prepared to change careers. But this is not yet the prevailing view, and the risk is that they never really integrate; they simply gather a collection of different expertises that remain disconnected.

While differentiation is a necessary step in the evolutionary process of anything and has created a boon for humanity across the board, it is not the final stage of evolution.

Integration (polymath integrator or bee)

In order for the insights that have been generated, as a result of differentiation, to become really useful, they must be fully integrated with each other. Thus, integration is about context and relationship and it is vital in an increasingly complex world. It is entirely possible to break a problem down into very clearly defined smaller issues but, unless there is integration, the danger is fragmentation or even dis-integration. Such collapse results in problems either not being solved at all, or only being partially solved. Fragmentation produces a great deal of activity but very little genuine change for the better. Pretty much any field you care to explore is awash with well-intentioned individuals trying to change the world. But when there is a failure to integrate effort and effectively collaborate across organisations, all this good intention is dissipated, leaving us in much the same situation we were before we started. What we lack is the ability to integrate and collaborate together to the degree that can solve and re-solve the wicked problems we have created.

Going back to our medicine example from earlier, we can see the unintended consequences that getting stuck at differentiation has created. Medicine has largely mastered the emergence part of the evolutionary process; we are pretty skilled at the differentiation element, but we have a very long way to go to master integration. In fact, 'integrated care' and 'interdisciplinary research' have only really emerged in the last 35 years as a concept, let alone matured as practices. The human system is an example of a complex system, and complex systems cannot be understood simply by understanding each part of that system because the whole is *always* greater than the sum of the parts.

Business is also another complex system. We have become reasonably proficient at the emergence of ideas, new businesses, new products and new strategies for growth. We have broken business down to understand its component parts and we now have different divisions and departments. We have specialists that manage those divisions whose area of expertise is limited only to that division or industry. And, of course, we have every type of business consultant and guru who will supposedly fix a specific corporate ailment.

What we have *not* mastered is integration. Even within the same business, divisions compete against each other; departments remain isolated and act as separate silos within the single entity. And without access to the "whole", the parts are not greater than the sum of the parts; they are just bits of the system generating bitty answers that often serve themselves but disadvantage other parts of the organisation. In such siloed organisations, strategic direction and tactics easily become stale. New ideas are no longer new ideas, new products are no longer new products, they are simply old ideas and old products, tweaked slightly, repackaged and re-launched. In desperation, we look around at the competition, only they are doing the same thing: regurgitating what already exists and spending vast sums of money trying to convince their customers that it really is something new, something better or something different. And yet if we look at disruptive innovators such as Apple, Sony, Dyson and Rolls Royce, often their innovations were made possible by looking *outside* their industry.

Rolls Royce for example completely changed their business model from manufacturing jet engines to the 'printer and ink' business model by appreciating the game changing nature of sensor technology. Printer manufacturers know that there is very little margin in the manufacture of the printer, the real money is in the ink that will make the printer useful long-term. Rolls Royce did the same. Now, instead of just manufacturing the engine, every engine comes with an on-board computer that is the brain of the engine, controlling it and collecting and monitoring data from thousands of sensors buried deep within the engine measuring 40 parameters 40 times per second including temperature, pressure and turbine speed. All those measurements are stored in the computer and streamed back to Rolls Royce Headquarters in Derby via satellite. If any of those sensors show anything unusual, it's flagged and dealt with before it even has time to escalate into a problem.[9] Amongst other advantages, these sensors allow for dynamic maintenance based on actual engine-by-engine performance rather than some time-based rota system. This is not only more cost effective but also safer too. Collectively, these sensors continuously monitor the performance of more than 3,700 jet engines worldwide, delivering engine-by-engine intelligence to their clients as well as generating long-term, recurring revenue over and above the manufacturing revenue stream. Rolls Royce now sells the engines *and* offers to monitor those engines too, charging customers based on engine usage time and repairs and replaces parts if there is a problem. This disruptive shift in focus now accounts for 70 per cent of the civil-aircraft engine division's annual revenue.[10] The jury is still out on how the company will recover from COVID-19 and the near global shutdown of air travel, but the innovation itself was brilliant.

Without this disruptive integration, this exploration of unusual partnerships and genuinely novel ideas, the business stagnates. It's like playing poker with half of a deck of cards; we are all constantly shuffling the same cards in an effort to find a new solution but unless we get access to the rest of the deck, it's impossible to create the hand we know we want to play or are capable of playing because we just don't have the cards in the deck. In our struggle to innovate, we invest in costly mergers or acquisitions in an effort to access the other 'cards in the deck' only to find we now have a duplicate set of exactly the same cards rather than the other half of the deck.

Innovation is more important now than ever before but genuine innovation is impossible without high quality differentiation and integration. The evolution of anything is an upward spiral of emergence, differentiation, integration and re-emergence. Today we are increasingly stuck because we have broken everything down so completely that we are innovating from the same, often duplicated, deck that everyone else is innovating from. Consequently, many companies are banging their heads against the same performance wall, or throwing good money after bad in a desperate attempt to unlock some new potential.

Differentiation certainly allows us to really dive into a topic and see what works, what doesn't, what's accurate and what's not. But those insights are often set against each other as we out expert each other, one expert refuting the other. What's needed is an ability to preserve. Preserve the useful and discard the dysfunctional; ingrate what's left to create something better in an endless upward cycle. And one way to help unlock that potential is to recognise and embrace the role of the bee, who works alongside the generalists and specialists with each helping to get the most out of the others.

The bee acts like a comb, having a broad, generalist knowledge to create the spine together with the depth of understanding of multiple topics to provide the teeth. The depth won't be as significant as the expert and not as broad as the generalist, but the bee is the person that can unlock the brilliance of both. The bee transcends and includes both the generalist and the expert. Bees do not replace experts or generalists; all three types of people are needed, especially if we are to come up with genuine innovation or solutions to the myriad of complex problems we face. But it's the bee who is able to harvest knowledge from the meadow of experts and convolve that knowledge with their existing expert and general wisdom to come up with possible solutions or innovations.

Harvesting and convolving knowledge

The bee adds value because he or she is able to harvest the wisdom of the crowd to come up with multiple possible solutions.

Since we are at a point in history where differentiation is still prized above all else, experts are still seen as the most important people in all systems. They are the pinnacle, the aspiration, in many careers. They are often, mistakenly, seen by society as the repository of wisdom from which answers will flow. We are not suggesting we no longer need experts — we will always choose a qualified brain surgeon over a GP if we have a brain tumour. We are simply suggesting that bees are the new sources of breakthrough innovations because they work by unlocking the wisdom of the meadow of experts while acknowledging the contribution of the generalist.

Such a view is supported by the research into the wisdom of crowds. Recently, social scientists discovered something quite surprising. Namely, that under the right conditions the crowd is remarkably intelligent and is often smarter collectively than the smartest individuals in that crowd.[11] And, the right conditions are not that the crowd is filled with experts or that the crowd should be particularly well-informed about the problem or even that the crowd is rational. The conditions for wisdom to emerge have been well described;[12] they are:

1   **Diversity of knowledge and opinion** – wisdom is enhanced by diversity. The exact type of diversity required to optimise the wisdom of a crowd is still unknown but it certainly includes diversity of expertise, gender, ethnicity, background, education, culture, age and how developed the individuals are. The best innovation is made possible if the bee accumulates knowledge and insight from a diverse range of experts (and generalists) in the meadow. The diversity of inputs may include intuitions, opinions or interpretations of 'facts' from any of the experts, generalists or indeed the bees themselves

2   **Independence of thought and collaboration** – wisdom is enhanced when each individual contributor is not unduly influenced by another person's opinion. Thus, there is no cross-contamination between expert flowers in the meadow. Effectively, the bee collects more pure nectar or knowledge

3   **Decentralisation of power** – the wisdom of the crowd is enhanced by the inclusion of opinions outside or away from traditional power hierarchies and where people impacted by decisions are free to share their local and specific knowledge relating to that decision without influence or impunity. This means that the bee collects nectar from a vast and varied meadow of experts

4   **Integration** – as we have already seen, the ability to combine separate views by transcending and including them to create a new view is a very sophisticated evolutionary capability. Such integration is not the same as averaging or aggregating existing views, both of which dumb down the output. Effective integration often requires a bee, not an expert or a generalist

The bee is a veracious consumer of knowledge and information. This may happen through meeting a diverse range of people in diverse industries or subject areas or reading a lot of books, scientific papers, journals or articles across a diverse range of topics. By accumulating ideas, knowledge and information, those data streams or information points bump up against each other or 'percolate' internally via a process known as convolving.

Convolution is a mathematical operation on two functions to produce a third function. However, the notion of convolution has spread to neuroscience (an example of convolution itself) and it is now thought to be a critical component of creativity. Many kinds of creativity result from combinations of mental representations. Creative thinking can arise from combining neural patterns into ones that are potentially novel and useful via a convolution, a process that interweaves structures and can support the cognitive and emotional processes underlying human creativity.[13]

In simpler terms, when a bee, who is by their nature a veracious consumer of information, adds new information to their data banks, all that data recalibrates and reorganises, largely unconsciously. The previous information bumps up against the new information and new patterns and observations emerge that can give rise to new thoughts and new ideas. The brain will automatically evaluate the relevance of the new ideas in relation to any existing goals or needs and stores the thoughts or discards them. Some will be useless and the convolution will put data points together that don't work or don't throw up anything genuinely novel, but sometimes those combinations or pattern recognitions will be ground breaking.

For example, Sir James Dyson's invention of the cyclone vacuum cleaner was undoubtedly a process of convolution. Dyson had brought what claimed to be the most powerful vacuum cleaner on the market but it didn't work – it just pushed the dirt around the room. It was a visit to an industrial sawmill that sparked the idea of the cyclone technology central to his success. The sawmill used something called a cyclonic separator to remove dust from the air. Dyson wondered if that might work in a vacuum cleaner. It did.

Charles Darwin probably also used convolution when he connected nature and selection, two ideas that seem at odds with each other. Darwin was amazed to discover that the novel concept of 'natural selection' could explain facts about species that had long puzzled him and his resultant theory is arguably one of the most important discoveries of all time.

It was the combination of unusual ideas or the stepping out of comfort zones or observations of different unconnected elements that, when combined with existing knowledge, triggered the new insight. The bee's accumulation of diverse knowledge and information can seem ad hoc or even indulgent or irrelevant, but when a problem or need is then applied to that data set or knowledge bank, potential solutions begin to emerge. The bee knows enough about a lot of things to be able to start to see the connections, but not too much to see the constraints and close those options down too early. So much of what we might call innovation is killed off before it's ever really considered because limiting beliefs, industry conventions or internal business culture squashed it. The bee rarely has these constraints.

Integration is the real challenge we face today. The knowledge available to all of us now is staggering, so staggering in fact that it has pushed many individuals in all walks of life into specialist subjects and intellectual silos. Whilst understandable, it's time to bring it all back together and it's the bee that can help us do that in business and government. Not only will this integration allow us to gain a more comprehensive and accurate understanding of complex systems such as business, medicine or government but it will become the wellspring from which genuine innovation will emerge.

Types of bees and their output

In the natural world, a honey bee hive is made up of:

- One queen
- 50,000 infertile female worker bees performing various tasks including making honey
- 300 male drone bees (whose only purpose is to mate with the queen)
- 9,000 hungry larvae needing to be fed
- 20,000 older larvae and pupae in sealed cells, needing warmth
- 6,000 eggs from which new larvae will hatch

For the first three weeks of a worker bees' life, they are 'house bees'. House bees are responsible for keeping the hive clean, feeding the growing brood of developing bees, building the honeycomb, packing nectar, water and honey into the honeycomb and taking care of the queen. They also act as guards, killing intruders and sick bees, if necessary, to protect the colony from disease. As worker bees mature, they become smaller and lighter as they take on the new role of foraging bees. Their increased strength and agility make them good at gathering nectar and water to bring back to the hive to add to the comb to make the honey.

Only these foraging worker bees actually produce anything.

The same is true of the bee. While there may be 20 or more bees in your business already buzzing around gathering information and knowledge, only the mature bee will be able to create or come up with potential solutions based on the knowledge they've gathered from the meadow of experts and beyond. Knowing how to recognise and nurture the bees in your business is therefore important for on-going success and developing innovation capability.

But how does the mature bee do it? What is happening in their brain that allows them to come up with potential solutions beyond the integration of disparate pieces of information gathered from the meadow? One systemic thinking tool that is useful is the Magnitude, Periodicity and Holistic (MPH) model created by author and consultant Mike Cope.[14] We've adapted it here to help facilitate faster solution assessment.

The Magnitude, Periodicity and Holistic (MPH) model

Originally designed as a way for consultants to assess clients and their needs to orchestrate a better professional fit and facilitate greater results, the MPH model describes three common filters that bees often use to see the world:

- Magnitude (M): is the altitude we see from
- Periodicity (P): the time period we include
- Holistic (H): the type of view we prefer

These three filters can be expanded to create a nine-grid assessment model (see Figure 4.1).

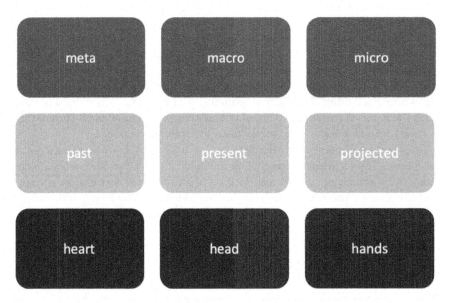

Figure 4.1 Magnitude, Periodicity and Holistic (MPH) Assessment Model

When the bee visits the meadow of experts, they may use these system frames to integrate their creativity with the expert knowledge to draft potential solutions quickly. They may not be fully fledged solutions but they are solid and coherent enough to allow for robust scrutiny and further investigation.

Meta

The bee absorbs the high-level information from the meadow of experts to get a big-picture sense of the problem and the environment and stakeholders it impacts. These are the narrative theme and parameters of the problem at the 'I', 'WE' and 'IT'/'ITS' levels.

Macro

Bees may drop down a level and gather mid-level information. Here the idea is to capture just enough information to be able to form a view on what the solution might look like and start to weave an answer together.

Micro

Once potential ideas begin to percolate from the macro information gathered from the meadow of experts, the bee will test those fledgling solutions using the micro information or details of the problem to quickly assess suitability and potential. This is where the solution may or may not pass initial thought experiment stage. It is also the point where it will become clearer as to what dimension of the problem the proposed solution is most likely to address.

One of the critical skills of a bee is the ability to shift levels from meta to macro to micro and perhaps, more importantly, know how, why and when to do so.

The ability of a bee to see the largest possible picture and embrace the biggest and most complex data sets is one thing that differentiates the ability of bees from each other. This 'meta-capability' of a bee is often manifested in their consistent use of metaphor. Bees will often energise themselves by considering "what is the *meta* for"? The simple answer is communication.

A carefully chosen and crafted metaphor is used by bees to convey some very complex or nuanced insights. A metaphoric story can have a significant impact by rendering complexity simple. Metaphors are a common way for bees to convey their wisdom. They will spend time considering and crafting their metaphors and often spice them up with paradox, humour and linguistic charm. For example, a bee may talk about the importance of moving from 'emergency to emergence', a small change, in this case a single letter, leads to a big difference. Such conceptual and communicational alchemy comes naturally to many bees.

Past

Via the meadow of experts, the bee will seek to establish what's happened in the past in terms of attempts to solve the problem. What have the experts learned from the past failures regarding the problem? Bees will intuitively assess whether the solution or solutions playing around in their mind are sufficiently different to past failures. Does the solution take into consideration what was learned from the past attempts or any changes to the issue?

Present

Where is the leading scientific or knowledge edge regarding this issue? How have the past successes and failures convolved to create the present situation? What are the current hurdles, threats or opportunities? Again, does the solution(s) that have already formed through the meta, macro and micro information provided by the meadow of experts consider the current reality around the problem?

Projected

According to the meadow of experts, where are we trying to get to? Does the solution or solutions that are forming in the bee's mind pass muster against this projected future? Would it actually solve the problem, mask it or only solve part of the problem?

A bee considers not only solving the problem as it currently appears but also how the problem and solution may look in the future. This futurologist ability to project into scenarios that have yet to materialise is particularly strong in mature bees, and draws on one of the most fundamental operations that is at the core of how the mind constructs reality.[15]

Heart

Does the prospective solution(s) feel right? Will it be possible to emotionally engage the various stakeholder groups around this solution? This filter along with 'Head' does require a level of vertical sophistication on the part of the bee so that they can embrace multiple perspectives and appreciate that often the best solutions live in the nuanced world of the perceptive rather than the absolute world of the definite.

Head

As you might expect, the head filter is the rational perspective. Will the solution(s) meet the need? Does it make logical sense? Is it possible and feasible? Can it actually succeed given market conditions, and will it add value?

Hands

Finally, the solutions that are playing around in the bee's mind must be practical. They must offer an executable solution that will solve a real-world problem rather than just an intellectual problem. Thus, the solution has to be emotionally engaging, make sense and be deliverable.

The MPH framework is a useful way of making explicit the systemic thinking of a bee and one of the ways they sense-check the potential solutions that emerge from speaking to the meadow of experts.

It is the integration of all the knowledge and expertise gained from the meadow of experts with the creative intuitive minds of bees that generate genuinely innovative solutions. Once those solutions emerge, it is actually very fast and inexpensive to test these ideas with a systemic tool such as the MPH filter to determine the breakthrough nature of the answer. Using further conversations with the meadow of experts, we can determine if there are any glaring errors of judgement or opportunities where that solution may create negative unintended consequences.

The bees are coming

We acknowledge that there may be a distinct shortage of bees in many businesses today (2020). Even if they exist, which they almost certainly do, there is currently very little appreciation of the value this new type of thinker can bring to innovation. In fact, we believe this shortage of bees or their dismissal is fundamental to why innovation is failing so frequently at present.

However, there is good news. We suspect that there are more bees than we might initially imagine. It's just that they have been in hiding or been forced into generalist or expert roles. In addition, and perhaps more importantly, there is a growing recognition across most businesses of the need for more integrative roles. With the increased demand and the flushing out of hidden capability, we can see that more bees are coming. And, if utilised properly, this will mean less innovation failure.

As the world speeds up, organisations are becoming increasingly aware of the need to break down their silos and work in a much more fluid and cross-functional fashion if they want to remain competitive. As a result, a few of the more enlightened organisations have begun to realise that silo busting is massively facilitated by the integrative thinking that bees offer.

At present, we understand and value the role of a generalist. In many companies, the general manager is still a highly regarded role. At the start of many leader's careers, individuals begin as generalists. To progress, they soon realise that they need to differentiate and become experts in some aspect of business. This specialism often takes them all the way to the C-suite, particularly if that specialism is finance or sales. But the value of the expertise ironically diminishes as a leader gets close to the top job as a CEO. In fact, if leaders want to be the CEO and manage the end-to-end P&L, then they often have to let go of their own expert discipline and embrace a more human-centric, integrative approach in order to reach the summit of their own organisation.

But it is not just in business where people are increasingly questioning the role of the expert. Many others are beginning to realise that experts are fallible and the role of the expert is under a much higher degree of scrutiny. People are much less likely to blindly accept expert opinions in any subject than they once were.[16] Of course, some of this is because we are in a post-truth meltdown, but some of it is due to a legitimate realisation that we must not blindly accept expertise and must be considerably more discerning about who we believe and why.[17]

One of the many things that can prevent a breakthrough is the hubris of an expert. Experts, often by their very nature, operate from a stance of certainty, deploying an "I'm right, so you must be wrong" stance. When two sides are pitted against each other (as the media loves to do), each side finds their own expert to 'out-expert' the other side instead of everyone finding the genuine merit in each argument, preserving that and collaborating to find workable solutions to complex problems.

This battle of the experts has become the very thing that now often blocks progress, particularly in the areas of innovation, religious reconciliation, ethnocentric culture wars, political divisiveness and excessive corporate competitiveness. The ability to reconcile differences, be they political, religious or commercial, has become one of the primary risks to the future of our planet.

We believe the recognition and understanding of the role of the bee could be the source of a potentially massive breakthrough in all fields of human endeavour.

There are also several contributing factors that we believe will fast-track humanity's leap to the third stage of evolution – integration – and the proliferation of bees that integration will bring. If you can already see a shift in the workplace and appreciate an emergence of a new type of thinker, then, again, you may want to jump forward to Chapter 5. If you remain to be convinced, then our suggestions as to why the bees are coming might prove illuminating. They are:

- The influx of Millennials into the workforce
- The acceleration of AI
- Shifting work practises
- Increased diversity
- The failure of leadership in a post-truth world

The influx of Millennials into the workforce

Even as recently as five or ten years ago, it would have been considered seriously career limiting to admit to 'gaps' in your C.V. Job hopping, especially between industries, was considered poor form and negative assumptions were made in recruitment discussions about the persons 'reliability' or 'professionalism'. But the working world of Millennials (also known as Gen Y) and younger is a very different one to the working environment familiar to Gen X or the Baby Boomers.

For a start, when Baby Boomers, those born roughly between 1946–1964, entered the workforce, a job for life was still a viable concept. Apprenticeships or working their way up was a common and accepted route to take and many people entered and stayed in the same company for life. Life was good for the Boomers; there was plenty of work, the swinging sixties and cradle-to-grave welfare. Unsurprisingly, Baby Boomers were idealistic and optimistic, opportunity was everywhere and many grasped that opportunity and enjoyed unparalleled prosperity.

By the time Gen X came along, those born between 1965 and 1980, things were not so rosy. They watched their parents work hard for their success, often loyally working for the same company for 40 plus years. This often took a toll on relationships and the Boomers were the first to divorce in large numbers. The Xers therefore learned to look after themselves early as both parents often worked, or they were raised in single parent households. Xers were shaped by major political events such as the Vietnam War, the fall of the Berlin Wall, the end of the Cold War and Thatcher's Britain. This made them more diverse, open to difference and more tolerant and self-sufficient than their parents, but also more skeptical. This open-mindedness, curiosity and self-sufficient experimentation was the beginning of bee-like behaviour; and a few of these new types of thinkers emerged, but they were the exception not the rule. Gen X still believed that the way to success was to get an education and work hard for a company but they were more frequently laid off, amplifying their distrust.

Today, jobs for life don't exist. Downsizing is common and a university degree is no longer a ticket to a well-paid job. And Gen Y knows it. Gone are the days where someone could enter a profession and move up the ranks in that profession. Today Gen Y is expected not only to have multiple jobs but actually to have multiple different careers. According to the Bureau of Labor Statistics in the US, the average young adult has held on average 6.2 jobs by the time they are 26 years old.[18] Most Baby Boomers wouldn't have had 6.2 jobs in their lifetime! This diversity of experience is not a weakness; it's a potential benefit as it nourishes bee-like behaviour and mindset.

Millennials won't stay in a job they don't enjoy and they don't think twice about completely changing industries. As a result, the very characteristics that have made them a handful to manage in traditional organisations are the very characteristics that make them more naturally bee-like. Their job hopping creates the much-needed access to diverse opinions, experiences and information. It is their way of visiting a meadow of experts.

This is especially important considering the sheer number of Millennials that are now entering the workplace. Born from 1981 to 2000, Gen Y belongs to a huge cohort of about 70 million people. The Intelligence Group predicted that 40 per cent of the workplace will be made up of Millennials by 2020.[19] A separate Gen Y study published in April 2011 noted that by 2025, Generation Y will make up roughly 75 per cent of the global workforce.[20]

This generation is often known as 'Gen Why'.[21] They questioned their parent's effort in relation to their reward. And, they realised that people are not always rewarded for their effort or loyalty. Gen Y is a lot more technologically sophisticated than their parents and are looking for purpose and fulfillment as well as a way to make a living. They don't necessarily feel loyalty to a company or brand and are happy to keep moving to new positions until they find one that suits them and their ideology. As more and more Millennials move into the workforce and progress in those businesses or start new businesses, they are looking for more than simply profit or a salary. They are looking for purpose, the ability to make a positive contribution to something they feel is important, all while achieving a healthy work-life balance. What could be more worthwhile and deliver more purpose than having an instrumental role in solving complex problems and coming up with game changing innovation that changes the world?

This is certainly backed up by the Intelligence Group studies of Millennials which found that:

- 64 per cent of them say it's a priority for them to make the world a better place
- 72 per cent would like to be their own boss. But if they do have to work for a boss, 79 per cent of them would want that boss to serve more as a coach or mentor. (Bear this in mind when we discuss the idea of bee 'in residence' later in this chapter – this new role may be an ideal work fit for Millennials.)
- 88 per cent prefer a collaborative work-culture rather than a competitive one. (By their nature, bees are collaborative harvesters of knowledge and experience. They are not competitive or combative)

- 74 per cent want flexible work schedules. (Again, bee 'in-residence' would offer such flexibility.)
- 88 per cent want 'work-life integration', which isn't the same as work-life balance, since work and life now blend together inextricably[22]

Millennials are not looking to fill a slot in a faceless company; they're looking strategically at opportunities to invest in a place where they can make a difference, preferably a place that itself makes a difference. "Good luck with that" is the cry of Gen X and Baby Boomers who often wrongly assume their needs and expectations are simply an excuse not to work. But Gen Y are a potentially disruptive, innovative, creative, technically skilled and purpose-driven bunch that are likely to accelerate the acceptance of the integrative bee approach, which will in turn enhance innovation potential. While integrative thinkers were rare and unusual in the Gen X and Baby Boomer cohorts, they will be much more common in the Millennials and the Digital Natives that will follow them.

The Digital Natives, born from 2000 onwards, have yet to enter the workforce in any number but they too will bring a positively disruptive influence. All they've known so far is a world proliferated by technology. They can't imagine their life without the internet and political and financial turmoil are 'normal'. They see technology not as the waste of time or danger that their parents often see it as but as an opportunity to bring equality, education and information that can help right some of the wrongs they can already see in the world.

Innovation has been failing to deliver for too long. At least part of that failure is down to the wrong people in the wrong roles. Either people who could make a positive difference squashed into roles that nullify their gifts or those who are forced to take on tasks in the innovation process they are wholly unsuited to. Neither is fair and both represent a colossal waste of human potential. But, the advent of this new Gen Y and Digital Native workforce could change all that. If understood, appreciated and managed properly they could transform innovation and bring much needed integrative insights to business and government.

The acceleration of Artificial Intelligence (AI)

Part of the opportunity inherent in Gen Y and the Digital Natives is their comfort and familiarity with technology. While technology existed before they were born, its growth and proliferation into every aspect of our lives has been exponential in Gen Y's lifetime. These generational cohorts don't know a world where technology isn't a part of their daily experience. Today, no industry is untouched by technology, from food production and manufacturing through to the service sector and beyond. Game-changing technology and AI is changing the nature of work itself, particularly in a post-COVID world. And this change too is likely to usher in a greater appreciation for the role of the bee. Consistent successful commercialisation of a novel idea starts with a bee. They are by no means the only role or the most important role but, to really turn the dial on innovation and convert the current failure rate of up to 90 per cent[23] to consistent success, we need those bees. And AI will further help to illuminate their role.

Behavioural science has suggested that despite the myriad of activities in any job or the massive variety of jobs that people perform, there are essentially two types of tasks: algorithmic and heuristic. As the name might suggest, algorithmic work is tasks which follow a set of established instructions down a single 'best' path. Heuristic tasks are essentially the opposite, there is no 'best' outcome, no algorithm; instead the individual must experiment with possibilities, remain flexible and use creativity to devise novel and frequently changing solutions.[24]

Technological innovation has been replacing human effort for centuries. Once the division of labour was mastered during the Industrial Revolution, those differentiated algorithmic, repetitive tasks were increasingly replaced by machines. Assembly lines in manufacturing have been steadily replacing human beings doing algorithmic tasks ever since. In 2016, Foxconn, the Apple and Samsung supplier, confirmed that they had replaced 60,000 factory workers with robots. In the two years prior, some 505 factories across Dongguan, in the Guangdong province of China, invested the equivalent of £430 million in robots, aiming to replace thousands of workers. This type of automation has prompted dire warnings, with one report from consultants Deloitte in partnership with Oxford University predicting that 35 per cent of jobs are at risk over the next 20 years.[25] In 2016, Robert Skidelsky, professor of political economy at the University of Warwick stated that, "Credible estimates suggest it will be technically possible to automate between a quarter and a third of all current jobs in the western world within 20 years".[26]

But technology is not just going to replace lower paid, repetitive or 'generalist' roles. It's also going to replace many of the highly skilled experts. Although we perceive these roles as completely different and society certainly values the latter more highly, they are both still algorithmic tasks.

A doctor may be highly educated, having completed years of study in order to make the best diagnosis based on how the patient presents to them, but effective diagnosis is still a data or information crunching activity. The doctor assesses the patient's symptoms, matches those against the doctor's knowledge banks and experience to arrive at the most likely or plausible diagnosis based on the patient's history and location. There are already computer programs and Apps that can diagnose better than a doctor simply because the technology can access *all* medical knowledge currently known, every anomaly, every symptom and every scenario including probabilities, crunch that data and successfully narrow down the likely diagnosis faster and more accurately than a human being.[27] The online service Isabel Healthcare is one such system offering professional tools for doctors and a free Isabel Symptom Checker for everyone. Starting out as a charity, the system was inspired by Isabel, the founders' daughter who contracted chicken pox. A common childhood condition which usually clears up in weeks developed into necrotising fasciitis and toxic shock despite assurances by doctors that nothing was wrong. Isabel went into cardiac arrest and experienced multiple organ failure, only pulling through after three weeks in intensive care and a further five weeks in hospital.

Isabel's parents were told they had a case for 'clinical ignorance', and that the diagnosis had been missed simply because it was rare. Instead of taking legal action they created the Isabel Medical Charity with the aim to improve diagnostic processes and help doctors with their jobs. The resulting paediatric tool brings up a list of all the possible diagnoses for an entered set of symptoms. This way no diseases, particularly the rare and more dangerous conditions, could be missed.[28]

The day isn't far away where we will initially 'self-diagnose', not with Google but by logging-on to a medical system, inputting our symptoms or situation and the technology will access our medical records and deliver a diagnosis together with instructions and appointment times for the next round of assessment. This type of technology may even replace some of a doctor's functions.[29] Whatever the outcome, it will change the nature of their role, encouraging them to foster more bee-like, integrative capabilities.

The same is true for other experts such as lawyers. They too are currently highly trained, highly paid experts, but technology is going to change their role too. Technology will be able to assess all the cases ever heard, all the variables and all the rulings to find a precedent that can be used in court; this will be done faster and more accurately than a team of junior lawyers in a library. We will probably still need human beings to represent us in court and deliver powerful closing arguments (a heuristic task) but the nature of the industry will change and the industry itself will require fewer human beings.

Algorithmic repetitive tasks are very easy to replace by machines. McKinsey & Co estimate that only 30 per cent of job growth now comes from algorithmic work, while 70 per cent comes from heuristic work.[30] A key reason for this is that algorithmic work can be outsourced either to cheaper physical locations or automated, whereas it's much harder to do so with heuristic work.

The growth and proliferation of AI is going to create a gap that may be best suited to bees, people who can see the big picture and have a broad understanding across multiple areas but also possess sufficient depth to be able to see connections and convolve unusual solutions to complex challenges. The people who will be most likely to thrive in an AI world will be the bees, those who can integrate and adapt. It is this capability that may become the most highly prized in tomorrow's world.

Many innovators who are tracking the impact of technology and AI are predicting that AI will completely re-shape the world of work, and the massive job losses that it will usher in may necessitate governments to pay everyone a Universal Basic Income (UBI).

In January 2017, Finland became the first country in the world to trial the use of UBI. A randomly selected but mandatory sample of 2,000 unemployed people aged 25 to 58 were paid the equivalent of £475 per month. It came with no obligations or stipulations. If the individual got a job in the two-year trial period, they would still receive the money.[31] Although much was made in the press when Finland announced they would not be extending the study, the truth is the intention was always to conduct the test for two years and then thoroughly study the results before deciding whether to find an alternative solution, tweak the approach or roll it out. Certainly, Elon Musk and Mark Zuckerberg have both stated they believe such an approach is valid and holds the key to tackling inequality.[32]

Too often automation and AI are pitched as the destroyers of jobs but, coupled with some workable form of UBI, they could be used for a transformational intervention for human beings.

Is it such a bad thing that machines replace all the repetitive jobs? What if all that spare human capacity was redirected toward innovation or solving the mounting challenges we face as a species? What if that liberation from the daily grind opened the door to new experiences, the acquisition of greater knowledge and the sharing of that knowledge collaboratively via constantly improving technology? Such a fusion of people, with increasing polymathic capabilities, working with collaborative technology could bring incredibly positive change to the planet.

Such a world, minus perhaps the AI, was predicted by philosopher and political economist John Stuart Mill in 1848. Mill believed that eventually economic growth would become a 'stationary economy', which would allow us to focus on human improvement:

> There would be as much scope as ever for all kinds of mental culture, and moral and social progress . . . for improving the art of living and much more likelihood of it being improved, when minds cease to be engrossed by the art of getting on.[33]

In other words, when we were no longer consumed by making a living, we could be liberated to make a life.[34]

Whatever happens, it's clear that those people who can embrace a more integrative outlook and demonstrate bee-like behaviour could be the ones in most demand. And frankly, this may be particularly appropriate given that the new workforce of Gen Y and younger naturally exhibit more of these characteristics anyway. They don't want to slot into a 'boring' job, so it's good news that those jobs are disappearing. They don't want to work insane hours, which is excellent because the amount of work needing to be done by a human being is decreasing; it just makes more sense to have more people working fewer hours anyway. The spare capacity they have can be used to pursue their own interests, amplify their collective value to the system and enjoy a more balanced, meaningful life. AI and automation will allow bees to flourish. And that increases the likelihood that we will become more consistently successful innovators and generate more creative and disruptive solutions to complex problems.

Shifting work practises

The third reason to suggest that bees will become increasingly common, more highly valued and better understood is necessity. Since we live in a complex and uncertain world, we are likely to fail in our attempts to solve the problems we face. The generalists and experts we currently turn to can't deliver. The escalating complexity we face will necessitate the emergence of bees in greater numbers.

The increase in wicked problems will be amplified by the rise in AI, roboticisation, and the disruption of tech-savvy Millennials entering the workforce. All three reasons will synergistically accelerate our need for more bees.

This will be further amplified by a change in working practices and a concentrated move away from traditional roles. Out-dated business hierarchies, entrenched organisational silos, excessive regulation and overly complex compliance are all giving way to more flexibility and more fluid ways of working, which are in turn more compatible with bees. The days where an individual enters a company as a project manager and stays a project manager until they retire have disappeared. As jobs become scarce or businesses have to adapt, people create their own jobs within that context. More and more, recruitment is happening around the individual rather than any specific role. When a business meets someone interesting, they are more likely to find a role for them. This is the trend and it is highly likely to increase over time.

Some of these new flexible working practices were thought to be emerging over the next five years but given the time compression that the COVID pandemic has inflicted on the world, many of the practices described are already being rolled out. For example, some more enlightened companies are making it possible for their employees to reduce their commitments while maintaining all the perks of full-time employment.[35] Some companies may even allow valuable employees to work for competitors. Larger companies are exploring how they share the employment of staff in 'Start Alliances' and certainly how they may share training or development budgets.

Such flexible working practices may be particularly interesting to bees, who may prefer not to be employed full-time in a traditional way, but rather take on an 'in-residence' role for several organisations. That way, they deliver value when they deliver value and are paid for that but are not eating up resources and office space when they are not. This is likely to build on the ideas of portfolio careers, where an individual no longer pursues just one career path in one industry but can bring more of their diverse knowledge and experiences to all their roles in all their portfolio contracts.

Innovative recruitment firms such as Forshay in the San Francisco Bay area are already matching highly paid, short-term roles with those seeking to work for a shorter time period, having a break to enjoy family or personal time and then repeating the process. When pushing into the data around whether there was a genuine need for this innovative approach, founder Sally Thornton found that it wasn't just working parents who were keen to pursue this type of solution but Millennials who simply didn't resonate with the daily grind of climbing a corporate ladder. Surprisingly, it was also being driven by Baby Boomers who had reached the top of the corporate ladder but didn't want to do it every day anymore. Thornton also discovered that creativity flourishes when there are design constraints. In other words, when boundaries are created about how much time is given to that work or the solving of that problem, we become more creative.[36]

This too is relevant to bees and innovation. A bee 'in residence' is likely to be much more innovative and creative if they have boundaries and are constantly buzzing around the meadow of experts in whatever form that takes – different companies, different industries, different colleagues. Again, shifting work practises are not something to be feared; they are likely to facilitate a faster and greater embrace of bee capability – liberating that capability to deliver results. The massive shift to remote and online working and the use of digital platforms such as Zoom and Microsoft Teams as a result of the COVID-19 pandemic is speeding up this willingness to embrace new ways of working.

In this new world, a great deal of the work will be project-based, spanning geographies and product categories, with swarms of employees rather than teams and co-ordinated by 'scrum masters' rather than team leaders.[37] Such roles will give individuals more flexibility about how and where they work and they will facilitate greater diversity of experience, meeting of new people and elevated knowledge gathering, which will further amplify the bee's maturity and innovative potential.

Increased diversity

At least part of the reason that bees have been ignored or supressed is that they rarely conform to society's expectations and established career tracks. They don't look or act like everyone else and, in the past, this was a problem. To succeed in business, you pretty much had to be white and male, certainly in most western countries.[38] There may have been a token woman or person of colour in middle management but very rarely at a senior level. People are naturally biased toward people who look like them, so it's not really very surprising that C-suites were populated by different versions of the same thing.

But this is changing.

Although there is still some way to go in the application of diversity and inclusion in business, especially in senior roles, there is a growing appreciation of the value of diversity in all its forms. Boards that consist of only white men from the same backgrounds, same type of school and same religious and socioeconomic demographic ('pale, male stale') tend to create an echo chamber where the same hackneyed ideas continue to circulate. Innovation becomes almost impossible in that environment. Plus, such a limited demographic does not mirror the diverse demographic mix of that company's customers, which means that whole swathes of customers are ignored when it comes to innovation and on-going product and service development.

A greater appreciation of what diversity can bring will further facilitate a greater understanding and appreciation for the role of the bee and the difference they can make. Instead of being sidelined, squashed into a generalist or expert role or ignored completely from the recruitment process, bees may finally be allowed to deliver their unique contribution.

Diversity is just the smart use of difference. And there is robust evidence, certainly in business, that diversity can bring significant financial gains to a business. Research conducted in 2014 by the New York-based Center for Talent Innovation (CTI), involving more than 40 case studies and 1,800 employee surveys, looked at 'inherent diversity' such as gender, race and sexual orientation and 'acquired diversity' such as experience and language skills. It found that publicly traded companies with inherent diversity were 45 per cent more likely than those without it to have expanded market share in the past year and 70 per cent more likely to have captured a new market. When teams had one or more members who represented a target end-user, the entire team was as much as 158 per cent more likely to understand that target end-user and innovate accordingly.[39] A 2012 Deloitte report looking at 1,550 employees in three large Australian businesses identified an 80 per cent improvement in business performance when levels of diversity and inclusion were high.[40]

Diversity allows us to see the same problems through fresh eyes, and a growing acceptance of that may also facilitate a greater understanding of the role and value of the bee.

That said, diversity, as it is often conceived of today in terms of physical characteristics, like gender, ethnicity or sexual orientation, can be a red herring. If is often this red herring that exacerbates innovation failure because an innovation team may look diverse on the outside but think almost identically on the inside with everyone sharing a similar worldview. This can lead to the project failing and everyone is left scratching their head saying, "But we have a diverse team"?

What is needed in business, if we are to innovate successfully and embrace the escalating complexity, is diversity of thinking, not just physical diversity. We need diversity in values or worldview.

The truth is we could have an ethnically diverse board with gender balance but if all those people were operating from 1st tier value systems (see later), they may look different on the outside but they may not be that different on the inside because they value the same things and operate from a similar worldview.

It was the pioneering work of Clare Grave that allowed us to appreciate the variety of 'worldviews' that are determined by our value system. His resulting model (see Figure 4.2) shows how value systems evolve and how the focus shifts from the individual to the collective and back again as we move up the expanding spiral. Table 4.1 provides greater explanation of the various worldviews. We should naturally become more sophisticated in terms of what we value as we grow up and mature as adult human beings, although this is not always the case. For example, Donald Trump is famously quoted as telling one of his biographers, Michael D'Antonio, "When I look at myself in the first

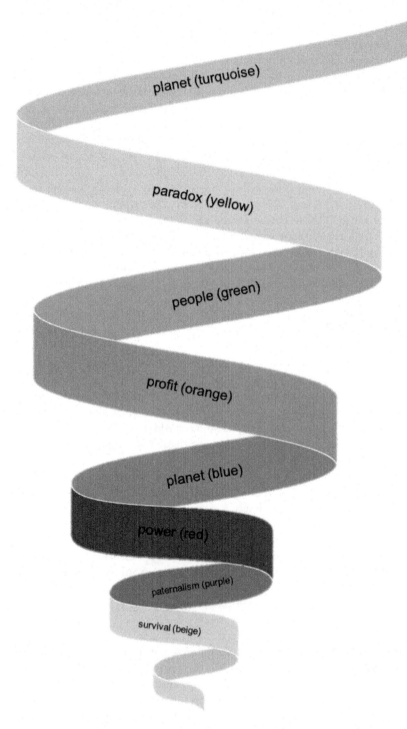

Figure 4.2 The Evolution of Values Systems

Table 4.1 Different Value Systems

Colour	What's valued	Common thoughts	Motivated by	Goal	Way of operating
TURQUOISE (collective)	System balance	Consider everything, balance everything, take the long view, be of service	Evolution and the greater good	Unity	Transpersonal and compassionate
YELLOW (individual)*	Innovation	Innovate the future, be flexible and spontaneous, learn and take responsibility	Ideas and genuine transformation	Variety, novelty and interesting life	Philosophical
GREEN (collective)	Social connection	Include others, take people with you, do it together	Affiliation and sharing	Building a community	Personal touch
ORANGE (individual)	Wealth	Make it work, achieve the target, succeed	Winning and success	Wealth	Pragmatic and competitive
BLUE (collective)*	Order	Stick to the plan, be loyal and respectful, do the right thing	Principles	Salvation	Disciplined and adherent to the rules
RED (individual)	Power	Go for it, work hard, play hard, take charge	Being	Power and pleasure	Use their own authority
PURPLE (collective)	Belonging	Don't risk it, stay vigilant, work together, look after the group	Reassurance	Safety	Tribal
BEIGE (individual)	Survival	Get through today, stay alive, 1 has what 1 need	Basic urges	None	Reactive, extremely short-term

Note: **Some authors refer to Blue as Amber and *Yellow as Teal.

grade and I look at myself now, I'm basically the same. The temperament is not that different".[41] For a man who had access to nuclear codes, that is not ideal.

Our evolution of values or our worldview impacts everything, including innovation.[42]

Initially there is no innovation, as the focus is simply survival (beige). Getting through each day is hard work. After some time, individuals discover that ganging together in groups makes survival easier, so their focus becomes collective. This shift from individual (I) to collective (C) repeats all the way up the evolutionary spiral. The first six values systems, from beige to green, are known as 1st tier value systems.

Yellow and above are known as 2nd tier value systems. The most striking difference between 1st tier and 2nd tier value systems is that those operating from the 1st tier believe that they are right and everyone else is wrong. Those that are operating from the 2nd tier appreciate that nothing is that simple or binary. They accept that there is merit in all levels and the key to collaboration, innovation and success in business, politics and beyond is to preserve and incorporate the upside of each value system while mitigating the inherent weaknesses at each level. Successful innovation needs those differing viewpoints and someone sophisticated enough to integrate them rather than allow them to degenerate into argument and hostility. Bees are ideally placed to integrate these diverse values, given that they buzz around and connect with the full spectrum of value systems.

Every value level has its merits. Given that orange is deeply rooted in pragmatic, rational objectivism, it can tend to be a little incremental in its approach to innovation. The orange value system lends itself well to an R&D environment. The green value system tends to be more pluralistic and as such can be very creative and an individual or team; operating from this value system tries to embrace a range of views. But the disruptive innovation doesn't fully fire up until you reach the 2nd tier. When the yellow value system comes online, it can create whole rafts of new ideas and spontaneously flex around those ideas. This is partly because, at 2nd tier, the individual significantly broadens their perspective and sees the merit and value in a much wider range of viewpoints and worldviews. They actively seek to integrate these diverse perspectives.

And all of this amplifies our first point about the influx of Millennials in the workforce. A larger number of Millennials are already operating from the more innovative 2nd tier value systems. The best bees operate from 2nd tier value systems. In fact, we would argue it's very difficult to be a bee when operating largely from the 1st tier.

When in the 1st tier, an individual is very invested in their own worldview which they believe is right and all others are wrong. Such rigid thinking makes genuine innovation and new thinking very difficult. First tier thinkers are much less likely to see the merit in alternative value systems or find novel ways to integrate alternative approaches into a viable solution. And, yet the ability to see value in different values is exactly the type of thinking we need.

The importance of inner diversity of value systems, rather than outer diversity of gender, ethnicity or physical appearance, was brought into sharp focus when Alan was asked to help break through with the culture of a pan-European governmental agency. The presenting problem was that the culture was in conflict. This was attributed to the fact that this agency was made up of people from 28 different nation states and every four years up to 50 per cent of the staff rotated for political reasons. So, Alan and his colleagues profiled the value system of the top 200 leaders. This revealed that the real problem was almost the exact opposite of what was suspected. Alan discovered that far from their being an extremely diverse culture that was in conflict because of the immense diversity of nations, there was in fact a monoculture of orange-green values. Every time Alan cut the data, the profile looked the same and it didn't matter whether he controlled for country of origin, gender, longevity in the organisation or seniority and pay grade, the source of the conflict was not excess diversity but a lack of diversity!

Being able to measure value diversity means that it is also possible to better identify the bees who may be in your organisation already.

The failure of leadership in a post-truth world

The final reason that we should see an increase in demand for the abilities that a bee can offer organisations is the current leadership crisis. Whether considering the ramifications of Brexit, the global political landscape and the generational regression that it will almost certainly create, the nationalistic division witnessed in many countries, climate change or how the world recovers from COVID-19, it is difficult to resist the conclusion that we are currently in the midst of a leadership crisis. But paradoxically, the failure of leadership may just be the stimulus we need to provoke the evolutionary jump from differentiation to integration.

Just to put this in context, the leading edge of leadership on the planet has been the orange value system for the better part of 660 years. Globally, orange values first became established during the renaissance in Europe in about 1300 driven by wealth and patronage. Over the years, it took various forms. From 1685 to 1815, it was considered the 'age of reason' or the period of enlightenment. This gave way to romanticism, liberalism, classicism and, by 1900, what become known as modernism. At the core of this modernism was a rational objectivism. Man could think about thinking. We were able to objectify everything in a glorious differentiated flourish. This ability to objectify ourselves peaked when we landed on the moon in 1969 and we truly saw ourselves from afar. But a new set of values had already started to emerge: pluralism or the green value system. In 1959, only about 3 per cent of the global population operated from green values but today about 20–25 per cent of the entire planet functions largely from this worldview.

Whilst green may now be the leading edge, the vast majority of people even in developed nations still operate well below green. The green value system really started in the 1960s and delivered some incredible 'green gifts' to the world, such as civil rights, feminism, environmentalism, corporate social responsibility, social entrepreneurism and an increasing focus on global and social inequality.

But in recent years, green completely lost its way and this cutting-edge leadership has failed profoundly to live up to its promise of finding new ways to embrace diversity. It has failed to create cooperation across stakeholders. In many nations, this failure to embrace diversity has led significant numbers of people to feel excluded and left behind. Ironically, making people feel included and heard is meant to be a strength of the green value system. But when people feel they no longer have a voice and those in power ignore them, then we create the conditions for backlash where there is a large-scale rejection of the status quo.

The failure to create a more inclusive cooperative narrative in society where we can transcend and include the immature, excessively competitive Darwinian model with its financial and social inequality is at the root of many of the disastrous divisions that are now appearing in many nation states – think Brexit, Catalonia, Italy's north-south divide, Trump's America.

The election of Donald Trump brought this green chaos into sharp focus. His ability to build a broad enough platform to win the Presidential race was in large part his ability to rally the anti-green lobby, a move that *may* have been accelerated by unregulated social media platforms and the proliferation of fake news stories by firms such as Cambridge Analytica and/or Russian interests who wished to see Trump in the White House instead of Hilary Clinton.[43] It's worth pointing out however that Cambridge Analytica originally supported Ted Cruz and their insight didn't do him any favours. Trump won, but he didn't win the popular vote despite being up against the most unpopular Democratic candidate in modern history who was vying for a third Democratic term (something that had not been achieved since the 1940s).[44]

Regardless of the outcome and why it happened, the reaction to Trump's appointment from the green cutting edge was extreme, visceral and loud. The same polarised, visceral and vocal opposition between two strongly opposing cultural views was also experienced in the UK before and after the referendum on leaving the European Union in 2016. Both sides pointed fingers and mocked the 'stupidity' and short-sightedness of the other side. Identical polarisation and extreme opposition have been seen in France, Netherlands, Italy, Austria and many other European countries who are seeking a regression back to a more insular, nationalistic value system.

The point here is that we are still operating from a largely competitive and immature 1st tier perspective and the green leading edge, which should help us unlock a more mature cooperative and collaborate viewpoint, is failing us. Green has tipped into its dark side and is operating from 'mean green' judgment. The net effect is that we are stuck. Every stage of development is elbowing each other for a position at the table. Excessive competition and domination are still widespread as each stage vies for supremacy.

So, what has this got to do with innovation and the rise of the bees?

As it turns out, everything. The turf war we are experiencing between worldviews is at a nexus point. We either leap forward into 2nd tier thinking or regress back to an earlier 1st tier worldview. If we look at the rise of authoritarian leaders, it would be easy to assume that regression is winning. But the Millennials and younger already operate more frequently from a 2nd tier perspective. As they enter the workplace in larger numbers, start businesses, vote and engage in adult life, they could fundamentally change the game for all of us. If that engagement swings the balance of power away from the authoritarian leadership and triggers a more widespread leap to 2nd tier thinking, then everything will change, not just innovation.

The 1st tier "I'm right and you're an idiot" thinking is exceptionally destructive to innovation and the ability to find novel solutions to complex problems. Bees only really come online in significant numbers in the 2nd tier; making that leap is hugely important to the evolution of our species – even the continuation of our species.

We need more bees to stave off the threats we face. If we make the transition, or enough of us make the transition, from 1st tier to 2nd tier, we will collectively have access to the types of people and types of thinking that can halt the division and disintegration we are now seeing in many nation states. Instead, bees, along with their collaborative, big-picture ability to harvest knowledge and integrate new solutions, will become commonplace in business, government, politics and beyond. Ironically, the current leadership crisis could be the springboard into the new future rather than the beginning of the end that many of us fear.

The dual nature of cutting-edge green leadership

All values systems or developmental levels have positive, constructive characteristics that can, if taken too far, flip into negative characteristics. These negative characteristics can block evolution and progress for generations, although they will ultimately be the catalyst for the emergence of the next evolutionary stage.

In its natural desire to be as 'inclusive' as possible, the green value system promoted the critical importance of 'context' in understanding any knowledge claims. Unfortunately, the positive, broad-minded inclusivity of green slipped into rampant and runaway relativism. Thus, all 'truth' became 'relative' to your point of observation. The notion that all truth is contextual (or gains meaning from its cultural context) eventually slid into the notion that there is no real universal truth at all; there are only shifting cultural interpretations. This loss of truth collapsed into nihilism: what's the point if there is no truth anymore? Such nihilism aggravated the outrage felt by the voiceless.

Really important ideals, which began as 'true but partial' differentiated concepts, collapsed into extreme and deeply self-contradictory views. One of the main victims in addition to truth was knowledge itself. The idea that all knowledge is, in part, a cultural construction began to become the narrative. As a result, people started to believe that all knowledge is context-bound. And this move away from truth and knowledge bought us into the deeply damaging view that there is no truth. This led to the conclusion that what passes for 'facts' are little more than fashion.

You may recognise this scenario as the 'post-truth' era we now find ourselves in where truth is whatever we want it to be, nothing more than a cultural fiction. Science, fact and rigor have been overtaken by fake news, click-bait, 'alternative facts' and endless Twitter feeds.

This nihilistic vacuum has created the perfect conditions for a leadership takeover. And who succeeds in such a vacuum? The biggest narcissist. Because if there is no truth, if facts are simply opinions, then the people who shout the loudest and who are masterful in attracting attention rise to the surface, from politicians such as Trump[45] to academics such as Jordan Peterson.[46] They seem to be saying something meaningful but much of the time it is empty rhetoric or narcissistic nonsense. But such narcissism is not confined to politicians and academics; it is rife in pockets of the media, music business and a generation of bloggers and vloggers.[47]

This collapse into a narcissistically driven 'post-truth', 'fake news' world brings with it extreme risk to our very survival as a species. Never in our history has that been more painfully demonstrated than with COVID-19. All the countries with populist, narcissistic and bombastic leaders who dismissed the threat and either suggested it was 'just the flu', or worse, 'fake news', experienced the worst death rates. Turns out COVID-19 doesn't care if its host believes its fake news or not.

In this post-truth environment, we have become even more lost, devoid of real leadership by the green cutting edge, not knowing who to trust anymore. According to the 2018 Edelman Trust Barometer, media has become the least-trusted global institution for the first time. So, if we don't trust our media, where do we go for the truth? There is declining trust in search engines[48] and social media.[49] People have retreated into self-selected information bubbles, reading only what they already agree with. Half have stopped watching or reading mainstream media and the majority believe news organisations are politicised and elitist. The US is enduring the worst collapse in trust ever recorded in the history of the Edelman Trust Barometer.[50] In effect, the meadow of experts that we have harvested knowledge from in the past has become fatally corrupted. We are facing an 'overgrowth' of narcissistic 'weeds' in the meadow that are killing off the value of experts and their true, albeit partial, facts. The meadow needs re-pollinating. The hope lies with the emergence of more bee-like behaviour from more of us.

In saying this, we are not ourselves excluding weeds. The problem is when weeds become dominant. When there is a monoculture emerging of political narcissists operating from the 1st tier and encouraging us to turn our backs on any expert who could help,[51] we are in danger of losing the diversity of the meadow that we need to innovate our way out of the problems we face. When the weeds overdominate, we are only left with a 'truth' that supports our own partial worldview, where we remain confused and disenfranchised in an echo chamber of our own making.

Like all other developmental stages before it, the green leading edge has created a monster. The 'green' monster, emerging from the collapse and failure of green leadership, is the 'post-truth' world with its evil twins of nihilism and narcissism.[52] The failure of green and the emergence of the dark under belly of green, with its green judgment and vocal denigration of early stages of development, are self-destructive and will not help us to evolve beyond differentiation or solve the wicked problems we face. Nor will it allow us to integrate sufficiently so we can innovate in new ways.

Evolution, whether it be our own personal evolution or the evolution of the society or organisation in which we live, has to experience each level before transcending and including that level in the journey of development. Judging and ridiculing people operating at earlier levels is a little like adults laughing at infants for their inability to construct an argument. In order to be able to argue, we all had to first learn to speak. Learning to argue doesn't mean we lose the ability to speak. So denigrating people who are still functioning at an earlier level of development is no more than denigrating our own development.

We have arrived at a uniquely confusing, albeit predictable, juncture in human history. This moment is equally laden with the possibility of triumph and disaster. It's widely acknowledged that postmodernism or pluralism as a philosophy is now dead. It has collapsed in on itself and shows no signs of recovering or healing the splits it has inadvertently created. The big question is what is going to come next? Are we going to make the desperately needed quantum leap up to 2nd tier thinking, which will facilitate an even greater emergence of bees and a disruptively innovative worldview, or are we going to collapse back down to egocentric, power-based, nationalistic systems?

Reasons to be cheerful

It can be incredibly challenging to know what to do to improve innovation. Even if some of the boxes are ticked, such as diversity in the innovation team, that won't necessarily translate into better results, especially if the diversity is only skindeep. The key is the inclusion of a different type of person, the bee, and a new way to approach innovation that starts with the solution.

Thankfully, the world is changing and this change will create an environment that makes new ways of thinking about and doing innovation far easier.

Millennials are in our businesses today. Instead of seeing them as a problem to manage, we will achieve more by allowing them to be who they really are. Foster the bees within.

If we are already using automation, AI or technology, to improve efficiency and get rid of the dull jobs, could we establish flexible 'bees in residence' positions to deliver better results, reduce cost and deliver more value and meaning to everyone involved?

If we are proactively seeking diversity of thinking to better understand the issues we face, then we are paving the way for better, more inclusive, disruptive and novel ideas.

If we already acknowledge that old-style power structures that used to work with the Baby Boomers and Gen Xers aren't working anymore, then we already know that business and operational models of business are being turned on their head. Embrace it. They represent a seismic opportunity (or threat) to revolutionise business, not just innovation.

And, the really great news is that all these changes are already happening in business right now. More Millennials in the workforce, technological advances, shifting work practices, increased diversity and the recognition of the value that that can bring together with a growing recognition that the old way is falling short are all already part of our reality. The only difference is that often we see these separate issues as threats to be contained or managed rather than actively brought together and utilised. If we recognise the individual gifts each change could deliver and embrace them as integral components of a new emerging business environment, we will be able to achieve far more with far less and genuinely transform innovation.

Notes

1　Martin RL (2011) *Fixing the Game: How Runaway Expectations Broke the Economy, and How to Get Back to Reality*, Harvard Business School Press, Boston.
2　Wilber K (2017) Trump and a Post-Truth World: An Evolutionary Self-Correction Integral Life https://integrallife.com/trump-post-truth-world/
Galloway S (2017) How Amazon Is Dismantling Retail YouTube www.youtube.com/watch?v=3MOwRTTq1bY
3　Cadwalladr C and Graham-Harrison E (2018) Revealed: 50 Million Facebook Profiles Harvested for Cambridge Analytica in Major Data Breach *The Guardian* www.theguardian.com/news/2018/mar/17/cambridge-analytica-facebook-influence-us-election
4　Cadwalladr C (2017) The Great British Brexit Robbery: How Our Democracy Was Hijacked *The Guardian* www.theguardian.com/technology/2017/may/07/the-great-british-brexit-robbery-hijacked-democracy
5　Watkins A and Wilber K (2015) *Wicked & Wise: How to Solve the World's Toughest Problems*, Urbane Publications, London.
6　Ahmed W (2020) This Is the Indispensable Skill That Will Future-Proof Your Career *The Fast Company* www.fastcompany.com/90516784/this-is-the-indispensable-skill-that-will-future-proof-your-career
7　Le Fanu J (1999) *The Rise and Fall of Modern Medicine* Little, Brown and Company, London.
8　Harari YN (2015) *Homo Deus: A Brief History of Tomorrow*, Vintage, London.
9　Marr B (2015) *Big Data: Using SMART Big Data Analytics and Metrics to Make Better Decisions and Improve Performance*, John Wiley & Sons, London.
10　Mayer-Schönberger V and Cukier K (2013) *Big Data: A Revolution That Will Transform How We Live, Work and Think*, John Murray Publishers, London.
11　Surowiecki J (2004) *The Wisdom of Crowds: Why the Many Are Smarter Than the Few*, Little Brown, London.
12　Watkins A and Stratenus I (2016) *Crowdocracy: The End of Politics*, Urbane Publications, Kent.
13　Thagard P and Stewart TC (2011) The AHA! Experience: Creativity through Emergent Binding in Neural Networks *Cognitive Science* 35 1–33.
14　Cope M (2003) *The Seven Cs of Consulting* (2nd Edition), Prentice Hall, London.
15　Hawkins J and Blakeslee S (2005) *On Intelligence: How a New Understanding of the Brain Will Lead to the Creation of Truly Intelligent Machines*, Henry Holt and Company, New York.
16　Nichols T (2016) *The Death of Expertise: The Campaign Against Established Knowledge and Why It Matters*, Oxford University Press, Oxford.
Pearl D (2018) The Death of Expertise *The Spectator* www.spectator.co.uk/2018/04/the-death-of-expertise/

17 Wilber K (2017) Trump and a Post-Truth World: An Evolutionary Self-Correction Integral Life https://integrallife.com/trump-post-truth-world/

18 Miller A (2015) 3 Things Millennials Want in a Career (Hint: It's Not More Money) *Forbes* http://fortune.com/2015/03/26/3-things-millennials-want-in-a-career-hint-its-not-more-money/

19 Asghar R (2014) What Millennials Want in the Workplace (And Why You Should Start Giving It To Them) *Forbes* www.forbes.com/sites/robasghar/2014/01/13/what-millennials-want-in-the-workplace-and-why-you-should-start-giving-it-to-them/#48ec1efe2fdf

20 Dhawan E (2012) Gen-Y Workforce and Workplace Are Out of Sync *Forbes* www.forbes.com/sites/85broads/2012/01/23/gen-y-workforce-and-workplace-are-out-of-sync/#3ec15d9d2579

21 Chester E (2002) *Employing Generation Why: Understanding, Managing and Motivating the New Workforce*, Tucker House Books, Boulder.

22 Asghar R (2014) What Millennials Want in the Workplace (And Why You Should Start Giving It To Them) *Forbes* www.forbes.com/sites/robasghar/2014/01/13/what-millennials-want-in-the-workplace-and-why-you-should-start-giving-it-to-them/#48ec1efe2fdf

23 Gourville JT (2006) Eager Sellers and Stony Buyers: Understanding the Psychology of New-Product Adoption *Harvard Business Review* https://hbr.org/2006/06/eager-sellers-and-stony-buyers-understanding-the-psychology-of-new-product-adoption Christensen CM, Alton R, Rising C, and Waldeck A (2011) The Big Idea: The New M&A Playbook *Harvard Business Review* https://hbr.org/2011/03/the-big-idea-the-new-ma-playbook

24 Pink DH (2009) *Drive: The Surprising Truth about What Motivates us*, Penguin, New York.

25 Wakefield J (2016) Foxconn Replaces '60,000 Factory Workers with Robots' *BBC News* www.bbc.co.uk/news/technology-36376966

26 Skidelsky R (2016) A Basic Income Could Be the Best Way to Tackle Inequality *The Guardian* www.theguardian.com/business/2016/jun/23/universal-basic-income-could-be-the-best-way-to-tackle-inequality

27 Olson P (2018) This AI Just Beat Human Doctors on a Clinical Exam *Forbes* www.forbes.com/sites/parmyolson/2018/06/28/ai-doctors-exam-babylon-health/#3b02f09c12c0

28 About Us Isabel Website https://symptomchecker.isabelhealthcare.com/about-isabel-symptom-checker

29 Finnegan G (2018) Your Virtual Doctor Will See You Now: AI App as Accurate as Doctors in 80% of Primary Care Diseases *Science Business* https://sciencebusiness.net/healthy-measures/news/your-virtual-doctor-will-see-you-now-ai-app-accurate-doctors-80-primary-care Moore-Colyer R (2017) AI Doctors on the Rise: British Startup Babylon Health Secures £50m for iOS & Android App Silicon www.silicon.co.uk/mobility/mobile-apps/robots-doctors-babylon-health-210215?print=pdf&inf_by=5a9183ed681db8dd608b509b

30 Johnson BC, Manyika JM, and Yee LA (2005) The Next Revolution in Interaction *McKinsey Quarterly* 4 25–26.

31 Henley J (2018) Money for Nothing: Is Finland's Universal Basic Income Trial Too Good to Be True? *The Guardian* www.theguardian.com/inequality/2018/jan/12/money-for-nothing-is-finlands-universal-basic-income-trial-too-good-to-be-true

32 Reynolds M (2018) No, Finland Isn't Scrapping Its Universal Basic Income Experiment *Wired Magazine* www.wired.co.uk/article/finland-universal-basic-income-results-trial-cancelled

33 Mill SJ (1848) *Principles of Political Economy*, John W Parker, London.

34 Watkins A and Dalton N (2020) *The HR (R)Evolution: Change the Workplace, Change the World*, Routledge, Abingdon.

35 Watkins A and Dalton N (2020) *HR (R)evolution: Change the Workplace, Change the World*, Routledge, Adington.

36 Thornton S (2015) Re-Imagining the Future of Work TEDx http://forshay.com/

37 Scrumstudy (2017) Importance of SCRUM for HR Scrumstudy http://blog.scrumstudy.com/importance-of-scrum-for-hr/#:~:text=Along%20with%20the%20Scrum%20

Master%2C%20it%20is%20also,Scrum%20Teams.%20They%20moderate%20and%20
facilitate%20team%20interactions

38 www.thecolourofpower.com/colour-of-power/

39 Smedley T (2014) The Evidence Is Growing: There Really Is a Business Case for Diversity *Financial Times* www.ft.com/cms/s/0/4f4b3c8e-d521-11e3-9187-00144feabdc0.
html#axzz3p0vNtogT

40 Deloitte (2012) Waiter Is That Inclusion in My Soup? A New Recipe to Improve Business Performance www2.deloitte.com/content/dam/Deloitte/au/Documents/human-capital/deloitte-au-waiter_is_that_inclusion-150615.pdf

41 Syracuse A (2016) Donald Trump Is a Mother's Nightmare *Time Magazine* http://time.
com/4187658/donald-trump-is-a-mothers-nightmare/

42 Lent J (2017) *The Patterning Instinct: A Cultural History of Humanity's Search for Meaning*,
Prometheus Books, New York.

43 Cadwalladr C and Graham-Harrison E (2018) Revealed: 50 Million Facebook Profiles Harvested for Cambridge Analytica in Major Data Breach *The Guardian* www.theguardian.com/news/2018/mar/17/cambridge-analytica-facebook-influence-us-election

44 Kavanagh C (2018) Why (Almost) Everything Reported about the Cambridge Analytica Facebook 'Hacking' Controversy Is Wrong *Medium* https://medium.com/@CKava/
why-almost-everything-reported-about-the-cambridge-analytica-facebook-hacking-controversy-is-db7f8af2d042

45 Graham DA (2018) Trump's Furious Tweetstorm Backfires *The Atlantic* www.theatlantic.
com/politics/archive/2018/02/trump-solipsism/553664/

46 Robinson NJ (2018) The Intellectual We Deserve *Current Affairs* www.currentaffairs.
org/2018/03/the-intellectual-we-deserve

47 Wyecroft J (2015) Vlogging: Making Narcissism Pay Since 2005! *Social Matters* www.
socialmatter.net/2015/12/31/vlogging-making-narcissism-pay-since-2005/

48 Cadwalladr C (2016) Google, Democracy and the Truth about Internet Search *The Guardian* www.theguardian.com/technology/2016/dec/04/google-democracy-truth-internet-search-facebook

49 Hern A and Sabbagh D (2018) Zuckerberg's Refusal to Testify before UK MPs 'Absolutely Astonishing' www.theguardian.com/technology/2018/mar/27/facebook-mark-zuckerberg-declines-to-appear-before-uk-fake-news-inquiry-mps

50 2018 Edelman Trust Barometer Executive Summary http://cms.edelman.com/sites/
default/files/2018-02/2018_Edelman_TrustBarometer_Executive_Summary_Jan.pdf

51 Mance H (2016) Britain Has Had Enough of Experts, Says Gove *The Financial Times* www.
ft.com/content/3be49734-29cb-11e6-83e4-abc22d5d108c

52 Wilber K (2017) Trump and a Post-Truth World: An Evolutionary Self-Correction Integral Life https://integrallife.com/trump-post-truth-world/

5 How to identify and create more bees

In time, bees are likely to become more common as a result of the influx of Millennials into the workplace, the proliferation of AI, changing work practises and diversity of that workforce plus the failure of leadership in a post-truth world.

It's also likely that a few bees are already in your business. Chances are, they are the individuals that annoy you, the 'weirdos', corporate mavericks or the outliers that never seem to stick to the plan. The bees are the ones that are always asking questions, pushing back against assumptions and questioning the status quo. This can be irritating for those around them that don't understand the value this curiosity can yield. But the Socratic 'question everything'[1] approach of the 2nd tier must be differentiated from the belligerent power-play of the red value system, the rigid challenge of the blue value system and the attempt to simply 'win' the argument by the orange value system.

The importance of bees goes way beyond simple pollination. Pollination or the spread of ideas and the connecting of assets and people is not confined to bees. They do this but their real value add is in the creation of solutions through the convolution of ideas.

As organisations increasingly recognise the need for more bees in their systems, they may well recognise that they may need a master bee or a chief integrator. This is an individual who can provide insights on a whole new level and potentially even orchestrate the wisdom of all other bees. The challenge is that such individuals are not easily employed. To be effective, they need to be free to roam the meadows of experts. As such, they don't tend to work well with a 'boss'. But how do organisations engage such individuals? The answer is they probably need a different model of employment. Organisations may need to consider employing bees full-time in a business to work on multiple products across multiple divisions or departments. Or they may consider an 'in residence' position where the bees are engaged on a 'retainer basis' rather than on a full-time employment contract.

When thinking about how organisations employ bees, it may help to use an alternative metaphor to the bee. Such an 'in residence' role inside a company could be likened to a *Joker* in the pack of cards. In card games, Jokers are the paradigm-busting trump card that can substitute any card in the deck. They are game changers, but most people are unsure what to do with the Jokers so they simply set them aside or leave them in the box, not realising their potential. They can only be used by invitation and agreement of all parties. The Joker needs to be invited into the organisation and engaged for as long as they add value. There must be a degree of independence and they must be prepared to lose their position to maintain their credibility. They must rely on their wisdom and wit, and that is how they add value. To really mine their value, a retainer model probably works better than a typical consultancy model, which is often entirely transactional and doesn't easily build trust and the sort of intimacy that is required for real innovation to emerge.

The whole idea of a Joker in a deck of cards was originally based on a court jester. Jesters were relied upon by the king (or queen) to tell the truth, often using humour or song to make their point. They are the antithesis of the 'yes-man' (or women) sycophants who often roam the C-suites and prop up the power hierarchies so common in many modern businesses. Such grey ingratiating survivors of the corporate world lack the courage to speak up; they serve mainly as echo chambers reinforcing the ego of their immature leaders. The Joker is different and is willing and able to 'speak truth to power' in pursuit of innovative breakthrough. And those breakthroughs come through their polymathic knowledge and ability to see patterns, connect previously unconnected concepts and integrate them into genuinely novel ideas or concepts. These people see the world differently.

The bee, whether employed by a business or taking an 'in residence' Joker role draws on their breadth and depth of knowledge in order to work their magic and spot unusual connections and novel ideas, patterns or potential avenues for exploitation. It is likely that existing bees in your organisation are being misdiagnosed as experts or generalists in order to maintain their own financial security, but unless recognised, they will probably leave to pursue something that fits their nature better. They will prefer more interesting pastures where they are less constrained and can buzz around and do their thing.

If we can better recognise bees and appreciate their gifts, we would be better able to prevent this departure and find roles and models of working, such as the 'in residence' model, that suit them better so that their gifts can fully benefit the business.

Attributes of a bee

Better understanding the potential attributes of a bee is therefore important to help stop the brain drain.

Although there is no set attribute list of an effective bee because the role itself is still differentiating, we would suggest that most bees possess at least some of these attributes.

- Bees are connectors, mavens and 'salespeople'
- Bees are effective communicators

- Bees trust their intuition
- Bees are completely curious and voracious harvesters of knowledge
- Bees are disruptively creative

Bees are connectors, mavens and 'salespeople'

In Malcolm Gladwell's debut book *Tipping Point*, he describes the three 'agents of change' that appear to 'tip' ideas, products, messages or behaviour over a critical mass threshold allowing that idea, product, message or behaviour to spread like wildfire. Bees have a good dose of all three qualities.

Gladwell suggests a tipping point is made possible by "people with a particular and rare set of social gifts",[2] namely:

- *Connectors*: These are the people who know large numbers of people, are incredibly well connected and are constantly meeting new people and adding them to their personal contact database. A connector is the social equivalent of a computer network hub. The real skill of a bee is not in the volume of connections but the diverse range of people they connect with across an array of social, cultural, professional and economic circles. They will carefully manage their network, keeping track of people who may be useful years into the future. This doesn't mean they stay in constant contact but they may seek out old contacts for new issues. They also make a habit of introducing people who work or live in different circles to each other. Gladwell attributes the social success of connectors to the fact that "their ability to span many different worlds is a function of something intrinsic to their nature, some combination of curiosity, self-confidence, sociability, and energy". Bees are uber-connectors
- *Mavens*: Mavens are similar to the expert in that they are "information specialists", although Gladwell considered mavens to be more akin to the geeky data collectors – the people you want on your team on a pub quiz. They are the "people we rely upon to connect us with new information". Mavens tend to have a more open attitude to sharing information than an expert does. One of the challenges with an expert or specialist is that they can become protective or defensive about the information they possess. Experts often make their living by trading in information and therefore are likely to see this as a competitive advantage. Experts therefore often get into turf wars and intellectual arguments with fellow experts. In contrast, a maven is more open and helpful. Bees possess this same attribute; they are "information brokers, sharing and trading what they know". Bees see the sharing as a way of creating new knowledge as they integrate the reactions to their sharing as an additional data set. They often don't need to plunge to quite the same depth of understanding as a traditional expert because their connector capability enables them to access other people who they can tap into if greater depth is required

- *Salesmen*: These people are the engagers, persuaders or storytellers that can create a tipping point. Not salespeople in the typical or traditional sense; they inspire an audience toward an idea or potential solution or sell the concept rather than a product or service. They tend to be charismatic with powerful communication and negotiation skills. They often bring some additional 'magic' that goes beyond what they say, which makes others want to agree with them. This ability to sell their narrative also exists to some extent in high-functioning generalists because bees and generalists both need to keep a lot of different types of people onside. Bees may know less than the people they must interact with but they interact with real flair. Being able to tell a great story is crucial in the innovation space because bees need to work with an innovation manager and his or her team to flesh out how viable the bee's prospective solutions might be. The bee must be able to articulate that vision well enough to take people with them and move forward. For the bee it's not really about selling or persuading in the way Gladwell describes it; it's more about passionate, effective and engaging communication. Ideally, the audience will buy-in but it's not seen as essential for the bee

The bee exhibits attributes of all three types and convolves these qualities into a potent resource. The bee can connect information and knowledge that may not normally be connected, cross-pollinating that knowledge across industry and sector to come up with genuinely novel solutions while selling that vision and working with the innovation team to inspire them to take the idea forward.

Bees are effective communicators

Effective communication has two basic aspects: transmission and reception. However, as children we are only ever taught half the formula. As we grow up into adulthood, our grammar, pronunciation and diction may be corrected by teachers and parents. We are taught to use the right word in the right situation. We might learn about the potency of a developmentally appropriate metaphor and how a story told as metaphor can really animate and impact an audience. This is in service of establishing a deeper understanding within the audience. As a result, we learn to transmit impactfully to a greater or lesser extent. Unfortunately, we are not trained in the flip side of communication, namely reception. We are not tutored in how to receive information with anywhere near as much focus. Our parents rarely gave us instructions and then asked us to repeat those instructions back to them to make sure we understood them. Instead they might simply enquire, "Are you listening"? To which most children say, "Yes" and carry on ignoring the parent.

As a result, children become adults believing that listening is simply 'waiting to speak'. To most people, listening is just the moment before *they* say something. In meetings or during dinner table conversation we imagine the other person's silence is them listening to us but that is not necessarily the case. The other person may have zoned out and be thinking about the TV show they plan to watch later or they might be building their counter argument to the first part of your transmission and not listening to anything you said after the first 18 seconds.[3] Either way, they are not actually listening to what is being said.

Genuine communication is about both transmission and reception. Dialogue literally means 'flow of meaning'. Unfortunately, most communication training is focused on transmitting with impact, using video feedback and media experts for example to help 'get your points across'. Or if it does involve the reception side of the equation, then it is often too superficial. The most effective listening must go beyond the simplicity of 'tone, words and body language' training (what we call 'level 1'). It must go beyond sensing the thoughts and feelings behind the transmission ('level 2'). The most powerful listening gets to the deeper level, 'level 3' or the meaning level. Since most people get stuck at level 1 or 2, the message never truly lands as it was intended.

Real communication actually occurs when we seek to establish what someone means rather than what they say or what they think or feel. The meaning level is also the domain of potent influence.

Bees are extremely effective communicators. They listen for meaning and ask questions of the diverse people they meet so that they can be sure that they have understood the transmission and have received the meaning accurately. They are less concerned with how something is said (level 1) or the reason why it is said (level 2). What they are most interested in is the implication of what is said (level 3 – meaning). They store the information gained from all three levels, especially level 3, in their intellectual honeycomb for later use or consideration. They will know who said what and when, what book they read the information in or who they might need to go back to for additional insight. Their mind is a massive web of connections, so each piece of newly stored information is loaded with multiple tags. Once stored and given time to convolve with the existing material in their data banks, they are able to come up with solutions and then transmit those solutions to others in a way that makes sense to their audience.

As such, their use of developmentally appropriate metaphor seems to be particularly enhanced. Bees are able to tell a story that encapsulates the essence of the message and ensures that their target understands the multiple layers of complexity wrapped up in what may appear a simple story or metaphor. They have a way of bringing others with them that allows anyone to grasp even the most complex thoughts.

Connected to this is the bee's ability to change the message depending on the audience to ensure that the message 'lands' with that particular audience. They will match the message to what the audience values. This is not to say that they will distort the message, they will simply choose a story or explanation of the message that will resonate with that audience.

Going back to the work of Clare Graves, his evolving values systems offers real insight into effective communication too.

A bee most powerfully operates from 2nd tier and as such can move up and down the evolutionary spiral to couch the discussion in a way that makes sense to the other person.

This evolution doesn't make the bee 'better' than those who operate at the lower levels of the spiral and it certainly doesn't mean they will be happier or more successful. It is simply an expression of the breadth and depth of their capability. The higher up the spiral the bee travels, the more options they have in terms of how they behave, interact with others and the number of different things they can see value in. All of which is vital in the innovation space.

This understanding of values also improves their communication skills and increases their influence. A few years ago, Alan did some work with TNT Australia who was trying hard to win a large account from their main rival DHL. TNT had tried everything to entice the customer to switch allegiance to TNT. They offered the customer various commercial incentives: buy one get one free, 'no fee Fridays', 5 per cent off, 10 per cent off and ultimately in their desperation 15 per cent off. The TNT Australia business, at that point, was very orange (1st tier) in its approach. The fact that their orange financial inducements didn't work for this client was baffling to them. "We are cheaper than DHL, why isn't the customer switching"? was the question they just couldn't answer.

In an effort to answer this question for them Alan explored what the customer's values system was and concluded that it was probably purple. And purple companies are not persuaded by the orange sales message that TNT was delivering. What matters to the purple value system is safety and maintaining the status quo. Purple is about survival and security (the client was actually an information technology security company). So not surprisingly, this customer was resistant to switching its logistics supplier. All TNT's messages were focused on what they did differently compared to DHL. Alan explained to TNT that what the customer needed to hear was the exact opposite of their current sales pitch. The customer needed to hear how similar they were to DHL. And that's exactly what TNT then did. They explained their similarities in offerings but then added that there was probably only one real difference – unlike their competitor they could guarantee the security of the parcel to the destination in ways that DHL could not match. When they pitched this story in a way that was couched in the values of the customer rather than their own value system, TNT won their business.

When an innovation team understands the worldview of the people they need to influence in order to move that innovation forward, they can alter their message based on that worldview to better 'land' the vision and get people on board. This is not about saying whatever will get someone over the line; it's about re-presenting the truth of the story and telling that story in a way that makes sense to the listener, not simply telling the story in a way that makes sense to the innovation team.

A bee can operate with this type of communicational flexibility because they intuitively understand how to transmit their message in a way that will make sense to the audience based on the overriding value system of the recipient.

Bees trust their intuition

Bees don't seek to possess the depth of knowledge that an expert can demonstrate but they have enough to be able to shape a solution or possible solutions. Most importantly, they are comfortable with their own depth of knowledge because they know who they need to connect to and involve to flesh out the solution they are building. They are not afraid to explore from a position of limited knowledge.

Ironically, too much information can stifle innovation because industry conventions or internal cultural rules or assumptions prevent those inside the system from looking beyond that system. The bee is often unencumbered by these constraints – many of which are untested. The bee doesn't care if something 'can't be done', has 'never been done' or 'won't work here'; they just start with solutions to the challenge or propose solutions to certain needs and involve the appropriate experts and generalists along the way to prove or disprove the idea.

This can appear confronting to the other members of the innovation team, especially if they are used to approaching innovation from an innovation funnel perspective. One of the unspoken fears for innovation managers or innovation teams when considering an impeller approach is, "If we in-source bee innovation capability, what happens to us"? The fear is that this weird bee type person will fly in with wacky, implausible ideas and they will all be pushed out the door. Nothing could be further from the truth.

The innovation manager and the innovation team, whether in-house or out-sourced, is still vital to the innovation plan. Rather than getting bogged down in problem definition or research, which is expensive, time consuming and rarely triggers genuine answers, they focus on what they are good at: testing, validation and implementation. The only difference is that there is a bee or a few bees upstream who can come up with potential solutions for them to progress, test and either eject or perfect.

Everyone plays their part. Bees are great at harvesting information, assessing trends, meeting diverse people and gathering data, which then percolates internally so that when a particular problem is applied to that data set, innovative and unusual ideas are created. But they are less focused on implementation. The innovation team is already proficient at implementation, but they are often implementing poor initial ideas born of a desperate desire to follow process rather than focus on results. Some of the bee's ideas will be terrible, some will be ruled out quite quickly because of time or budgetary constraints but others may rumble through verification gathering evidence and momentum, all without months of expensive problem diagnosis and research.

Bees are also rarely bothered by social conventions. This is often why they are perceived as outliers, especially in traditional organisations. They might be the person with the strange hair or the weird dress sense. They don't take the traditional path and don't do what everyone else does. And they are absolutely fine with that; they trust their own judgement and have a relatively unshakable faith in their own abilities.

Completely curious and voracious harvesters of knowledge

Bees are completely curious knowledge collectors in all forms – books, meeting people, articles, industry journals both inside and outside their sector, TED talks, you name it and they will consume it. It doesn't matter where the information comes from; the bee hoovers it all up and stores it.

Bees are naturally curious and they will dip their toe in all manner of knowledge ponds across the arts, politics, history, health and whatever sparks an interest. And it is those interests that will determine what problems or innovation teams they are best suited to work with.

Albert Einstein once said, "I have no special talents. I am only passionately curious". It's hard to accept that he had no special talent but certainly curiosity seems to play a significant role in brilliance. Leonardo da Vinci was perhaps the most famous polymath or bee of all time and was someone who was also well known for his curiosity. da Vinci loved to investigate areas that interested him.

In his notebooks, he would list things that he must do or learn about and the items on these lists tell us a great deal about the way da Vinci's mind worked. In one of his lists he wrote, "Observe the goose's foot: if it were always open or always closed the creature would not be able to make any kind of movement". Or what about, "Why is the fish in the water swifter than the bird in the air when it ought to be the contrary since the water is heavier and thicker than the air"? Or our personal favourite, "Describe the tongue of the woodpecker". As da Vinci's biographer Walter Isaacson rightly points out, "Who on earth would decide one day, for no apparent reason, that he wanted to know what the tongue of a woodpecker looks like"?[4]

That is curiosity taken to a whole new level. Bees certainly exhibit a natural curiosity – whether they muse about woodpecker's tongues is unclear but they ponder about things that never even cross the mind of the general population.

Bees are able to use this curiosity to harvest knowledge from all manner of typical and unlikely sources. They then use that to present a coherent argument and sell their idea because the ideas have not just come from them. Their solution is the integration of many people's views. This enables the bee to be less attached to the solution, as, strictly speaking, it is not their 'baby'. The solution has had many parents, including the bees themselves. The bee is not saying, "Hey what about trying X – that sounds interesting"? They are bringing a huge amount of prior information to bear against a particular challenge. That information may have come from a myriad of reputable and well-known sources or people as well as obscure observations. Knowing that the bee has spoken to ten university professors and various leading lights in the industry also fosters trust and faith in the proposition being presented.

Bees are disruptively creative

Although implied by the earlier attributes, it's worth pointing out that bees are also disruptively creative. They are not simple pollinators visiting various flowers in the meadow spreading knowledge and information around; their curiosity and ability to harvest knowledge convolves with all their existing knowledge, information and experience to come up with novel disruptive thoughts and ideas that the flowers alone would probably never have imagined.

Whilst the gathering of knowledge from diverse sources is an essential asset, it's what the bee then does with that information that makes them so valuable. They see what others don't.

The mind of a bee

We suggested that bees are voracious knowledge harvesters, trust their intuition, operate from the altitude of the 2nd tier value systems and are powerful communicators, as well as being effective connectors, mavens and 'salesmen' or persuaders. But they also tend to operate with a different type of thinking in the way that they innovate. Some bees may not be fully conscious of the way their own minds function, but when they do understand their own minds, they can step change their own innovative capability.

In order to explain this, think for a moment about anyone you believe is 'creative'. Often, we think of artists, performers, musicians or even comedians. The ability of a Cirque du Soleil acrobat to come up with a new trick or Gary Barlow to come up with a new hit song requires the creation of a new concept. This 'concept formation', as it is known, is exactly what most strategists do in any business or government. It may be invisible within the confines of their own mind or it may be visible as a behaviour, as people 'work out' an answer on a white board or in a series of 'brain storms' in post-it laden, green-walled, well-lit 'creative spaces'.

But as many people have noticed when tasked with coming up with new ideas, some days they can do it and some days they can't. Strangely, most people are not very curious about why their performance is so variable. Most mistakenly attribute their creative ability to something random or some external condition. In the absence of knowing how their mind works to generate a good idea, they often live in fear of failure.

If your career depends on coming up with ideas, this fear can be very disabling. Many comedians worry about 'writer's block' or are anxious that one day they will wake up and will no longer be funny. A songwriter fears that they may never write another hit. The music industry is littered with 'one hit wonders'. The creative industries likewise contain lots of people who were wonderfully creative then somehow lost that ability.

If the creatives, innovators, thinkers or strategists reflect for any length of time or to any depth on their own ability at concept formation, they may start to identify that there are some conditions that enhance their ability. This is an important developmental insight. They are moving from 'concept awareness' to 'context awareness'. As a result, they can extend their career significantly. Thus, if a musician is in the Barbados recording studio with the right entourage and range of 'stimulants', he or she may be able to continue to 'work their magic'. But unfortunately, contexts often fade in terms of their ability to continue to deliver.

The ultimate breakthrough in the mind of a bee is to transcend context. If the bee develops their mind sufficiently, they can move from concept to context to something called 'construct awareness'. This is a quantum leap forward in their mind's ability to convolve data. Their innovative capability is not tethered to any context. It is truly liberated. Ideas now flow thick and fast. Their mind is free. In fact, when bees operate from construct awareness the problem often becomes too many solutions are being created. The most powerful bees have either consciously or inadvertently developed their mind through these three developmental stages:

- Concept awareness
- Context awareness
- Construct awareness

How to identify a bee

Although we've identified a few attributes of bees, there are likely to be a range of different types of bees. Some bees may exhibit all of the above attributes and others may only exhibit only one or two or there may be more we are yet unaware of.

The power of the human mind is built on its pattern recognition capability and how it uses this to anticipate the future. The core capability sitting at the centre of the mind of the bee is the disproportionate ability to see patterns in the relationships between things. This is why they are adept with complexity, chaos and change. All require a sophisticated pattern recognition capability.

It has been argued that the relationship between things may be more important than the things that relate. For example, as you sit reading this book if we handed you a photo of yourself aged six you would instantly recognise this as 'you'. This is despite the fact that there is hardly a single molecule in your body today that was there when you were six years old. Virtually every single cell that makes up you today is new (often several times over since you were six). So why is it still 'you'? It is the unique relationship between these things that has remained constant and is at the centre of your identity.[5]

Given that bees are exceptionally gifted at pattern recognition and understanding the connections between things, it should come as no surprise that one of the best ways to identify bees in your organisation right now is to use network analysis technology.

Network analysis

Network analysis technology provides powerful insights into how your organisation really works as opposed to how the organisational chart suggests it works. Based on complex social network theory, this technology objectifies the connections between people and the patterns of interaction within the business and beyond. Alan has developed a tech platform that asks employees nine simple questions, generating thousands of data points, which can reveal invaluable insights about how your organisation does and does not function, in a matter of minutes. The questions look into three critical networks:

1   **Functional network**

Q1: Name the people you typically get work related information from.
Q2: Name the people you collaborate with on a regular basis.
Q3: Name the people you go to, to get things done quickly.

2   **Social network**

Q4: Name the people you feel energised by when you interact with them.
Q5: Name the people you feel you can be open and honest with.
Q6: Name the people to whom you turn to for support when things are tough.

3   **Strategic network**

Q7: Name the people you feel personally stretch your thinking.
Q8: Name the people to whom you turn to for leadership or guidance.
Q9: Name the people that support your development at work.

Understanding the existing internal network may help to identify the bees that are already in your business.

Alan has seen repeatedly, across multiple industries and geographies, using network analysis technology, that most leadership teams are only aware of about 50 per cent of the innovators within their business at most. People who are good at stretching others' thinking and energising them to action are easily identified with this approach. In addition, it's possible to quantify the scale of the impact of one innovator compared to another based not on the view of management or external consultants but based on the wisdom of the crowd. It is possible to see who is most socially and functionally influential and who operate as key information hubs. The best bees, or course, tend to be impactful simultaneously across a number of dimensions.

Because network analysis can identify hidden talents, when we do this across a whole team, division or company we see all the 'dendritic connections' that spread out and can easily identify who the 'budding bees' might be and target customised investment and support to develop them. Such insights can be incredibly useful not just for identifying the bees in your business right now but for succession and driving improved performance and developing innovative capability.

Rather than simply jumping to conclusions or assumptions about who might be a bee or where your bees might be hiding in your business, or worse still guessing who the bees are based on some spurious personality trait, network analysis allows you to identify people who are already exhibiting bee-like behaviour according to those who know best – everyone they work with.

How to help a bee fly

Since bees are almost certainly in your business already, albeit possibly unknown to you, once organisations have developed the ability to identify them, the company then needs to help them fly. This will enable the bees to work their magic to enhance the business and improve innovation results.

The first step to change anything is awareness. Acknowledging that there is this third type of thinker, the bee, and they are very different from experts and generalists is where the journey to innovate innovation starts. Network analysis can go a long way in identifying the bees in your system just by looking at the way they connect to others or metaphorically buzz around the internal meadow of experts. The more mature bees will be having the greatest impact, but the budding bees often have a similar connectivity profile.

Bees can also be identified by the type of behaviours they manifest. Mature bees use these behaviours to an advanced degree and the budding bees are still developing these behaviours.

The potential of any particular bee can be quantified using what we call the Four A's approach:

- Aptitude – what range of polymathic skills does the bee currently exhibit
- Amplitude – how widely is the bee applying these skills? (e.g. markets, geographies and seniority)
- Attitude – how strong are the bees' relationship bonds in their networks
- Altitude – what is the level of vertical development or sophistication of the bee across the eight lines of development mentioned in Chapter 2 that matter in most businesses[6]

Being able to quantify these four aspects of a bee enable an organisation to create a plan of how to develop their bee population and make them more effective. Such an approach is independent of the different types of bees that exist. As we said earlier some bees integrate certain types of information and visit certain meadows of experts. Other bees integrate completely different data sets, sometimes from a much more limited set of generalists and experts, but integrate the answers more deeply. But what they all do is collect nectar and create solutions to difficult questions.

Notes

1 Shingler T (2017) What's Next for Heston Blumenthal www.greatbritishchefs.com/features/heston-blumenthal-interview
2 Gladwell M (2000) *The Tipping Point: How Little Things Can Make a Big Difference*, Little Brown, New York.
3 Beckman HB and Frankel RM (1984) The Effect of Physician Behavior on the Collection of Data *Annals of Internal Medicine* 101(5) 692–698.
4 Isaacson W (2017) *Leonardo Da Vinci*, Simon & Schuster, New York.
5 Hawkins J and Blakeslee S (2005) *On Intelligence: How a New Understanding of the Brain Will Lead to the Creation of Truly Intelligent Machines*, Henry Holt and Company, New York.
6 Watkins A (2015) *4D Leadership*, Kogan Page, London.

6 Other players in the innovation system

Although the bees are at the heart of this new way to innovate, they can't do it alone. Not only do the bees need access to the meadow of experts but the innovation system needs other very distinct roles to function. In order to successfully commercialise a novel idea, we need an innovation team just as much as the traditional approach needs an innovation team.

Each team member must understand their specific remit, including their objectives and how they contribute to the whole process. And they must work well together. Not every role will be involved in every innovation. Some will be more involved than others, and some may only act in an advisory capacity.

In addition to the impeller specific roles of bees, meadows of experts and entrepreneurs, the innovation team also needs to work with the more familiar roles. Namely:

Research & Development (R&D)
Government
Private sector
Analysts
Designers

Research and Development (R&D)

The remit of R&D is to discover new things. They are not necessarily interested or focused on solving problems, and nor should they be. They explore and invent. Graphene is a good example of something that emerged out of R&D. Graphene is a form of carbon consisting of a single layer of carbon atoms arranged in a hexagonal lattice. Graphene has many unusual properties. It's the strongest material ever tested, it conducts heat and electricity very efficiently and it's nearly transparent. Scientists theorised about graphene for years. It had been unintentionally produced in small quantities for centuries but despite countless people working on Graphene – probably in R&D departments and science labs all over the world – there is, as yet, no commercial application for it. Although there are doubtless many people trying to find the right product for graphene, that product has not yet emerged. This fact however is not relevant to R&D. Their job is to explore, invent and go where the science or new thinking takes them. Many of those explorations will lead to dead-ends. Many will uncover funky stuff like graphene that while incredibly interesting doesn't yet have any commercial applications. This ability to pursue invention unencumbered by traditional measures of success or failure is key to R&D. R&D people are not and should not be commercially aware of what they are trying to achieve. An awareness of commercialisation is not required in their job to be a good R&D person. In fact, such awareness is likely to impair their ability as an R&D professional.

We believe that it is this awareness that has often muddied the waters of innovation. In a push for quantifiable results, where everyone is 'paying their way', businesses have put pressure on R&D to deliver commercially viable outcomes. Worse, they have often charged the R&D professional responsible for the discovery with making it a reality in the business. This is a profound mistake because the skill set needed to be an outstanding R&D professional is not the same skill set that is required to validate or implement that solution. R&D has also been used by companies to tout innovation focus with the R&D budget being used in shareholder data and messages to the city. This has created its own set of problems as mentioned in Chapter 1. Companies become locked into a specific R&D expenditure regardless of whether that expenditure makes any commercial sense or not. They can't reduce it because it will be viewed negatively by the market and it may create a public relations disaster if positioned as causal to a perceived product failure.

Where possible, R&D should be left to get on with their exploration and invention, free to spend time and money on their pursuit of discovery. They should be given the flexibility for everything from a targeted piece of research to develop something specific or needed to an element of serendipity where they simply do experiments in the hope of finding new things out that lead on to new ideas and inventions. It is the activity *not* the outcome that is vital for successful R&D, although that reality has often been lost in the noise of market narrative. When left pure and unencumbered, R&D activity creates an intellectual storeroom of concepts, knowledge, ideas, experiments and results that can be called upon in the future. Trying to envisage what R&D might come up with is pointless in a complex world. Instead, we just need to allow R&D to do what they need to do so the rest of the innovation system, including the bees, analysts and designers, might draw on their expertise and rummage around in that R&D storeroom to pull though a concept or fragment of technology that could address a current need.

Government

There are innumerable problems to solve in most businesses and societies. When the bee is buzzing through the meadow of experts, accumulating knowledge and insight, they also need to know what government is doing. Government makes rules, regulations and policies which may therefore impact the solutions that the bee brings forward, even though they are, by their nature, subject to change. There is no point in suggesting a solution that the government doesn't adhere to or support. At the very least, the solution must not contravene government policy or present a solution that is actively working against policy.

Ideally, the bee needs access to a range of connected public servants (the higher the better) so they can gauge as early as possible whether a proposed solution would be supported or encouraged by government. The solution being proposed may already fit with something that a government is already thinking about or exploring. Being able to tap into that resource or pour over their existing research would clearly be beneficial. Such conversations might also lead to funding opportunities and alert the bee to whether the solution is inside existing policy. It's also pertinent to stay abreast of political changes and how those may impact policy in the future.

Obviously, the impact of government will depend on the proposed solution and the area of the challenge. If you are creating the next flavour of cornflakes, you will only need to ensure that the process doesn't include any banned substance or problematic flavourings. The government will also probably stipulate the amount of sugar that the new cereal can have per 100gms; so there may be government involvement along the line. But, if someone has come up with a tasty, healthy breakfast snack that is beneficial to children, then it might be more advantageous to go further and seek to influence government policy, perhaps to make healthy breakfast cereal a recommended action to improve children's health or at the very least get some sort of government credibility or endorsement.

Private sector organisations

The role of the private sector in the impeller approach is acceleration, utilising strategic private sector collaborations to access technology or markets very quickly. A 'go to market' (GTM) partner.

What often happens in innovation is that an idea that has merit is packaged, put in a start-up and someone unsuited to entrepreneurial activity is charged with making it happen. More often than not, the enterprise tries hard but fails. Alternatively, an idea that has merit is wrapped in a start-up and sold as a concept only. This is especially attractive if the owner of the innovation doesn't have ready access to markets or only has access to limited markets. The bigger business may then purchase the start-up or idea and take it forward into more markets. This may make the idea more attractive and more valuable, which might attract the attention of a larger company to take it to global markets.

Private sector organisations can help solutions to take real form and grow quickly. They may not be very good at innovating themselves, but most are continually on the look-out for a novel solution that may ignite their growth particularly if those solutions deliver synergies in markets, product categories or geographies. The GTM company might have identified a space that is of interest to them, but they don't know very much about it and therefore part-nering or joint-venturing with someone who has created a solution in that space has value because they get to learn fast.

Rather than buying the solution outright, the private sector organisation can add value by investing in a venture as it develops. This approach carries less risk and offers benefits to both parties. Increasingly, this type of investment is utilised with incubators and corporate accelerators, but they don't always work. Primarily, investment and partnerships require a new mindset, one which moves away from competition toward mutually beneficial collaboration. Too often this route to accelerate the solution is dismissed by the inventor because they assume that the private sector organisation is a competitor and their fear about protecting company secrets or IP arise. But if managed properly with well thought out contracts, the payoffs can be significant.

Say a car manufacturer is behind on their electric car program because their battery technology is not good enough. The answer to that challenge may not be to step up investment but to partner with another private sector organ-isation that specialises in battery technology. Not only does this benefit the car manufacturer, because it solves the problem faster, but it also benefits the battery manufacturer because they get to play in a larger market, test, learn and improve their batteries in partnership with the car manufacturer. Such 'in-sourcing' is now widespread in most market sectors. It may include large multi-national corporations, SMEs or medium size companies, whatever is best suited to fast tracking the solution into the market. The private sector organisa-tions are crucial in the successful commercialisation of novel ideas. They allow the invention owner to move quickly so they can either confirm validation or kill the project and focus on another invention.

A word on corporate venture capital (CVC)

It's easy to assume that if private sector organisations are so crucial in the suc-cessful commercialisation of novel ideas, then the notion of CVC, corporate venturing or strategic venturing makes sense.

And yet it doesn't.

Remember the story of the FTSE 100 company that had invested £800 million in a corporate venture fund and had nothing to show for it. And yet the company still authorised an additional £400 million. Even if we asked this company why they did this, all we would hear would be waffle and buzz words. "It's strategic". The assumption is that they invest in start-ups that augment their current business. The narrative is "we unlock huge strategic synergies by connecting our portfolio of start-ups to the mothership". Or, "if we invest strategically, we can increase the probability of success and the expected returns to the Group". Or, "there's a huge potential for return on investment, while hedging against the future".

And, clearly, big corporates believe this story. In 2019, 107 CVC funds made their debut, with corporate investments climbing to a crazy $57.1 billion globally! According to CB Insights, active CVC more than doubled from 2012 to 2016.[1]

Granted, the logic is relatively sound. Big business has deep pockets, tons of expertise and an established brand. It's an attractive combination and perhaps only reasonable that those in the C-suite of these companies believe that they can do innovation better than any outside resource. Such venturing also allows them to tick the innovation box, keep the markets and stakeholders happy and demonstrate front-foot innovation activity, regardless of output. But it almost never works – it never delivers any output. Like so much of doomed innovation, there is an overreliance on process and the result doesn't even seem to matter that much as long as the company can be seen to be investing in innovation.

According to Jordan Schlipf, co-founder and partner of Rainmaking, the reasons for this disconnect are obvious. Seventy-five per cent of venture capital completely fails, and corporate VC is not an exception. If we look at the 25 per cent that does deliver a return, 95 per cent is generated by the top 20 funds – the Andreessen Horowitz, Union Square Ventures and Sequoia Capitals of the world that have been in business for decades. Why? Probably a few reasons but primarily because they have a monopoly on deal flow. It's a numbers game; these corporate venture funds would need to be investing in a lot of innovations or start-ups to ensure that the one or two that might hit the jackpot deliver the goodies.

VCs don't just set a minimum of 10x target for every investment for the bragging rights; they do it because they know if they do succeed in getting a positive return on their fund, it will likely be from just one or two of their portfolio investments. Minimum cost to play for each foray into innovation is around £50 million. That would allow for £1–£3 million per idea, maybe ten ideas, with the remaining investment going toward further exploration of the one or two ideas that show promise. £50 million of investment capital therefore offers a realistic chance of making a profitable return. But is there sufficient deal flow in CVC? Probably not. All the really good ideas are going to these top-tier VC funds, not the FTSE 100 companies. And this is regardless of the size of the corporate venture fund or the recognisability of their brand. The ideas are certainly not coming from inside big businesses – at least if past performance is anything to go by.

The odds of genuinely unlocking the strategic benefits everyone talks about are seriously low. Why? Because in order to do so, those involved in the innovation must wade back into the corporate treacle, fight their way through legal and procurement and quickly find themselves once again reliant on the BUs. Now they have to ask themselves if this start-up is aligned to that BU's strategic objectives and its senior management key performance indicators; because if not, senior management won't be giving the start-up any of their resource any time soon, or worse they may see the start-up as a risk and actively block it.

In addition, corporates don't have the venture capital skill set in-house to take the innovation to market successfully. There is no top tier, proven entrepreneurial VC talent sitting around in-house. If they were that good, they would be in the much more lucrative VC world. Hiring talent usually doesn't work because a company has the wrong incentive structures in place. What's needed is best in class talent to assess the start-ups, craft a successful investment thesis, make investments and manage the portfolio if they're going to have any chance of success. In the open market, top talent expects a 2 per cent management fee and aim for a 20 per cent stake in carried interest, i.e. once the fund has returned its target internal rate of return. Typically, corporates do not feel comfortable offering this level of remuneration to their managing partners. So, they are left with 2nd tier talent trying to achieve something that is already stacked against them, regardless of their ability.

And finally, even if that team does miraculously create a significant return on investment, that investment won't be realised for ten years, five to seven years best case; and by that point, the actual net profits generated are still going to be equivalent to a rounding error compared to the company's total revenue, especially, when considered over a five to seven year period! And that's best-case scenario!

Considering all the drawbacks, how severely the odds are stacked against CVC and the track record of zero return, Schlipf's conclusion is that the only purpose of a CVC is to create a cushier job – a better Monday to Friday. These corporate venture funds give those involved in them the chance to drop the corporate tie, relocate to a nice new office in a start-up hub and escape the daily corporate politics all while still enjoying the comfortable base salary and plentiful big corporate perks without the stress to actually deliver anything meaningful for a few years. This may be a smart move for the people involved but they are rarely a smart move or smart use of resources for the company or their shareholders.

There is a better way to harness the power of the private sector than CVC.

Analysts

Traditionally, in the current innovation model analysts are only brought in once a significant amount of money and time has been spent assessing the problem. That problem assessment will then identify a single favoured option which may be assessed by an analyst. The analyst will know where the solution comes from and what data sets point to that solution. They will understand the genesis of the proposal. The analyst is ambivalent on how the proposed solution has been formulated. Their role is simply to assess that solution for validity. They don't want to know or need to know how the solution has been arrived at. And the less they know about the area the solution sits in at the start of the assessment the better. This means that they approach the assessment with less natural bias or preconceived ideas and attitudes. They just do the analysis and allow the results to indicate whether that solution has legs or not. In addition, the analyst involved in an impeller approach can apply their analytic ability much earlier on in the innovation process.

In the old model, it's not uncommon to have three-year development cycles where the analyst will only get involved in year three. In the new model, the analyst can look at the solution as soon as it has been identified. Their role is to prove or dis-prove any assumptions that the bee and the innovation team may have made, verify data and basically pick the idea apart to establish if it has verifiable merit or not.

The way the system works now, an innovation project goes for a few years and findings are presented to the board. The owner of the project documents everything up to that point and the board is the arbiter – they say yes or no and ask whether the business can afford it. By starting with the solution or solutions and involving an analyst early, the evidence is gathered quickly rather than having to wait for the board to meet and decide if it's a goer or not. By the time the board meeting comes around, the analyst will have already established what works best or dismissed it based on evidence, not opinion. That way the innovation team is only ever taking projects that have a very high likelihood of success to the board. Besides, the analysts are a lot easier to access than having to constantly wait to be squeezed into a board meeting.

In the old innovation model, analysts are used in a traditional business ana- lyst role where they are asked to investigate price points, markets and eco- nomic and product trends. Often the 'analysis' ends up going to the finance department to crunch some numbers, but the numbers are just one small component of what the analyst could bring to the table. The analyst in the new model drills down into the *solution*, not the market, environment or potential opportunity. Their job is to figure out if that solution is doable, possible and potentially commercial or not. Where the designer is interested in desirability and usability, the analyst is interested in feasibility and viability. The analyst is a key player in ensuring that the proposed solution(s) have com- mercial promise.

They are not attached to the information they find but they are able to find the information needed to instruct the innovation owner whether the inven- tion is worth pursuing or not. They bring structure and order to the innova- tion process, something that is not often thought of as part of the innovation process. Where the bee can tell a great story, the analyst breaks that story down, verifies its accuracy and presents evidence as to whether the story stacks up. Credibility of the evidence is key and often an external analyst will be used to review the potential solutions and therefore starting with even less bias than if they were in-house.

Designers

Designers are vital because their key skill is to see into the future. They are also the experts of desirability and usability. We all have the capacity to 'time travel' and imagine the future. The designer is able to imagine what they think the future could be and communicate that so that others can share the vision.

This can be done digitally, traditionally with old school media (pen and paper) or perhaps through video or moving image. Either way designers can help the audience get a fuller understanding of what the bee envisaged.

They can take a verbal or anecdotal solution and craft something more tangible. They are not necessarily worried about what something has looked like; they are more interested in what something *could* look like. This ability to communicate a solution early on in the approach means that there is less chance that any misunderstandings will develop at a later stage.

The designer will be responsible for ensuring that the solution remains desirable and usable. Basically, the consumer/user must want the new product or service more than the existing offer; and that requires an early design input. Good design becomes disproportionately important in early adoption and the creation of the market for the product or service. In the tech space for instance, this makes the user experience (UX) and user interface (UI) central to the successful adoption of the solution.

Usability comes into play nearer the delivery of the product or service, but it needs to be considered all the way through the development of the solution. If the user cannot understand how to use or engage with the solution or finds the solution uncomfortable, then they will not adopt it.

The designer either in-house or external works with the bee to translate what they have created as a solution and is able to develop the solution to a point where it can be communicated without the need for the bee.

Designers are crucial for the communication of the solution to other stakeholders. This is especially relevant for a service-based solution, which can easily remain intangible. For example, several years ago Simon developed a cardboard optician's practice for a client in Santa Monica to reconfigure the way that a pair of glasses from a UK manufacturer should be sold in the United States. The team hired an office and converted that blank canvas into an optometrist using large panels of cardboard that visualised the inside and outside of the 'store'. That way, the customer was able to experience the proposed solution without investing in a full refurbishment and the team was able to test customer receptivity to the store and the product before significant capital investment. If Simon and his colleagues had taken them into an existing practice, it would have made no sense because they were trying to create something new based on an established approach to buying glasses. When buying glasses, we visit the optician, have an eye test, get the prescription, chose some frames and get the glasses. Simon and the design team were proposing something very different and yet without the designer's input to create the 3D-alternative, the client would have viewed the new idea through the lens of the old and it wouldn't have made sense. The designer's role is to bring the solution to life to better 'land' the idea.

The designer is not asked to come up with the solution at this point but to craft a way of communicating and putting across new ideas that people haven't necessarily thought about and can't envisage because they've only got the reference of the existing state to go on.

Innovation teams that work

Ultimately the successful commercialisation of a novel idea requires a whole team of contributors, as outlined previously, working to a new operating model, using the impeller approach. Each team member brings something unique to the party; they all work in different ways and to different timeframes. To help synchronise their efforts and disparate capabilities, we often use a 'gearbox' metaphor.

Every team member moves at a different speed with different leverage abilities. But if the team is locked together with enough skill, it is possible to move through the gears and create incredible speeds to market, solution generation and commercialisation. Of course, making a gearbox work to unlock the power of a team is not an easy task.

Most corporate leaders come up through the ranks having managed teams of various sizes. They have learnt on the job how to work with others. Some have developed an ability to get the best out of others; some have simply learnt how to tell people what to do. But very few team leaders have been formally trained in the nine stages of team development or even know much about this topic beyond some generic clichés about 'norming, storming and performing'. Alan has written extensively on these nine stages of development in *Coherence* and *4D Leadership*.[2] As a result, most people don't know what is required to take a team from one level of development or capability to the next level. Few team leaders have studied team dynamics as a discipline or dug deep into the qualities that characterise truly high performing teams and what distinguishes them from average teams. And that is true of any team, including innovation teams.

That said, an understanding of the stages of team development can make a massive difference to the effectiveness and ability of a team to deliver innovation in any meaningful way. Most work teams are operating at level 2 or level 3 of nine possible levels of sophistication.[3] However, if an organisation invests in team development, they can massively speed up the innovation process. This allows ideas to be verified and taken to market or discounted much faster than normal. Such investment will not only build team capability but will also deliver a team of people who are proficient in an impeller process.

Experience has proven that once a leader has a deeper appreciation of the stages of team development and has mastered the behaviours, practices, methodologies and disciplines required to drive a team forward to more advanced levels, then they can deliver a greater competitive advantage across the board – not just with innovation.

Consequently, making a strategic decision to properly invest in team development is one of the most commercially important moves an innovation leader can make and such investment can step change the performance of the innovation team and beyond.

Better team working cannot be mandated. In fact, leaders who demand team engagement are having the opposite effect and inhibiting team development. This is especially true in innovation teams that consist of people who are by their nature very different people. Mandating engagement may work when the team is made up of similar types of people who get on with each other; it's impossible in teams where the members have very little in common.

There are certain factors that if worked on drive a team's development, moving them from suboptimal functioning to world-class and even ultimately world-leading. These six factors, which are measurable using the Complete Team Development Index, can be used to identify exactly where a team is in terms of its development and more importantly what a team needs to do to reach the next level of capability. The six factors are:

1 **Activism** – All good teams need a laser focus on priorities. In fact, a team's ability to prioritise naturally improves as the team matures through the nine stages of development. For innovation teams, the priorities change depending on the people involved in the team at any one time and the stage in the journey from invention to commercialisation. More mature teams are characterised by the degree and speed with which they can individually and collectively take responsibility for the critical outcomes and deliver their promises. As part of this prioritisation ability, mature innovation teams continually reset their metrics to track their own trajectory and drive their own improvement.

   This team activism must occur in the context of the team's autonomy. Every innovation team needs to be clear on its degree of autonomy and the ability to determine its own destiny within the limits of its authority. An innovation team that is clear around what delegated authority it has and what it can change is able to cohere around such authority. This is why we advocate that the team charged with commercialising the invention create a stand-alone autonomous BU (more on that in the next chapter). This allows freedom and the license to operate within an agreed governance framework

2 **Strategic power** – In addition to driving the short-term priorities, great innovation teams needs to continually develop their ability to create and re-create a powerful vision and strategy that is compelling and exciting, distinctive and unique as well as achievable and sustainable. This requires an ability to understand how the world is changing and have a differentiated view of how to maintain competitive advantage

3 **Entropy** – One of the tell-tale signs of an immature innovation team is its inability to deal with conflict effectively. Conflict is almost inevitable when a group of dissimilar people are pulled together to achieve a goal. Undeveloped innovation teams often waste time in endless rounds of debate as team members jockey for position and status. Some immature innovation leaders foster such 'internal conflict', although this is often just a shallow power play borne of outdated 'divide and rule' thinking. Sometimes the power play is subtle, passive aggressiveness masked by a thin veneer of surface bonhomie. Occasionally the desire for social cohesion is so great it creates a diplomatic politeness and the tough conversations never really

occur. A team that is unable to address difficult questions will never reach the advanced stages of team development. More mature innovation teams surface and process differences of opinion rapidly and find integrated answers. In such teams, differences of opinion and diverse views get heard and are seen as a valuable source for innovation

4   **Coherence** – The counterbalancing force to entropy is the innovation team's ability to cohere. This ease with which a team can find common ground and truly align changes as a team develops. This is however often made harder in innovation teams as the people in the team will change as the invention moves to market commercialisation. There are several ways innovation teams can create common ground. Aligning behind a collectively developed and shared version of a team vision, purpose, ambition and strategy can serve as an incredibly powerful unifying force. If there is alignment across all these differentiated concepts, then these are strong building blocks for the team's development. Such strategic architecture can be further enhanced by co-creating and agreeing to a way of working, a set of values, business principles and a flexible decision-making process

5   **Relationship quality** – As an innovation team matures, the sense of psychological safety also matures. This is borne of strengthening personal connections and the willingness to support and develop each other. Such things take time to cultivate and are not the inevitable consequences of a few team away days. Relationship quality needs careful cultivation by someone well-trained in relationship dynamics and interpersonal development.

We are often asked whether team size is important in terms of a team development. The answer is that team performance is less to do with size but more to do with the relationship dynamics in a team. With increased size comes increased complexity. Larger teams, of say 18 people, can work extremely effectively but the governance and discipline required is much greater. The optimal size of any particular team really depends on several factors, such as the team's purpose and the range of capabilities required in delivering its purpose. Many organisations think six is the magic number, but we have seen dysfunctional teams of four people and highly effective teams of 18 people

6   **Personal engagement** – Strength of personal commitment to each other, the innovation team itself and its development as well as commitment to what the team is trying to achieve is vital if the team has any ambition to be world-class. Commitment starts with the leader of the innovation team and specifically their commitment to developing their team. This commitment to team development is perhaps one of the single biggest determinants of that team's success. If the leader is not behind the 'team journey' then the innovation team will never really develop. Even if the leader is committed to the team's development, the team members themselves must also commit to their journey together

Most executives' experience of team development events is pretty mixed and there is a justifiable scepticism to 'team away days'. However, a shared commitment to improving the innovation team's effectiveness and enhancing the team spirit, dynamics and interpersonal relationship can be a game changer. This commitment must be sincere. Fake commitment, lip service or 'box ticking' will not suffice. Of course, this is made a little harder by the changeable nature of an innovation team.

In addition to the leader and individual team members being committed to their development as a team; they must also commit to each other individually. We often spend a considerable amount of time with teams building their 'team spirit'. One of the most vital aspects of team success is the cultivation of the idea that all team members are 'in this together'; One Team, One Boat. For innovation teams, despite different people getting into the boat and getting out of the boat at various times, the team must remain committed to the end goal of successful commercialisation.

Rowing is the most widely used corporate metaphor for teamwork partly because it illuminates the point that no one member of the team is any more important than any other. The 'stroke' in the stern of the boat sets the rhythm and direction for the boat. This is the equivalent of the CEO or innovation team leader who is responsible for direction and injecting pace. But everyone in the boat has their role and no one role is more significant than any other role. Everyone must play their part, and if someone tries to 'be a hero' in their function then actually they will usually slow the boat or team down. Organisational status or hierarchy is irrelevant in the team; what matters is the team result, not anyone's individual expertise or contribution. Often leaders who are keen to exercise their own power or authority are the primary reason why the team does not develop beyond level 3 of team development.[4]

In a rowing boat, each person's success is dependent on the other team members' input, thereby creating interdependency across functions. An impeller approach advocates some form of shared incentive that can foster this mutual gain.

There are literally thousands of books on how to improve teamwork, every single one offering a partial answer to an extremely complex problem. We believe that what really game changes a team's ability to deliver results is a deep understanding of the nine levels of team development and the ability to coach the innovation team through every stage to becoming world-class.[5]

Notes

1 Schlipf J (2019) Betting Your Innovation Budget: Why Risk It on CVC? Rainmaking blog.
2 Watkins A (2014) *Coherence: The Secret Science of Brilliant Leadership*, Kogan Page, London. Watkins A (2015) *4D Leadership*, Kogan Page, London.
3 Watkins A and Dalton N (2020) *The HR (R)Evolution: Change the Workplace, Change the World*, Routledge, Abingdon.
4 Watkins A (2014) *Coherence: The Secret Science of Brilliant Leadership*, Kogan Page, London.
5 Watkins A (2015) *4D Leadership*, Kogan Page, London.

7 Getting to market

The way that we currently think about innovation, using the innovation funnel as a frame of reference, is designed to re-draw the finish line immediately after the initial testing and validation of a new idea or invention. This is why innovation is often perceived to be successful; initial trial data may be positive and there may be a verification of need or desire in the market. But those positive indications, while necessary and encouraging, are not proof of concept. No money has been made. The resulting product or service has not yet been sold to customers. It has yet to deliver value in the market.

Even if the innovation team recognises that some type of market success is required, their ability is invention. Just because they can invent it doesn't mean they can magically become great salespeople or masterful entrepreneurs and get that invention to market. And frankly, even if they could they would almost certainly fail to appreciate the gaps that exist between the different customer types described by Geoffrey Moore – specifically the gap between the enthusiastic *innovators* and *early adopters* and the chasm between the *early majority* and *late majority*[1]. As mentioned in Chapter 1, it is only when a new idea or invention has been sold into this latter 'mainstream' market that it can be considered a success. In most sectors, there are simply not enough *innovators* and *early adopters* to warrant the claim that what has been invented has bridged the commercialisation chasm and become a genuine innovation.

To add to the complexity of getting to market, more recent research has demonstrated that there is not one large chasm and a few cracks that every new idea or invention must navigate to cross the valley of death – there are three chasms.

Triple chasm model

By collecting quantitative and qualitative product adoption data for various technologies across many different market spaces in Europe, North America and Asia between 1995–2015, authors Uday Phadke and Shailendra Vyakarnam illuminated the triple chasm model.[2] Although their research focused on technology products and services, their insights are universal and offer us a practical way of perceiving the various challenges we must address in getting to market and achieving successful commercialisation. The three chasms are:

1   **Prototype chasm** – The transition from a product or service concept to a working prototype. To cross this chasm successfully you need a working prototype
2   **Commercialisation chasm** – The transition from an early working prototype of the product or service to a fully functional offering together with a commercially sustainable business model. To cross this chasm successfully you need to attract the attention of innovators and early adopters and have a proven business model that makes money
3   **Scalability chasm** – The transition from early customer adoption to mainstream customers as the business scales significantly. To cross this chasm successfully you need to attract the buying interest of the early and late majority

The first chasm (Prototype) is actually pre-market. It appears toward the end of the development phase where the team must convert promising concepts and initial trial data to a working prototype. Without that working prototype there will be nothing to sell. Many a great idea has failed because it couldn't convert from idea to working product or service. Electric cars are a great example of this. The idea for electric cars has been around for decades. The cynical amongst us might assume they didn't emerge into the market because there were too many vested interests in maintaining our reliance on fossil fuel-powered cars. But the technology and the logistical infrastructure to make electric cars a viable option for the mainstream market simply didn't exist until recently. If people couldn't easily plug in their cars or find a charging station as readily as a petrol station, they wouldn't buy the cars. Conversely, unless they bought the cars in enough numbers the manufacturers couldn't justify the outlay to create those charging stations. It was a chicken and egg situation. What would come first – the cars or the infrastructure to make them viable?

The second chasm (Commercialisation) is more closely related to the first 'crack' in the product adoption curve proposed by Moore. It is however viewed from a slightly different angle. Moore talked about how there was a gap between the uptake of the *innovators* and the uptake of the *early adopters,* which, if unappreciated, can cause the whole venture to fail. Phadke and Vyakarnam didn't find any specific evidence for these customer types but they did find a corresponding gap between working prototype and fully functional offering. There are some people, especially in tech, who just want to buy the new thing. They don't care that it has flaws or bugs. In fact, they are keen to be part of the de-bugging process. They want to give input and improve the product or service. They love being Beta users. But those people are rare. Assuming early sales from these types of customers is a positive sign of things to come can be a fatal error in the product's evolution and successful commercialisation.

The differentiating factor between Moore's initial gap in the adoption curve and Phadke and Vyakarnam's second chasm is the importance and relevance of a profitable business model. Previously, the issue of a viable business model was ignored, buried or blurred within vague descriptions of the valley of death. A term the authors consider to be "a singularly unhelpful metaphor".

Interestingly, once pointed out this chasm makes sense. In the current model of innovation, the inventor is frequently the person who is charged with leading the team and getting the idea to market (remember our poor Boffin). Only a Boffin is an inventor. Even if, by some fortuitous miracle, they have a sense of the importance of sales, it's incredibly unlikely that they will be suitably familiar with entrepreneurship to appreciate the multiple ways a product or service can be monetised. Successful commercialisation is as much about *how* to package or monetise the product or service as it is about the product or service itself, hence the importance of the entrepreneur in the innovation team. In this context, it is perhaps not that surprising that Phadke and Vyakarnam's research also demonstrated that the second chasm is the one that takes the longest to cross. Establishing a viable business model to underpin the sale of products or services to customers is a key factor that contributes to this extended timeframe. It is therefore little wonder that the authors also acknowledge that in addition to the "availability of skilled human capital is the need for a deep pool of experienced entrepreneurial talent with the right mindset and experience".[3] One of Rainmaking's key points of difference is access to exactly this deep pool of experienced entrepreneurial talent. They even have a set of unwavering principals that govern that talent, including passion and prior experience. Every entrepreneur chooses to work on the idea and is focused on its successful delivery full-time. And they must have prior venture backed start-up experience as a founder or key employee.

Typically, the founding talent is in their mid-30s with families. As a result, they are less willing to take on the same level of risk they may have done in the past. But they don't want to leave the entrepreneurial way of life by taking a senior role in a large corporate. The Rainmaking model therefore offers a very attractive entrepreneur alternative with less risk but still the potential for venture returns if successful. Win/Win/Win. It's a win for the corporate, a win for Rainmaking and a win for the entrepreneurial talent.

It is the entrepreneurial talent that is much more likely to appreciate the importance of the right business model from the start, thus potentially reducing the size of that chasm.

The third chasm (Scalability) corresponds closely with Moore's main chasm between *early adopters* and the *early majority*. The challenge any new product or service faces is to transition from the enthusiastic early customers who just want to be first to own that product amongst their peer group to the larger mainstream market who wants something flawless and functional. Figure 7.1 shows Moore's original cracks and chasm with Phadke and Vyakarnam's additional observations.

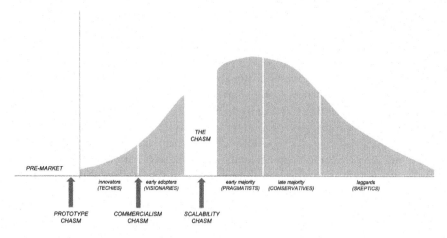

Figure 7.1 Chasms to Cross on the Way to Market

We need a way to appreciate these chasms and configure the innovation team accordingly. That way, we can make sure we bring the right team of people together to successfully cross these chasms and reach successful commercialisation as quickly as possible rather than simply assuming that the person who came up with the idea is the person that should lead the team from start to finish, even when experience tells us that this approach is ineffective, unfair and usually ends in the project and/or various members of the team disappearing into the various chasms.

How the impeller approach can help to cross the chasms

We believe that Phadke and Vyakarnam's work has added significantly to the understanding of how invention matures into commercial success and the hurdles that invention must navigate to reach fruition and add value in the marketplace. Not only does the qualitative and quantitative data confirm many of Moore's initial assertions but their research adds new granularity to the journey, which can be incredibly useful to everyone involved in innovation.

In fact, we believe that it is an appreciation of the journey or context of that journey that is the key to success rather than the content of that journey. We could talk about leadership or marketing or market segmentation or any number of tactics that must be addressed to successfully cross the valley of death. But there are literally hundreds of thousands of books on these topics. This isn't one of them. What we are seeking to do is to help people appreciate the relationship between innovation events and effectively navigate their journey to innovation. When innovation teams are stuck in the business-building stage, languishing in one or more chasms and their go to market activity isn't working well, reading another innovation book won't help. What is needed is a greater understanding of the journey. They need to understand why, not how, i.e. 'why' their approach is not working rather than the 'how' to make it work.

In this section, we will unpack why an impeller approach clarifies the steps on the journey and significantly improves the chances of successfully crossing the three chasms. Not only does this solution-focused approach to innovation provide a map for crossing those chasms but it does it at speed.

Crossing the prototype chasm

What makes an impeller approach so advantageous over the current innovation funnel approach is speed. By starting with the solution, made possible by the inclusion of the bee and the meadow of experts, the team is able to analyse those prospective solutions faster. At this point, the innovation team may consist of the bee (buzzing around the meadow), R&D professionals, analysts and designers. The solution(s) that have been proposed will be thoroughly vetted by the analysts to verify legitimacy. Those that stack up will be explored more fully and those that fail will be discarded. There is no need to investigate the problem when the investigation of the solution will reveal more about the problem anyway. In the course of the analysts work, they may draw on input from government representatives to ensure the solution complies with regulatory frameworks and is aligned with current policy in the appropriate areas. Public sector organisations may also be consulted to see if the technology for the solution already exists somewhere.

A designer will then seek to convert all the solutions that show promise from all the agnostic investigations into workable prototypes. It's time to make the vision tangible. According to Phadke and Vyakarnam, the biggest focus in seeking to cross the prototype chasm is the technology itself or the ability to physically make the product and whether it can be produced competitively enough to make it appealing to the market. Having a winning concept and even a doable prototype is one thing. being able to make that product competitively is often quite another.

An impeller approach does not use the Minimum Viable Product (MVP) philosophy. Our view is that customers don't want the minimum viable, they want the whole package. Or at least they want what appears to be the whole package, which may in effect be an 80 per cent solution. An impeller solution proposed by the bee should be predicated on design, specifically usability and desirability. From a commercialisation perspective, that usability and desirability must then be connected to feasibility and viability. Just because a solution appears to be needed and is usable doesn't mean that it is technically or financially feasible or viable.

Starting with the solution speeds up the entire process and allows an innovation team to get to a working prototype or offering far faster and with far less cost than the traditional approach, where much time is spent on diagnosing and dissecting the problem. With an impeller approach, the bee has usually understood the diagnosis and is already working the solution at speed with the help of the meadow of experts.

Once the innovation team has a working, viable prototype that can be produced competitively enough to make the offering viable, then this first chasm is successfully crossed. This landmark represents the end of the journey for some in the innovation team and marks the start of a new phase with new players.

Crossing the commercialisation chasm

This is the hardest to cross and can take the longest time. Largely, this is because too many people in the innovation field are unaware of the chasm and how it restricts growth. Plus, it is this chasm that corresponds to the highest area of commercial risk. Phadke and Vyakarnam suggest that it's vital to understand the market that the product or service is going to enter, appreciating how that offering will be framed in the competitive and regulatory environment and where it fits into the value chain. Being clear about who the customer is will also make a difference.[4]

This second chasm is an in-market hurdle. Not only is the focus on how to attract more than simply the early adopters but how will the offering make money. In order to successfully cross this chasm at speed, the team needs an entrepreneur.

One of the key differences in the impeller approach is the recognition that the people in the innovation team best suited to invent a solution, verify it, design it and build it to a working prototype are *not* the same people who can sell it and ensure commercial success. Entrepreneurial ability and experience are required to cross the prototype chasm onwards. In the impeller approach, the entrepreneur would ideally be involved in the final stages of testing and verification so they can bring their market focus to the prototype, but they *must* be involved to cross the commercialisation chasm successfully. The entrepreneur is needed to shape and package the right product or service; often that shaping can take multiple iterations and tests in the market. How is the product or service being received in the market? Could changes to the manufacture or delivery of the product or service improve customer engagement? Is the business model making money or could a different business model be more beneficial to the customer and the business?

The need for a separate, stand-alone delivery vehicle

One of the most critical components to an impeller approach is the creation of a stand-alone delivery or commercialisation vehicle to take the product or service to market. Usually it will be set up by the innovation team when the analyst has the cost information to determine an ROI and the team has recommended the best way to get to market. Exactly what type of vehicle is set up will depend on the business's situation. As we mentioned in Chapter 3, it may be a new division, department, special project, new business or special purpose vehicle. The form of the vehicle is less important than the autonomy of that vehicle.

When costs are shared across multiple existing divisions, it is easy to lose track of expenses or never have a true grip on costs in the first place. Consequently, it is easy to fudge expenditure and therefore results and return on investment. A stand-alone, autonomous business vehicle equipped with the right people makes the commercialisation journey transparent and easy to assess. The products and services that demonstrate merit can be ramped up and those that don't can be closed down quickly to avoid wasting more resources. Speed to market is critical. A stand-alone, autonomous unit also facilitates faster decision making. The team doesn't have to wait for weeks or months to speak to the board; instead the leader, usually the entrepreneur, is given the freedom and decision-making control at the start of the commercialisation project so they can get on with the job. This is not to say that we advocate a blank cheque approach – far from it. The rules of the game are set out clearly within a governance framework so that everyone knows the budget and what they are allowed and not allowed to do within that business framework.

Just think about it for a moment. An innovation team inside a big company can go away and research a problem for three years and decide on a particular strategy, by which time they may have spent, typically, £1–£3 million. Or they can try a different approach: start with the solution, get a working prototype and allocate that £1–£3 million to the innovation team led by the entrepreneur to make it happen. Because the entity that's been created to commercialise the invention is a stand-alone unit, it will be easy to view costs and results. If it doesn't work or demonstrate significant progress after six months, then it's closed down. Six months of operation will almost certainly have spent a fraction of that £3 million, so the remaining financial, human and other resources in the entity can be redirected and redeployed into the next more promising invention.

A speed-up, not a start-up

The entity created to commercialise the invention and led by the entrepreneur is not an incubator, accelerator or pilot. This is a fully functional BU or stand-alone business, selling a real product or service that has been verified and successfully crossed the prototype chasm. Done properly, the team will already have spent a fraction of what would have been spent using the traditional problem-focused innovation approach.

Unlike a start-up that usually starts on a budget, operates on fumes and pizza and expects all those involved to work insane hours for very little money on the promise of huge rewards once the business takes off, the impeller approach is a speed-up. The purpose is to get a viable, usable and desirable product or service to market as fast as possible. And that means getting the right people from the start.

Unlike a start-up which is often actively seeking to find people to work on the project for as little as possible, the speed-up is committed to putting the right people in place from the outset. That may mean a higher wage bill because not everyone wants to or can live on a promise of a future pay day. Some, very capable people have mortgages to pay and just want to come to work and do their job. Successful commercialisation needs those people just as much as the inventors and entrepreneurs. This creation of a stable, more robust and capable team from the start means that the speed-up also misses some of the more treacherous stages of a start-up.

The start-up is a state of mind. It involves testing, trial runs and pilot projects that need people who are creative and flexible. These are challenging times. On the other hand, a speed-up is about creating a team of people with mixed skill sets who are genuinely capable of running, managing and growing a business right from the word 'go'.

The speed-up is not about being in the market for three to nine months testing a theory living on rice and beans. It's about getting a viable product to market, integrating customer feedback to improve the offering in real time while growing and managing the business. There is no need for energy drinks and crazy breakout sessions, seat of your pant management and constant firefighting because everyone knows their role and is just getting on with it.

Where a solution has been created but there is no experience in the route to market, no pre-existing customer engagement and previous product or service sales, a partner will be required to add the speed needed to access the market successfully. In a traditional start-up, the time for customer acquisition is typically slow, as the business is new and the focus has been on product or service development (as well as fundraising) to get to the point where it has something physical to sell.

The speed up relies on identifying the best 'go to market' partner to give them fast access to the market when they need it rather than having to build their customer base from scratch.

Invitation, incentive and the founder mentality

By now you might be thinking, "Hang on, that all sounds fabulous but how do you create a separate entity, how do you find an entrepreneur to lead the new entity or entice employees from their existing roles to join the new untested delivery unit'?

The answer is invitation, incentive and a strong focus on the 'Founder's Mentality'.

There is a growing recognition that the way innovation is being done right now is not working. Increasingly, businesses are seeking to commercialise their IP and are actively looking at what group of people is needed in order to achieve that. Instead of leaving that IP languishing in an IP or commercialisation department, the business is strategically looking at who needs to be involved to cross these commercialisation chasms.

Of course, creating a new entity does have its challenges. It may allow for more transparent reporting and commercialisation assessment to better manage resources, but it needs to be positioned and managed carefully. For many people the memo informing them that they have been recruited into a 'special project' is seen as the career kiss of death. It is often considered as the first nudge toward the door. People also get used to working with certain colleagues and are especially productive because of those working relationships. Having those people leave their comfort zone to join a 'special project' or be part of a new entity that is going to take this exciting invention to market may not be something they want to do. It carries risk. Therefore, it's important to eliminate as much of that risk as possible. This can be done through invitation and incentivisation.

It's imperative to recruit the right people into the innovation team at all stages of the journey; but it is especially critical for commercialisation. The entrepreneur and everyone else need to believe in the project. The right people may therefore suggest themselves or apply for the position in the special project. Positioned as something exciting with potential financial upside can also help to entice enthusiastic believers to the team.

If you can find a group of believers, they will begin to corral together and create momentum. If there is also a financial incentive where the team will enjoy a share of the upside, then it's possible to amplify and reward that belief and hard work.

Smart incentivisation can also help to solve the inevitable challenges that can come when creating a new working group. When you get 20–25 new people in a speed-up, even if they are the right people, the group can run into difficulties because the people in the team can't get on with each other ('WE' problems). This is due largely to the different worldviews, beliefs and value systems we discussed in Chapter 5. The people in the team, by nature of their skill set, are different. That difference is needed to successfully commercialise the invention, but that difference also causes friction in the group. In most cases, the newly formed group doesn't know how to reconcile those differences because they don't understand the value the difference and diversity brings to the group and their collective ability to get the job done. Having a shared reward or goal that is bigger than the individual disagreements can help to break down those barriers. Appreciating the role everyone plays in the bigger picture outcome and understanding value systems and the various stages of team development can also have a profound impact on the group cohesion and eventual success.

Unless this interpersonal dynamic is better understood and actively managed, or the team includes someone who is ensuring that the relationship dynamics are maintained, and conflicts are resolved quickly, the commercialisation project may de-rail. And it will de-rail not because the invention wasn't brilliant or it wasn't possible to make money; it's de-railed simply because the team ends up fighting each other.

Isn't it ironic that even if the entrepreneur has the flexibility of mind to appreciate that the team *needs* a mix of assets and skill sets, the inclusion of different types of people can create hostility that ends up killing the project anyway?

The upside of getting this right is significant. It is also the model that Virgin has successfully deployed. A new idea or venture is proposed and investigated. If there is merit in the idea, a group of up to 10 people from the existing business create something new. If it doesn't work, the initial members go back to their original roles or on to other projects. If it does work, the team grows to about 50 people, which is the optimum number, and the group is either re-absorbed back into the parent business or is floated off to create something new. Getting this right, something that Virgin has been exceptionally successful at over the years, is partly due to the founder's mindset.

When Bain & Company's Chris Zook and James Allen researched why profitable growth is so hard to achieve and sustain, their findings illustrated that 90 per cent of the time the root cause was internal, not external. They also discovered that companies experience a set of predictable internal crises, at predictable stages, as they grow. Interestingly, these crises largely correspond to the various chasms we are discussing.

According to Zook and Allen, the first crisis is *overload*, which occurs when a business is seeking rapid scale. Too much to do and not enough people to do it makes the project start to derail. This is usually experienced when seeking to cross the commercialisation chasm. The second is *stall-out*, which refers to the slow-down that many companies suffer as their rapid growth gives rise to layers of organisational complexity and bureaucracy. This is a scale issue and is often faced when seeking to cross the scalability chasm. The third crisis is *free fall*, when the company has stopped growing. This relates to the stage when the mainstream market for a new product or service has been saturated and sales are in decline (more on that later).

Zook and Allen's research suggests that managing these choke points requires a 'founder's mentality' – behaviours typically embodied by a passionate, bold, ambitious founder.[5] But as we have seen, they may not necessarily be referring to the person who gave birth to the original idea. They are more likely referring to an 'entrepreneurial mindset' or enterprise- or solutions-focused mindset. And such a mindset should not be restricted to one original founder'. It is necessary to instil this way of thinking across the company rather than it being contained in one or two people who are attached to the company or idea for whatever reason.

In traditional innovation, the 'founder' or person who first comes up with the invention or new idea is often the Boffin or R&D person. In an impeller approach, the 'founder' is the bee – as they are the person who came up with the proposed solution. However, neither of these individuals should be the person who leads the commercialisation team. But, as Zook and Allen point out, it is possible to transfer that 'founder exuberance' and passion to all of the team. Indeed, that is exactly what happens in all the companies they researched that demonstrated significant long-term profitability and sustainability.

We recognise that there is an endowment effect and an attachment between the inventor and their invention. It's their baby; they are more passionate and enthusiastic about the invention than possibly anyone else in the team. This has its advantages, such as drive, commitment and perseverance, but those qualities can blind the inventor's assessment of the invention as it progresses through the various stages. This can mean that a mediocre idea is allowed to live on, with all its associated costs long after it should have been put out to pasture.

The key is to facilitate the upside of this attachment, enthusiasm and passion so that it can be transferred to the rest of the team while eradicating the downside which is not necessarily good for the business.

According to Zook and Allen, companies that achieve profitable sustainable growth share a common set of motivating attitudes and behaviours that can usually be traced back to a bold ambitious 'founder' who got it right the first time around. Sir Richard Branson is a classic example of this, and we can see that common set of motivating attitudes and behaviours used time and again in the Virgin model. These businesses often consider themselves insurgents – there to disrupt the status quo on behalf of the beleaguered customer. Again, Virgin fits that role. And finally, these companies have a special ability to foster employees' deep feelings of responsibility. Something that Virgin also gets right.

The three component parts of the founder mentality are further broken down as follows:

- Owner's mindset

    - Strong cash focus (attention to cash and costs, willingness to redeploy people and capital to wherever they are needed and better utilised)
    - Bias for action (people are empowered to make key decisions faster)
    - Aversion to bureaucracy (deliver value, reallocate resources, get on with the job)

- Insurgency

    - Bold mission (clear about the big 'why' and unique purpose which is personally motivating to staff)
    - Spikiness (clear about one or two differentiation capabilities with a repeatable business model that can capture and extend market growth)
    - Limitless horizon (focused on long-term instead of quarterly results, embrace turbulence and experimentation with products and business models)

- Front-line obsession

    - Relentless experimentation (innovate and experiment in the field, efficient feedback process that drives learning and improvement)
    - Front-line empowerment (sought after employer of top talent, treating front-line people as heroes)
    - Customer advocacy (clear about core customers and seek their loyalty, messaging tailored to this audience)

The creation of the stand-alone, autonomous commercialisation vehicle facilitates these factors and allows the enthusiasm of the founder to be instilled in everyone else who can get behind the invention and the team taking it to market. What makes the entrepreneur so crucial is his or her commercialisation experience and, ironically, their lack of attachment to the invention. This distance allows them to remain agnostic to the best way to commercialise and get to market successfully or close it down early.

Too often the inventor of the novel idea is looking inwardly at what already exists or could be achieved and may inadvertently close multiple doors of exploration as a result. For example, if the inventor thinks that only they can innovate around the production process then the inventor is not open to the full spectrum of potential solutions. So right from the get-go, the inventor is filtering the solution through those parameters and limiting the possible outcomes. Whilst there is nothing inherently wrong with a traditional innovation process, an impeller approach is much more agnostic and nothing is off limits.

For innovation to be truly disruptive, it should forget about the existing business and what can and can't be done. This is why the bee is so important – they bring potential solutions that no one will have thought of before. This is especially important when considering technology solutions. An experienced entrepreneur will be able to fast track the good ideas and validated prototypes because they will always find the technology if they look for it. When they know what they are looking for, it's easier to find. Too often R&D professionals try to shoehorn their existing technologies into the proposed solutions or seek to make changes to existing technologies to make something work. But an agnostic entrepreneur is not attached to the invention or the way it might best be commercialised and can often get to market quicker by finding technology that already does the job and partnering with the organisation that can make it happen.

The entrepreneur and the business model

There are literally thousands of ways to sell something. The default position, especially to those inexperienced in entrepreneurship, is direct sales. But direct sale is only one type of business model. There is franchising, licensing, wholesale, leasing, etc. New distribution channels and technology have also opened up new ways to reach markets and new ways to monetise products and services. An experienced and capable entrepreneur will know this and will understand the market and the customer profile well enough to experiment with the business model and find the winner relatively quickly.

You could argue that by the time a team has reached a working prototype they should have already considered the most appropriate business model for the product or service, but, as we've said before, what if that team doesn't include an entrepreneur? The chances of the team looking beyond a traditional sales approach are limited.

In addition, there is always some elements of trial and error in taking a product to market that not only explores the best business model but the best marketing messages and the best channels to reach those customers through. The entrepreneur can therefore significantly shorten the length of this chasm because of their prior experience. The challenge at this stage is to use customer feedback to improve the 80 per cent product or service to a fully functional product or service and test the water on what business model will yield the greatest long-term results. The entrepreneur is best equipped to do that.

Business outcomes, not creativity, are the drivers now. It is the entrepreneur along with any mentors or 'grey hairs' they may wish to consult that will determine how best to make money from the invention. Once this is known and has been demonstrated with a greater uptake in the mainstream market, the commercialisation chasm has been crossed successfully. And it usually requires specific talent in entrepreneurship and leadership.

Crossing the scalability chasm

Moore's chasm (as opposed to the cracks he identified between various segments of the market) is between *early adopters* and the *early majority*. However, Phadke and Vyakarnam's research suggests that it's not customer type but customer behaviour that matters. When customers have bought into the business model and are sharing experiences (hopefully positive), the mainstream market opens up. The risk of a less than optimal product or service has been surmounted and customers feel confident they are getting a fully functional, useful and desirable product or service.

In many ways, crossing the scalability chasm is the easiest. It's simply about changing gears. The team knows how to reach their market, they know what business model yields the greatest revenue and they have fine-tuned the product or service successfully using early customer feedback. Now it's about how to make real, sustainable cash over the longer term. Accurate customer segmentation, distribution, marketing and sales activities take centre stage for the entrepreneur and his or her team.

The chasm here is one of scale – how to successfully scale the business and take the offerings mainstream to where the big money is. The entrepreneur's role is also critical in crossing this chasm successfully because it requires knowledge across several business-related fields, such as manufacturing and packaging optimisation, the development of channels to market and negotiating deals with channel partners or marketing promotions. Leadership continues to be important – keeping the right team in place focused on the right goals. As scale is critical, ensuring that the sales and marketing arms of the new entity are adequately resourced and are following a proven strategy becomes increasingly relevant to secure market traction.

The entrepreneur, along with the business-focused team that they have gathered around them in the stand-alone entity, is paramount in crossing this chasm successfully.

Notes

1 Moore GA (2014) *Crossing the Chasm: Marketing and Selling Disruptive Products to Mainstream Customers* (3rd Edition), Harper Business, New York.
2 Phadke U and Vyakarnam S (2018) *Camels, Tigers & Unicorns: Re-Thinking Science and Technology-Enabled Innovation*, World Scientific Publishing, London.

3 Phadke U and Vyakarnam S (2018) *Camels, Tigers & Unicorns: Re-Thinking Science and Technology-Enabled Innovation*, World Scientific Publishing, London.
4 Phadke U and Vyakarnam S (2018) *Camels, Tigers & Unicorns: Re-Thinking Science and Technology-Enabled Innovation*, World Scientific Publishing, London.
5 Zook C and Allen J (2016) *The Founder's Mentality: How to Overcome the Predictable Crises of Growth*, Harvard Business Review Press, Boston.

8 Sale or scale to sustainable growth

Once the product or service has proven itself and is generating significant income in the mainstream market, some key decisions must be taken, not least because the new business, that has been created around that solution, is likely to be approaching its highest valuation at the top of the adoption curve.

This triggers crucial discussions on the future of the SPV entity. Who will be involved in those discussions will depend on the nature of the business and who ultimately owns it. In most situations, the autonomous, stand-alone entity will have been created within a larger business that is keen to pursue viable opportunities while ring-fencing their eventual outcome and impact.

As we mentioned in Chapter 1, there is often significant risk attached to innovation for most businesses, especially large, publicly listed businesses because any failure or perceived failure can have a detrimental impact on the share price. Creating a separate entity, with its own budget and governance framework, therefore allows the larger business to distance itself from the innovation. If it fails, it fails quickly and quietly and doesn't negatively impact the share price. If it is successful, then the larger business can decide to sell the new unit which is now worth significantly more than it was as an untested idea. This is most likely in a situation where the new unit is no longer on strategy or has limited fit for the company's portfolio going forward. They could still partner with another organisation to take it forward. Or, where fit is still relevant, they could decide to absorb the entity back into the larger business.

Which is the best option will again depend on the entity and the infrastructure and skill set that already exists in the business. If the innovation (and it is an innovation by this point because it's been successfully commercialised) is a significant departure from the existing business and requires a different skill set and infrastructure to maintain and develop into the future, then selling that entity and reinvesting that profit back into new innovations may be the smart play.

However, if the product or service has proven successful and can be maintained and managed within the larger business' existing portfolio, then bringing that business back in-house may be the wiser option. This is especially true as most businesses are already proficient at creating new iterations or variations on existing products or services to create additional revenue and appeal to different market segments. They are proficient in customer service and logistics. They are skilled in brand management and operations and can successfully engage the customer and upsell and cross-sell between the rest of the larger business offerings.

The entrepreneur and their team who successfully took the invention to market and demonstrated its worth can now hand that product or service over to the existing business as they move on to a new invention. The entrepreneur's job is to prove the invention works or prove it doesn't as fast as possible. If commercialisation doesn't work or there is no market or too small a market, then the unit is closed and the team and any unused budget is re-purposed to focus on commercialising the next validated solution. If it does work, their role is still over. The stand-alone unit is absorbed back to the existing larger business because it already has the necessary infrastructure and people to service that innovation going forward.

The impeller approach means that the novel idea or invention stays with the people best suited to support and develop it throughout its product or service life cycle. This is the exact opposite of what currently happens. Typically, the person who comes up with the idea in the first place – the Boffin – is the person who stays with that idea through its life cycle even though that person's skill set is only relevant or useful at the creative birth of that idea. Not only does this approach usually kill the idea, it often also kills the Boffin's career and does a great disservice to both. The impeller approach attaches the right people to the invention at the right time. If it fails, it is not the kiss of death for those involved. They are not pushed out of the business. Instead everyone in the team, including the entrepreneur, starts the process again and seeks to get the next proposed solution to market as fast and efficiently as possible.

There are now several companies that are offering a different way to innovate. As we said at the start, the impeller approach is just one possible solution. Another is the Rainmaking model.

The Rainmaking solution

Seeking to answer the question, "how can we confidently take informed bets that advance our innovation agenda"?, Rainmaking focuses on big corporate innovation; specifically large companies that are currently seeing little return on significant corporate venture capital funds, offering a novel partnership solution where both parties have skin in the game. This approach combines the best of out-sourced innovation with existing brand, reputation and reach.

Start-ups are the canary in the coal mine for big corporations. Used properly, start-ups become a proxy to identifying trends, disruption and opportunities and offer early warning signals for changes that are taking place in the marketplace. In particular, they look at where and how these early signals disrupt their client's innovation trajectory in the form of technology convergence, digital play or value chain disruptions.

Their process involves two phases. Phase one identifies key focus areas and 'where to play'. Phase two consists of planning and outlining 'how to win'. There are four steps in each phase and both phases usually take six weeks.

Phase one consists of:

- Step 1: Research the landscape
- Step 2: Assess the start-up ecosystem
- Step 3: Identify opportunity spaces
- Step 4: Assess and select opportunity spaces

Essentially, phase one consists of gathering data points and trends to form a view on how the industry is reconfiguring. This is followed by assessing opportunities where learnings can be applied to identify potential opportunity spaces where the company could play. This is their way of starting with the solution.

Phase two is focused on how to win and involves the process of selecting and executing strategic options. Phase two consists of:

- Step 1: Define the innovation thesis
- Step 2: Outline potential roles
- Step 3: Develop business cases
- Step 4: Outline execution roadmap

Multi-nationals tend to stick to what they know, despite the fact that some of the biggest opportunities sit in adjacent industries to where they're currently playing. Phase one is about looking for innovative ways to leverage their core competencies and their core capabilities to go into new markets where they, arguably, have a better right than start-ups to take big chunks of new revenue from the existing incumbents.

For example, working with a major banking group Rainmaking discovered that the bank were the largest spender on legal services in the UK. Unsurprisingly, they had their own in-house law department, which was essentially an internal law firm. Of course, originally the purpose of that department was to reduce the banks costs but it also offered some interesting opportunities.

There is still very little tech innovation in the law industry, although the tech does exist. The reason is obvious: most law firms work on billable hours. The more lawyers are involved, the more money they make. They don't want fast solutions and standard contracts. They don't want transparency. But the market does.

Combing their existing knowledge base with technology means that this banking group could easily automate standard contracts because that tech already exists. Instead of just solving their own problem and reducing their costs, the bank could take a sizable chunk out of the law industry. As a brand-name bank, they already have the right to play in that space, including significant in-house capabilities. Plus, as a bank and not a law firm, they don't have the barriers that law firms do. And they already have relationships with customers, SMEs and business accounts that would appreciate the new offering: cheaper legal services. And those customers already trust them for their banking needs, so it's a small step for them to also trust them to provide automated legal templates for their business.

Phase one is therefore about looking for the innovation opportunities in white spaces that may be adjacent to the current industry. The incumbent executive mindset doesn't always see these because they are too busy looking at their own feet. Phase two is then about making those opportunities happen.

Rainmaking identifies, on average, 25 new ventures and pilot opportunities per engagement. So far (2020), those innovations have led to the co-building of 30 companies with big corporates, nine to exit including one IPO. Their approach is also focused on fast solution or innovation identification coupled with the right team. Lean start-up methodologies combined with proven founder talent means that this approach has managed to convert getting to market and successful commercialisation into a repeatable science. It combines the best of the corporate world with the best of the start-up world. Using the corporates unfair advantage, i.e. the ability to provide access to advantageous corporate assets such as infrastructure, regulation, data, brand, distribution or logistics, etc. together with proven founder or entrepreneurial talent and external governance, the new entity is a new co-created, co-funded partnership with aligned incentives that work for everyone.

A word on sustainable growth

Throughout this book we have proposed that innovation is not the creation of novel ideas. It is the successful commercialisation of novel ideas. As such, sustainable long-term growth is not a hurdle that needs to be navigated before innovation can be deemed successful. If your novel idea in the shape of a new product, service or process has captured the attention of the mainstream market, then it has almost certainly made money and delivered value. Job done.

But what about longer-term sustainable growth? Does a business simply bow out of a market once that market is saturated and sales are in decline? We would argue that the answer is no. It simply presents another crisis – the one Zook and Allen refer to as *free fall*.[1]

Too much effort has been expended simply to allow a cash cow product or service to turn into a dog (Boston Matrix). Once a new venture reaches the point of decline it's worth looking at different ways to flatten out the product or service adoption curve into a continuous S curve (Figure 8.1).

Such an approach (Figure 8.2) therefore provides a business with a much more sustainable way to milk innovations toward long-term sustainability.

Conventional growth

When companies seek to grow their business, their first instinct is to engage in 'conventional growth' manoeuvres. They look for new or adjacent segment and

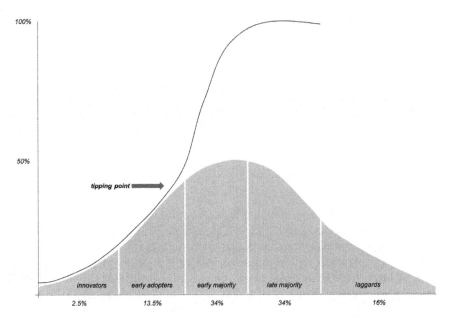

Figure 8.1 Flatten Out the Adoption Curve Into an S Curve

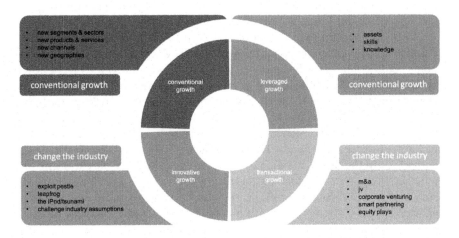

Figure 8.2 Opportunities for Growth

sectors, new products and services, new channels and new geographies. Much of the time, such manoeuvres are simply incremental variations of existing thinking and, as such, are not terribly innovative. A great deal of this activity is simply 'me too' copying of the best practice of competitors. A sort of 'innovation karaoke' or doing a really bad impression of someone else's original. That does not mean to say that they can't generate significant revenue. In the current digital world, for example, companies that did not have a digital dimension of their business can see significant growth when they first go online. Similarly, setting up in new territories can add significant incremental revenue. However, all such manoeuvres can become graveyards for companies that don't execute the strategy properly. The main value of conventional growth is that they don't require too much in the way of innovative thinking.

When companies are struggling for additional revenue beyond the scalability chasm, it can really help to realise that conventional growth is just one of four different types of growth manoeuvres.

Leveraged growth

Leveraged growth involves stepping back and considering what assets the business has or can tap into and leverage. This may range from physical assets such as office space and real estate, to digital assets such as customer email or databases, or people assets within their internal talent pool or external alliances as well as more traditional brand assets. Leveraged growth looks at how all the existing assets can be re-bundled in novel ways to attract a different audience. Viagra is an almost mythical example of leveraged growth. The assets of Pfizer included a medication designed to reduce high blood pressure and angina. However, the mediation didn't prove that effective in trials. It did however have one rather unusual side effect. The product was tested and repackaged around that side effect and Viagra makes Pfizer billions.

Another example might be British Telecom (BT). Around about the time the internet was developing and modem dial up was the primary way households could connect to this new opportunity, BT set out to leverage a novel bundle of assets. At that time, BT was a highly trusted brand in the UK. This allowed their engineers to turn up at customers' homes, knock on the door and most households would let the engineers in to do something technical to their phone line. When such brand trust was combined with the fact that they had a nationwide coverage of skilled engineers, they could set up their own equipment in the home at a moment's notice. The third key asset was a highly efficient billing system, which meant that the service went live almost immediately and started turning a profit shortly after. Leveraging those existing assets allowed BT to move, at speed, into broadband, making the company millions in the process.

Transactional growth

If companies don't engage in traditional growth manoeuvres, then they tend to drive growth by simply buying it. For most companies this means M&A. Despite consistent evidence that M&A activity is notoriously problematic in terms of ensuring it adds value to the bottom line, most multinationals continually look for targets that will increase their market share. Often there are whole divisions or subdivisions of large corporations looking for such deals.

Significant analysis goes into defining the 'right purchase price' for potential targets and whether the potential can be realised from a strategic point of view. Much less analysis goes into the risks of effective cultural integration, despite this being the most common reason for M&A failure.[2]

But M&A is not the only type of transaction possible. There are several other relationship dynamics that are possible. Effective transactional growth starts with listing all the people or organisations your business could potentially partner with. This list can include competitors and companies from completely unrelated market sectors that are well established or even rapidly growing start-ups. For example, Samsung makes many of the parts used to make the iPhone X. It is estimated that Samsung will make $110 from every iPhone X sold, which could result in Samsung making more money from the parts it produces for the iPhone than it made from its own Galaxy S8.[3]

Once potential partners have been identified some disruptive thinking is then required around what those transactional opportunities might look like in terms of how the relationship may be structured. It could mean taking an equity stake in the partner organisation, creating a new joint venture or simply injecting capital in a purer venturing manoeuvre. It may not even involve a direct cash transaction. Either way new partnership models that can provide greater commercial flexibility than a simple equity play are worthy of consideration.

Disruptive growth

The fourth growth manoeuvre is much more radical, again perfectly suited to an impeller approach. This involves a deliberate attempt to change the industry or market itself by disrupting all market assumptions, perceived wisdom or best practice. One way of doing this is to consider the mega market trends using the acronym for Political, Economic, Social, Technological, Legal and Environmental (PESTLE). Thus, when considering the PESTLE changes in any market and seeing how they may influence the future can provide rich insight that can then change your thinking about the new solutions that can be created.

One of the ways to be more innovative and change the industry is to 'leap-frog' existing offerings that are already leveraging PESTLE trends. This is what Samsung did when they nearly doubled their market share from 2007 to 2012, capitalising on the implosion of Nokia and Motorola to snatch the biggest share of the smartphone market. They looked at the accelerating success of the iPhone and identified the key benefits that had created traction and then simply leap-frogged all of them. Thus, their Samsung Galaxy provided greater storage capacity than the iPhone, their model offered a longer battery life, upgraded the camera technology and they innovated the design elements.

Speed and nature of decision making

The critical advantage of an impeller approach over current innovation models that follow a process though the innovation funnel is speed.

Everything about this solution-focused approach is designed to build speed into the innovation system so proposed inventions can fail fast or flourish fast. Not only is the approach designed for speed, but the entity that is created to take the invention to market is also designed for speed. Such an approach allows the innovation team to see results quickly and make better decisions as a result. Rainmaking, for example, builds speed into the co-created business. The founding talent is in charge, but a mix of directors from corporate and Rainmaking, together with a strict governance protocol, means speed is baked into the new company from the start.

Commercial success ultimately depends on both the speed and quality of decision making. These two concepts are not mutually exclusive, although many would suggest that decisions taken in haste are often less effective. To ensure that all decisions are optimised for both speed and quality, it is necessary to understand a little about the nature of how human beings make decisions in the first place.

The common assumption is that all decisions, particularly business decisions, are rational, based on logic and rooted in data analysis. Thus, the best information available is analysed and the most beneficial option is chosen. Certainly, this is the way we think about innovation – assess the problem, analyse data and choose a direction based on the analysis. But that's not now we make decisions.

There is now widespread agreement, even amongst the most hard-bitten reductionist neuroscientists, that rationality doesn't really exist as a separate cognitive process from emotional processing. Such an understanding is based on the research of neuroscientists such as Antonio Damasio, who has written extensively on the consequences of brain injury and its implications on decision making. Damasio cites the well-known story of Phineas Gage. Gage was a railway construction foreman who suffered a traumatic brain injury in 1848. Although he survived, Gage, perhaps unsurprisingly, was never the same again.

Based on medical records and subsequent reconstructions of the brain damage Gage received after an iron pole cut through his brain and disconnected the logic centres in his frontal cortex from the emotional processing centres located deeper in his brain, scientists changed the way we think about decision making. After the injury, Gage went from being one of the most capable men in the company to being unable to make even basic decisions, or he would make decisions and abandon them almost immediately.[4]

This patient and many other brain injury cases led neuroscientists to realise that decision making requires emotion. The disconnection of the 'rational thinking' in the frontal cortex from 'feeling' in the emotional processing centres rendered decision making almost impossible. We might like to believe that all our business decisions are rational, considered, intelligent decisions based on data, but what really happens is we have a 'feeling' first and then we simply look for rational data to support that initial feeling. As a result, all decisions we ever make are really just "feelings justified by logic".

An impeller approach recognises this fact and allows the bee to buzz around the meadow of experts to get a feel for the problems through the eyes of the experts who know the most about it. Then when solutions start to emerge based on a constellation of intuitions, either their own or the integrated intuitions of the meadow, the viability of the answer determines its 'validity' rather than any specific piece of data or evidence. The emergence of the answer isn't therefore constrained by the same level of 'proof' that slows down most R&D cycles. The ultimate evidence in an impeller is what we call 'self-evident', i.e. does it work or not. The same is true in the Rainmaking approach where the founding entrepreneurial talent brings their business *nous* and experience, but the ideas are still thoroughly vetted for quick, accurate validation or exit.

The bee's experience and intuition as well as all the evidence of the meadow of experts plus their intuitions and experiences are all factored in to generate better and faster solutions. On their own, bees don't necessarily have enough data points, context or a deep enough appreciation of the complexity of the situation. On their own, the meadow of experts can be blinded by their experience, not realising that experience is also emotionally laden data stored in parts of their brain to resurface when asked to make a decision. But when integrated together, fast solutions and fast decisions are possible, which can then guide further exploration.

Fifty years of neuroscience tells us that it is impossible to separate emotion from thinking, so we must factor in emotional data as well as logical data into our decision-making algorithms. For example, gut feelings or instincts, which are generated in the neural networks contained within the enteric brain in the gut, provide non-cognitive data that can facilitate the generation of innovative solutions.[5] Intuitive data are quite different and may have more to do with the neural networks in and around the heart. Instincts tend to have a more 'negative', fear-laden valence compared to intuitions, which tend to be more 'positive'. Both types of information represent 'non-cognitive data' and can facilitate a 'knowing without knowing', a 'felt-sense' without objective data.

Both types of data, instinct and intuition, generate an output in the form of an insight – which literally means 'sight' from within. The impeller approach seeks to tap into the insight within the entire meadow of experts and harness them in the generation of much better answers.

Speed of decision making is thus partially a function of the processing that exists within a single mind; and we have explored how the mind of a bee may confer very specific advantages over the mind of an expert or a generalist as far as innovation is concerned.

Speed is also a function of the maturity of a single mind. Thus, a six-year-old who thinks largely in concrete terms and has yet to develop the ability for abstract thought would take hours to solve a simple algebraic equation, if they could do it at all. But a 12-year-old who has developed the ability to think in abstract terms could solve the same problem in a few seconds.

The importance of maturity also constrains group decision making. A group of immature adults are likely to fight over an answer or even a definition of a problem much more than a group of mature non-egoic individuals. If a new entity is created to take the invention to market and is led by an aggressive entrepreneur, they may trigger all kinds of conflict or passive aggression in their support team that could significantly slow down, delay or even prevent their product launch. Autocratic overrule may speed up the process but it risks creating failure unless the autocrat has effectively considered all the various options correctly and come to the wisest conclusion.

If the problem being addressed needs a more nuanced solution, then it is necessary to integrate a diverse range of views, experiences and insights. Such high-speed integration is often beyond the ability of most autocrats. What is required is a much more sophisticated governance framework that can handle much greater levels of complexity and involve a more diverse bunch of people who all believe in the project and are incentivised toward its success. In addition, the process of reaching a collective decision also needs to be similarly sophisticated to ensure the wisdom of the crowd is unlocked at speed.

As people and teams mature, they gain access to different ways of reaching a decision. These different decision-making processes can be related to the evolution of the value systems we explored in Chapter 5. Figure 8.3 illustrates the evolution of decision-making sophistication in line with the eight value systems.

Innovation teams need to make daily decisions, and the way they do so is a function of their individual and collective maturity. When teams start to work together, there is often a brief period of anarchy where it is everyone for themselves. Survival within the innovation team is the first priority, which is not unreasonable, as their career may depend on it. But soon enough innovation team members realise that for the team to commercialise their novel idea, they will need to work together to succeed. As a result, cliques and alliances begin to form within the team. At this still very early stage of team formation, the decision-making process is still pretty tribal. But at least the innovation team can make decisions. Decisions at this point are imposed by the two or

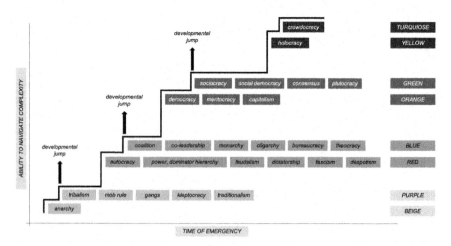

Figure 8.3 Evolution of Decision Making

three loudest or most forceful characters and claimed to be in the service of the innovation team's goals. In truth it is still largely a 'mob rule' process, but at least decisions are being made, so this is a step forward compared to the initial anarchy when innovation team members first showed up. When decisions are made based on tribal dynamics, they almost always privilege safety and security above all else. This is far from innovative; and if the way of deciding doesn't improve quickly, then there will be little progress, minimal innovation and the innovation team will collapse or be disbanded.

For an innovation team to have half a chance, someone needs to take charge. This may be an appointed team leader or someone within the group that assumes natural authority. This enables the innovation team to move quickly from mob rule to autocracy. When the decision-making power sits with one individual, the team can start to function. Although, as most executives have experienced, putting all the decisions in the hands of one person may be faster, it is incredibly fragile as a way of deciding; and this is also true in the field of innovation.

The very nature of innovation requires the convolution of ideas from many sources and many phases of the commercialisation process if 'fail fast', agile, waterfalls and valleys of death are to be navigated. An innovation team led by an autocrat may work in terms of quickly defining what needs to happen but there is always the risk that the autocrat makes the wrong call or their personal desires or biases distort the outcome. The extent of these flaws and the size of the risk to the innovation team depend on the maturity of the autocrat themselves.

If the innovation team can quickly establish some 'ground rules' for how to make decisions, then the risk of a single individual, the autocrat, inadvertently killing the project diminishes. Whilst the risk of making the wrong call decreases, the time it takes to make any call can increase, slowed by the rules that may have been put in place to reduce the risk.

If the loss of momentum in the team's ability to innovate, that occurs when the team introduces rules and process to help govern its decision making, becomes too great, then the stage is set for the emergence of a more pragmatic team decision-making process. If this occurs, then the innovation team moves to a democratic or meritocratic mode. In a meritocratic process, the quality of the idea is meant to trump all other considerations. In a democratic process, volume becomes the organising principle. Thus, if you can garner enough votes then you win the argument.

An innovation team that operates with this level of decision-making sophistication only partly integrates the rash of ideas that now exists either through the process of popularity (democracy) or persuasion (meritocracy). This is because, despite the rhetoric that surrounds democracy, the power sits with the minority that swing the vote. Democracy is absolutely not a majority rule. Not all perspectives are integrated; most are either outvoted or ignored. Clearly these decision-making processes are not optimal. Whilst both types of decision making are more sophisticated and therefore more helpful to innovation teams than the bureaucratic or autocratic process of earlier levels, there are still risks. Both democracy and meritocracy foster game playing and manipulation simply because if you want your answer to succeed you have to win the popular vote and persuade people that your answer is in everyone's best interest, even though this may not be the case as we have repeatedly seen in the political world in recent years.

Democratic decision making is pretty effective in creating or reinforcing inequality, and this can be damaging to innovation teams. But as with every level of decision-making, the dysfunction is what spawns the emergence of the next level of sophistication. It is the recognition that some views are being excluded that drives the emergence of a more sociocratic decision-making process. For most innovation teams, this means some form of consensus building.

Since this level of decision making is designed to embrace diverse perspectives, it can handle much greater levels of complexity and generate significantly better-quality answers. But as with every level of decision making, this comes at a cost. The cost, as many executives who may have experienced some form of consensus building knows, is a loss of speed. Debates can get stuck in the swamp of consensual deadlock. This is why new entities charged with the commercialisation of an invention must pay particular attention to interpersonal dynamics. Difference of opinions must be actively managed and understood. Everyone must recognise their role and do their job while simultaneously unlocking the power of the collective and keeping focused on the outcome.

The increase in quality but reduction in speed is partly what drives the emergence of the next level of decision-making sophistication which takes us into tier 2 values. The decision-making processes that have emerged in tier 2 have been called holacratic[6] and crowdocratic,[7] both of which bring speed and quality.

Taken from the Greek word *Holos*, meaning whole, a holon recognises that everything that exists is simultaneously a unique whole entity in itself and also a part of something greater. Every idea can have its own integrity while still being part of a greater suite of solutions. Holacracy embraces a range of practices that need to be installed into the innovation team or SPV to fully unlock their full potential. Much of this is a tidying up of governance processes within the innovation team or entity. In addition to tightening up governance, holacracy also includes a decision-making process, 'integrative decision-making' (IDM), designed to deliver a complete answer to any complex problem. But even in doing so, there is a recognition that this whole answer can always be part of a lager puzzle.

The value of IDM is that it transcends democratic decision making, which often produces a sizable minority that is disenfranchised with the outcome. The goal of the IDM process is to create 100 per cent alignment within an innovation team, and this can be achieved without getting stuck in consensual hell. Being able to rapidly reach a genuinely collective, mutually agreed upon decision within the new division or impeller commercialisation vehicle saves a huge amount of time and energy. It is no longer necessary to neutralise the effects of the minority that are unhappy with the decision because no one has to 'tow the party line', compelled to plot against the outcome.

Beyond holacracy is crowdocracy, which taps into the wisdom of the crowd and embraces everyone's ideas in innovating the answer, and therefore avoids decision-making by an elite, self-selected few.[8] Crowdocracy can deliver a significantly greater level of engagement right across the innovation team, organisation or nation. It could be very useful when the impeller invention has demonstrated success in the market and the entity is looking to scale as quickly as possible. Bigger ambitions usually mean more people, more work and greater corporate complexity.

We touched on the nature of crowdocracy and how to access the wisdom of the crowd in Chapter 5. Just as the bee must access the wisdom of the crowd in the meadow of experts, the entrepreneur must access the wisdom of the collective crowd involved in commercialising the invention to seek better and faster decisions.

Notes

1 Zook C and Allen J (2016) *The Founder's Mentality: How to Overcome the Predictable Crises of Growth*, Harvard Business Review Press, Boston.
2 Hodge N (2017) Why Do M&As Fail? *Risk Management* www.rmmagazine.com/2017/04/03/why-do-mas-fail/
3 Price E (2017) Samsung Will Make $110 for Every iPhone X Sold *Forbes Magazine* http://fortune.com/2017/10/04/samsung-apple-profits-iphonex/
4 Watkins A (2014) *Coherence: The Secret Science of Brilliant Leadership*, Kogan Page, London.
5 Gershon MD (1998) *The Second Brain*, HarperCollins, New York.
6 Robertson BJ (2015) *Holacracy: The Revolutionary Management System That Abolishes Hierarchy*, Penguin, London.
7 Watkins A and Stratenus I (2016) *Crowdocracy: The End of Politics*, Urbane Publications, Kent.
8 Watkins A and Stratenus I (2016) *Crowdocracy: The End of Politics*, Urbane Publications, Kent.

9   The impeller future

We believe that it's time to think differently about innovation. The current iterations of the innovation funnel are simply not working. In the UK alone £64.7 billion is wasted every year on innovation that goes nowhere.[1] And that may not even account for the hundreds of thousands of collective hours of human endeavour that delivers no value *or* the opportunity cost of that wasted effort and investment. It's time to innovate innovation.

An impeller approach offers an alternative to the innovation funnel process. When viewing innovation not simply as the creation of novel ideas but their successful commercialisation, most managers and business leaders would concede that their innovation budgets rarely deliver a consistent return on investment. In the old world of innovation for innovation's sake, some might argue that delivering a consistent return is not their objective and the very act of innovation is what matters. In the same way that venture capital firms only need one or two investments to pay off or publishers only need one or two bestsellers a year to make a significant profit, innovation is often viewed in these terms. In other words, those involved in innovation know that even if one or two ideas are successfully commercialised it may be enough to pay for all the ones that don't make it.

Certainly, the purpose of innovation is not always to create that billion-dollar idea, it is also to push out into the unknown, to shape and potentially disrupt markets or industries or simply to learn more that can be used or applied next time around. But until a novel idea is successfully commercialised, it's just an idea or invention. And while invention might be interesting and useful knowledge may be gained during the process, it's not innovation. Unless that invention can be produced or delivered successfully to a significant enough market and provide a solution or meet a need within that market then it's not fulfilling on its promise. If companies and countries want to remain competitive and relevant and find practical solutions to the myriad of complex problems we face, then we need to revolutionise innovation.

We believe an impeller approach is one way to innovate innovation. We are not suggesting that it is the only way to revitalise and reinvent innovation. Our deliberate inclusion of the Rainmaking approach should demonstrate that. Both offer a credible alternative to the wasteful innovation process many of us call innovation today.

Impeller innovation is fast because it allows us to start with the solution, not endless problem assessment. Currently, a huge amount of time and money is poured into analysing the problem so that an accurate diagnosis can be made about the causes and symptoms of that problem. An innovation team, along with R&D, is then charged with coming up with some sort of 'killer idea' that will solve that problem or meet a certain need. This is incredibly wasteful because often the people involved in that assessment have to first 'get up to speed' in relation to the issue or need. They are effectively investigating and assessing an issue that other people already know all about. Stage one in most project plans is typically research.

An impeller approach just goes straight to the knowledge via the meadow of experts. Not only does this massively speed up the process so that we can arrive at potential solutions faster but it also elevates the quality of the answer. Those involved don't have to understand the nature of the problem because they are already deeply familiar with different aspects of that problem. The bee integrates all the various aspects and views to come up with a number of prospective solutions which are then agnostically assessed by an analyst either in the innovation team or externally. The analyst doesn't care how the solution was formulated; their job is to prove or disprove it's potential for solving the issue as quickly as possible. That way the proposed solution can fail fast or flourish fast, saving time and money in the innovation process.

There will always be innovation teams inside organisations, the only difference is that their roles may shift slightly and there may be a few new players. We are already familiar with the idea of generalists and experts and they already deliver value in innovation teams. An impeller approach also calls for a bee – a third type of thinker who can harvest knowledge and insight from a vast range of sources and then convolve and integrate that information into ideas and solutions.

Impeller is also unique because the membership and leadership of that team changes as the innovation progresses from initial idea through to commercialisation. Too often in the traditional approach to innovation, the person who comes up with the idea, usually an R&D person, ends up leading the project. Although understandable because that individual knows the most about the idea and is also often the most passionate about the idea, it's a recipe for disaster. R&D people are R&D people. They are happiest and more productive in a lab or formulating ideas and solutions, testing hypothesis and determining viability. They are often not commercially minded and they are certainly not entrepreneurial. Once the idea has been validated, then the R&D person steps back to allow an entrepreneur to step into the leadership role and take the product or service to market. It's still a team effort but everyone stays within their area of expertise and delivers their part before handing the developing solution on to the next sub-group in the team to take it further toward commercialisation. Too many great ideas die because an R&D person was expected to become a completely different person with a completely different skill set and then commercialise an idea. Such a process does a huge disservice to the R&D person and the potentially brilliant solution he or she came up with. An invention must be able to successfully cross the 'valley of death' between viable prototype and market penetration before it will ever deliver value to customers and shareholders.

When it does, the rewards are significant, not only financially for the business but also in generating innovation capability into a fluid and interchangeable innovation team that steps in and steps back as needed while staying focused on the end goal of commercialisation. Having this interchangeable leadership within the innovation team also further speeds up the process and prevents waste. We are all more attached to an idea we came up with. It's human nature. And whilst that passion and commitment can be a blessing, it can also be a curse if the idea or solution starts to falter. Instead of recognising the flaws and killing the project to divert resources to another potential solution, an attached leader can allow the project to limp on for months, even years. The passing of the baton from the R&D professional to the entrepreneur can prevent this waste of time and money.

Imagine if genuine innovation capability was perfected and baked into all organisations across all departments, where everyone in the organisation was on the lookout for problems to solve, processes to improve, product or service innovations or new markets to enter. Imagine what could be achieved when an innovation team used the impeller approach on a number of solutions, seamlessly passing those solutions to those players in the impeller model that could accelerate the process from the initial idea, through analysis, validation, prototype and testing to design and delivery. Solutions that show the most promise are passed on to an experienced stand-alone commercialisation team, led by an entrepreneur skilled at turning ideas into commercial reality. Not every solution will succeed. There will always be an element of the unknown in innovation; however, if that conclusion can be arrived at quickly then neither business nor government will waste the time and money that is *inevitable* in the traditional innovation funnel approach. The innovation BU will simply be rolled up and the staff and remaining budget dispersed to commercialise the next invention or novel idea.

The impeller approach brings speed to the innovation process so that viable improvements and game changing inventions can be implemented or brought to market quickly. Isn't that why innovation exists in the first place?

But the possibilities don't just exist in business; they exist across society. Imagine a point where the role of this third type of thinker – the bee – is common place. We could install Joker's in residence or employ 'bees' in government departments or public-sector organisations who could come up with proposed solutions to the multitude of complex or wicked problems we face. Innovative solutions for social care, improvements to health care, sustainable energy, carbon capture, criminal justice, social housing, escalating inequality, education – the list of issues that need to be addressed is endless. The need for an innovation revolution is not just to deliver financial benefit to organisations keen to stay competitive. It's much bigger and potentially more important than that. Genuine innovation, where smart solutions are successfully brought to market to deliver value and solve problems, has the capacity to improve the lives of millions of people around the world.

A cursory glance at the evening news reminds us of the challenges we face globally. And yet, those challenges present opportunities not just to the businesses that can solve them effectively but to the politicians and governments who can institute those changes and support those solutions. Business can be a force for good while also delivering shareholder value – at least it can when that business is adept at impelling innovative answers into the market.

In conclusion

Our argument is simple: the innovation funnel approach may have worked or been acceptable five or ten years ago but it's not working well enough now. Businesses simply don't have the capital to endlessly throw at the innovation wall in the hope that something might stick.

Increasingly we are faced with incredibly complex and diverse challenges that are crying out for innovative solutions. In the UK, businesses are facing unprecedented opportunities and simultaneous threats as UK plc seeks to find its place in a post-Brexit, post-COVID global economy. Our ability to ensure that it is an opportunity rests largely in our ability to successfully commercialise the inventions we have traditionally been so capable of creating.

There are two key parts of real and successful innovation: the creation of the novel idea AND the successful commercialisation of that novel idea. Each part involves different people with different skill sets. The companies that are making this work, including Impeller Ventures, recognise these differences in team makeup, leadership and focus and are adjusting the mix to suit the outcome, not the other way around.

We need to build an ability to impel innovation into business for on-going prosperity. By creating that capability, we can ensure that we have the expertise in the business with bees, access to the meadow of experts, R&D people, analysts and designers, entrepreneurs – all the people we need to take an idea to market successfully – and that those people can step in and out of the process across multiple projects as they are needed. There is no one size fits all approach, but you can get more information including different configurations and case studies at www.impellerventures.com.

Developing capability in any skill or process takes time. But if we reverse the innovation funnel, start with bee-generated answers and let the market pull rather than R&D teams push products and services to the market, then the rewards are significant, and we may just change the world.

Note

1 Chandraker A, Houmas H, Hogg J, and Reilly C (2015) Innovation as Unusual PA Consulting.

Index

Note: Page numbers in *italics* indicate a figure and page numbers in **bold** indicate a table on the corresponding page.

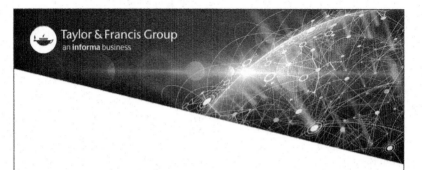